Wrixon James (Jim) Gasteen was born in 1922. He grew up on sheep and cattle stations in Western Queensland and has spent much of his life working as a farmer and grazier. He briefly left the land to become a diesel fitter in Sydney, but the lure of the outback proved too strong. His passion for the environment saw him awarded Membership of the Order of Australia (AM) in 1993 for his work in the fields of nature conservation and balanced land-use management. He is a life member of the Queensland Wildlife Preservation Society. He is retired and lives on a hobby farm in the New South Wales town of Lynwood.

UNDER THE

A Bush Memoir

JIM GASTEEN

First published 2005 by University of Queensland Press
PO Box 6042, St Lucia, Queensland 4067, Australia

www.uqp.uq.edu.au

Typeset in 12/15.5pt Bembo by Post Pre-Press Group, Brisbane, Queensland
Printed in Australia by McPherson's Printing Group

Distributed in the USA and Canada by
International Specialized Books Services, Inc.,
5824 N.E. Hassalo Street, Portland, Oregon 97213-3640

Cataloguing-in-Publication Data
National Library of Australia

Gasteen, Jim, 1922– .
Under the mulga: a bush memoir.

ISBN 0 7022 3445 1.

1. Gasteen, Jim 1922– . 2. Country life – Queensland – Anecdotes.
3. Queensland – Social life and customs – 20th century. I. Title.

994.3092

This book is dedicated to the original occupiers of Australia, the Aborigines. And bush settlers like my parents who opened up and worked the land through drought, dust, heat and flies. Their dogged persistence has shaped the destiny of this country.

Contents

Map 1: Southern Queensland and Northern New South Wales – where the properties Thrushton, Clonard and Dalgonally are situated

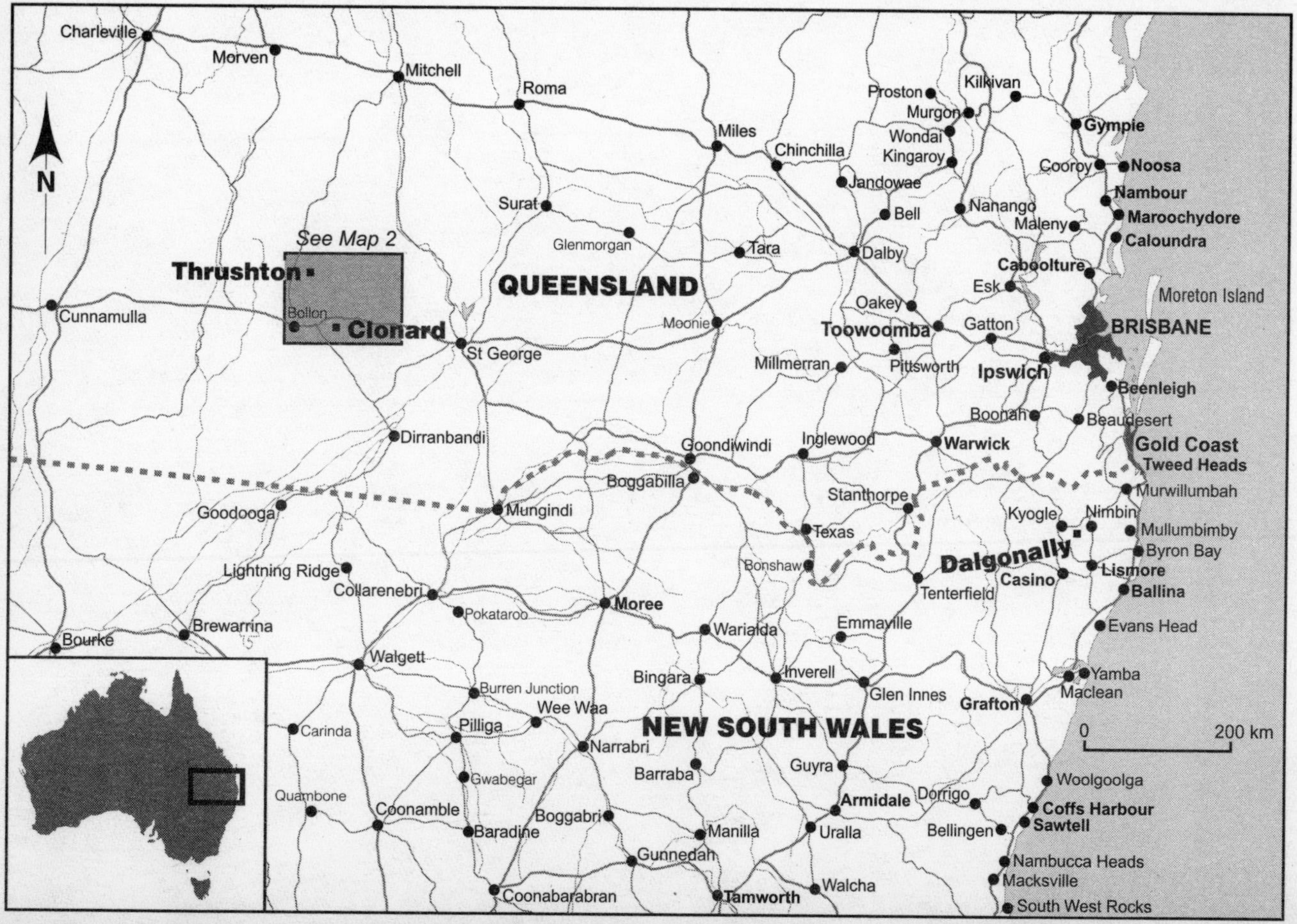

Map 2: Thrushton, Clonard and surrounding areas

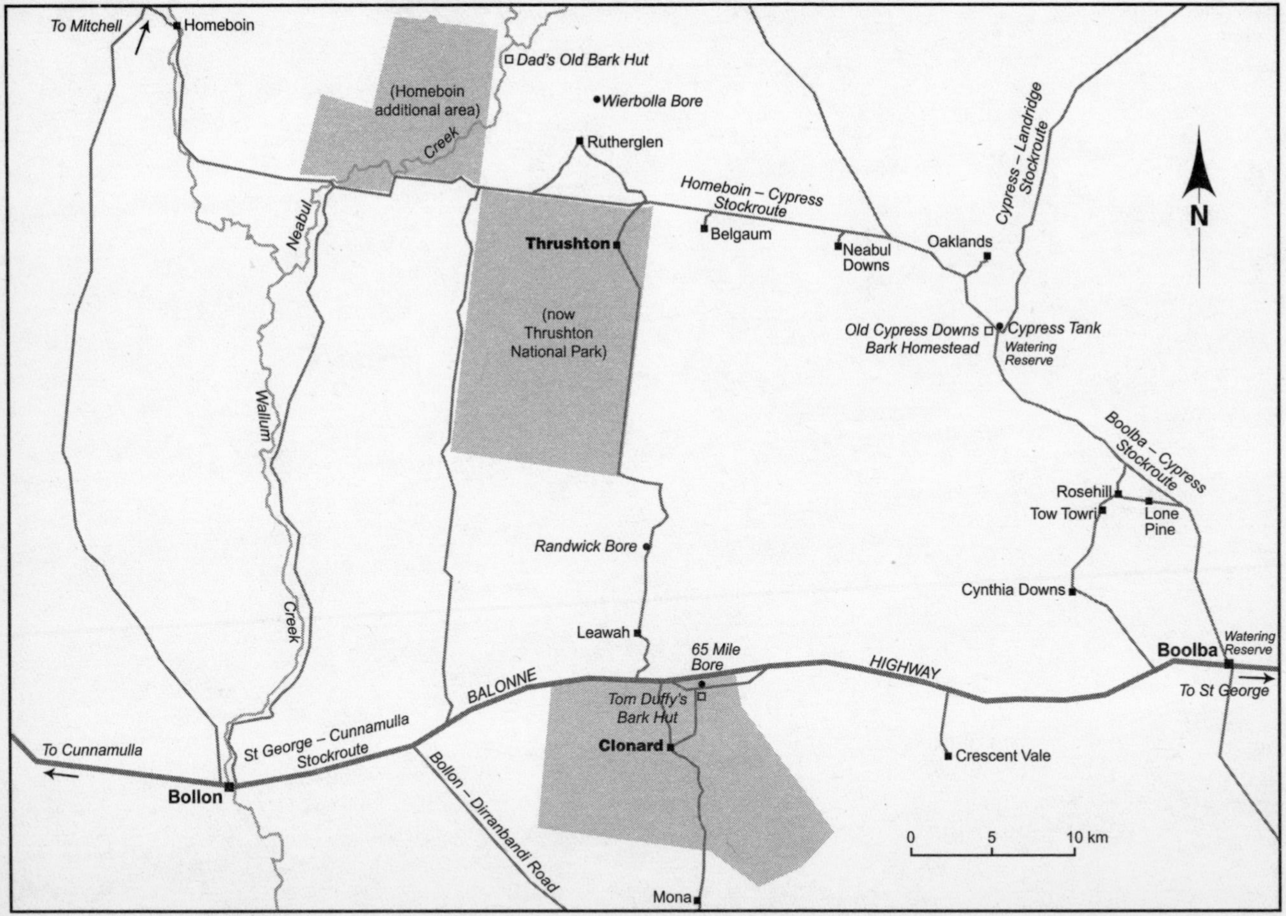

N

To Mitchell

Homeboin

Dad's Old Bark Hut

• Wierbolla Bore

Rutherglen

Cypress – Landridge Stockroute

Oaklands

Neabul Downs

Belgaum

Homeboin – Cypress Stockroute

Old Cypress Downs Bark Homestead

Cypress Tank Watering Reserve

Thrushton

(now Thrushton National Park)

(Homeboin additional area)

Neabul Creek

Wallum Creek

Boolba – Cypress Stockroute

Lone Pine

Rosehill

Tow Town

Cynthia Downs

Boolba

Watering Reserve

To St George

Crescent Vale

Randwick Bore

Leawah

65 Mile Bore

Tom Duffy's Bark Hut

Clonard

Mona

BALONNE HIGHWAY

Bollon – Dirranbandi Road

St George – Cunnamulla Stockroute

Bollon

To Cunnamulla

0   5   10 km

Preface

A number of people have asked me over the years to compile an account of our family's involvement with the land; to describe the changing times and life as it was lived during that earlier period. Always too busy, and doubtful that anyone would want to read it all anyway, I purposely put it out of my mind and tried to forget about it.

But in 1990 the same thing cropped up again. I was with the PATA (Pacific–Asia Travel Association) Task Force investigating Cape York and coastal regions from Port Douglas to Cooktown. The work terminated on Thursday Island with a round-table discussion in the old pub. John Courtenay, Chief Executive Officer of GLADA (Gulf Local Authorities Development Association) was the meticulous and able organiser of the outfit, and three four-wheel drive vehicles and a light aircraft transported us all over the place and carted the camping gear, swags and tuckerboxes wherever we went.

'When are you going to write your memoir?' John asked.

'Never, I couldn't bear to see *I, I, I* on every page.'

'Well,' he said, 'you'd better start thinking about it because someone else is going to do it for you.'

So it was John's ultimatum that finally stirred me into action, and the writing began a couple of years later. At first I didn't know where to start, but, as the story progressed, things I hadn't thought about for years gradually surfaced to fill in the gaps.

The story begins with my father leaving the Brisbane Grammar School and becoming a jackaroo on one of the big sheep stations in

Central Queensland prior to the 1914–18 World War. He joined up and, shortly after returning from the war, selected a block of waterless virgin mulga country in south-west Queensland. After marrying my mother, he set about developing it.

The book describes three wild bush kids growing up amongst rough and tumble old swag-carrying bush wanderers who added a little colour to those hard times in a hard country. Some couldn't read or write, some had big bushy beards, others smoked battered bent-stemmed pipes or chewed black plug tobacco and spat out of the corner of their mouth with stunning accuracy and dexterity. It was an art form perfected with the years. They had acquired their own special kind of lingo too, which was adequately descriptive for their simple bush lives and needs, but generally not suitable for ladies. They didn't talk much but, when they did, they were very amusing, dry-witted old scrubbers whose wit was simply part of them and flowed out as naturally as quandong seeds from the exhaust end of an emu in the quandong season. They may seem crude to some, but their hearts most certainly were not. In any case, authentic portrayal means you describe them as they were, warts and all. In doing this, my hope is that I will not offend.

The story follows our own early married life on the land on our two properties, Thrushton and Clonard, our move to St George, then to Sydney, then back to the land again in central and northern New South Wales. The book terminates as we leave our farm between Nimbin and Kyogle in mid-1950 and head for Brisbane to begin a new life in a foreign environment. But, of course, we were never city people. The bush was so deeply embedded and firmly established that it was soon back to the land again.

On looking back now, I realise what a chauvinistic, male-oriented life it was, yet in those days, nobody out in that country ever thought of questioning the distinct division between the sexes; it was accepted by both. Men had their work and women had theirs, and each was a quite separate entity. Men tended to stick together like a mob of kangaroos at the occasional mixed gatherings and, because there were so few women, they tended to be clumsy and uncomfortable in their presence — they generally buttoned up and became silent on-lookers. There were no women in the mustering camps, and only very rarely did the boss drover take his wife on the road with stock. A woman was rarely seen out in ringbarking, scrub cutting or fenc-ing camps either. It was the same, too, in the bullockies' camps while delving bore drains, tank sinking, horse breaking and yard building. The camp life was as rough as bags and so were the men. It certainly was no place for women and, although women were looked up to and respected far more then than they often are today, most men would have felt hemmed-in and restricted if women were in the camp. They probably would have rolled their swag and pulled out had someone introduced a woman into the men's domain.

It's hard to imagine life was so restrictive such a short time ago. Society is much more open and equitable now, with highly qualified young women participating with men in all branches of science, busi-ness and technology. They are equal partners with men in biological field studies, resource information gathering and similar modern ven-tures, often working from isolated bush camps with men in remote places. It's good to see their talents now being used and appreciated.

CHAPTER 1

Starting from Scratch

MY father, Wrixon Gasteen, had two brothers, Jack and Hugh, and two sisters, Elsie and May. Born in Brisbane in 1892, he was the eldest son of John Gasteen who was born in Navan, County Meath, Ireland, and sailed to Australia from Ireland with his family in 1863. Dad was educated at the Brisbane Grammar School and, on leaving school, took his first job as office clerk with Fenwicks' Brisbane Wool and Skin Store. Always more interested in the land than the city, he left Fenwicks after a short period and persuaded his father to help him become a jackaroo on one of the big western sheep runs owned by James Clark, an old family friend. At that time James Clark was probably better known as *The Pearl King* with a fleet of pearling luggers working Torres Strait and Northern Australian ports from their base at Thursday Island. In addition, he had extensive land holdings in Central Queensland in the name of Clark and Tait, Clark and Whiting and others.

James Clark also owned the Enniskillen Pastoral Company, a noted sheep station in the Blackall district to which he sent my father as first-year jackaroo in 1911. After about 18 months on the head station he was sent as overseer in charge of the stock camps on Castlevale, another of Clark's large properties adjoining Mantuan Downs at the junction of the Drummond and Great Dividing Ranges between Tambo and Springsure. When the 1914–18 World War broke out, Dad rode into Tambo, caught the Cobb & Co coach to Charleville and train to Brisbane. He joined the A.I.F. and was allocated to the 2nd Division's 5th Artillery Brigade Reinforcements. He was sent to Egypt, due to the withdrawal of the ANZAC forces from Gallipoli, then on to France. Badly gassed at the front near the Somme in 1918, he spent the first three months of 1919 in hospital before returning to Australia later in the year.

He and my mother (old Pappy and Doolie as we later called them) were engaged right through the war and were married early in 1920. Doolie was born in 1891 at Tent Hill, a small mining village near Tenterfield, where her father was secretary to the mining company. Shortly afterwards, the family moved to Brisbane for the children's education at better schools and after leaving school, she went into training and became a nursing aide at the Pyrmont Hospital. She also was a violinist with George Samson's Brisbane Concert Orchestra. This was one of Queensland's first orchestras, which eventually became today's Queensland Symphony Orchestra.

Dad was keen to get back on the land again, this time with a block of his own. He took up a 60,000-acre block of unoccupied rough mulga and poplar box country between Adavale and Quilpie, northwest of Cheepie. Within weeks of his discharge he was on the train with a reject tent from army stores, a swag, riding gear and pack saddle full of camping gear and tinned tucker, headed west on the weekly train to Cheepie. At that time there were only two blocks available for selection in Central and South West Queensland: the one north-west of Cheepie and a mulga block near Bollon. He probably selected the Cheepie block because it was closer to the country he had worked prior to joining up. He got a couple of horses from a droving plant camped on the stock route outside Quilpie and rode, leading the pack horse forty or fifty miles out to his block. Recent storms had brought up some low herbage that gave a green tinge to the country and filled a shallow hole in a small creek that drained the hard gibber ridge country comprising the bulk of the block. He would have been so excited at becoming a land holder with 60,000 acres of Queensland under his feet that he would barely have noticed how poor the country was, with gravelly breakaways and miles of scalded scrubby gibber plains. The few areas of better country were melon-holed black soil hollows with gidgee scrub so thick you couldn't drive a nail into it. He used to tell us that all he could think of was that the war was over, he was still alive and back on the land again. He lay in his swag at night and watched the stars and listened to the scrub cattle and brumbies coming into his waterhole to drink.

It was all too much and, within a few days, he started the long trip back to pick up Doolie to show her the wonders of the new block. But it was hot as blazes with dry scorching westerly winds from the day he left. By the time the return journey could be made from Brisbane, the herbage had withered and blown away, leaving the red gibbers shimmering on the surface like a furnace. They bought a bit more gear before heading off and rattled for days through drought-stricken country with water in the railway carriage water bottle almost too hot to drink. In those days Cheepie was a ramshackle collection of galvanised iron sheds that, from a distance in very hot weather, floated about in the mirage thirty feet above the scrubby plain.

They camped at the little railway siding while Dad scouted around for a bit and eventually bought an old cart horse and dray with patched-up bits of harness from some Afghans camped down the paddock behind the siding.

They started out before daylight next morning with their gear, as many four-gallon petrol tins of water as would fit in the dray and a couple of bags of chaff. The old mare, poor as a crow, knocked up every mile or so and had to be given a nosebag of chaff and some water out of the tins before she could be led off again. The occasional stock route bores were miles apart, generally the distance stock could travel in a full day. While this was going on, they shared the meagre shade from half-dead trees on the plain with the ants and flies. Dad reckoned Doolie had become pretty quiet and he tried to cheer her up by telling her about the beautiful waterhole they'd be camped on out at the block if the old cart mare could stay on her legs long enough to get there. After battling for days against the scorching westerlies and whirlwinds, with heat blistering up from the scrubby plains, they at last hit the creek and followed it down to the 'beautiful waterhole'. But by now, drought and hot summer temperatures had dried it back to a shallow puddle of red muddy water with a dead mare and foal half-submerged in the middle. Crows had picked their eyes out and their bodies were blown up as tight as a drum with white streaks of crow droppings all down their sides.

Things fell apart a bit after this disappointment, especially for Doolie, who had not been away from the city since arriving in Brisbane as a youngster. She realised she couldn't live away out in this dreadful heat in such depressing surroundings. Also, there was practically no shade as the old reject tent, erected at the hole on the previous trip, had been flogged to threads by battering westerlies and whirlwinds. They only had a couple of tins of water left and most of that had to go on the horse to get it to a bore they had passed about ten miles back before leaving the stock route. With tucker and spirits at a pretty low ebb and every day seeming hotter than the one before, they decided to head back to Brisbane. They forfeited the Cheepie block in favour of the mulga block near Bollon in the South West Queensland mulga lands, if it was still available. Reselling the turnout to the Afghans for half the amount they'd paid on the way out, they waited in the shade of the siding for the next train back to Brisbane a few days later.

The first explorer to traverse and describe a portion of the 22 million hectare mulga lands of South West Queensland was Sir Thomas Livingstone Mitchell (1792–1855). In 1845–46 he explored the headwaters of the Maranoa, Warrego, Belyando and parts of the Balonne rivers, charting large areas of previously unknown country. Journeying northwards from Sydney, he appears to have crossed the Barwon River below where Mungindi is now and struck the Balonne River about where Dirranbandi is today, following that river upstream to the present site of St George. At this point he found a flat rock bar extending the full width of the Balonne River which had dammed it into an excellent deep waterhole. The present town derives its name from the rock bar he named *St George's Bridge* when he crossed the river there on St George's Day, 12 April 1846.

Edmund Kennedy (1818–48) accompanied Mitchell on his 1845–46 expedition into Central Queensland and returned in 1847 to investigate the course of the Victoria River (later named Cooper Creek) that Mitchell had found. Kennedy hit the Warrego north of the present site of Charleville and followed that stream south to the present site of Cunnamulla, then south-east across the other Darling River tributaries, Nebine, Culgoa, Bierry to eventually cross the Bokhara about where Brewarrina is now situated.

Robert O'Hara Burke (1821–61) and William John Wills (1834–61) traversed the extreme western sector along the Bulloo River and across the Grey Range on their ill-fated expedition to the Gulf of Carpentaria. Becker, the artist of the expedition, was buried on the banks of the Bulloo River at Kooliatto Waterhole north of the present Bulloo Downs homestead.

William Landsborough (1825–86) was the only other explorer to enter the mulga lands. He led an expedition in 1861 to search for the missing Burke and Wills. Commencing at the Albert River near the present site of Burketown, Landsborough travelled south over the north-eastern rim of the Lake Eyre Basin. Continuing south, he struck the head of the Barcoo, which he named, and, keeping on a southerly course, crossed Nebine Creek and the Warrego River west of Bollon, thence south along these streams to the Darling and on to Menindee in New South Wales.

Soon after the separation of Queensland from New South Wales in 1859, the first settlers began fanning out along the tracks of the explorers. In slow stages, their wagons and stock spread across the trackless arid plains in search of good grazing land. Water was their preoccupation and the further they went, the scarcer it became; just occasional small holes in otherwise dry creeks. The few lakes and swamps encountered amounted to little more than shallow dints on the featureless plains, short-lived and generally brackish or salt by the end of each dry season. Only those who had experienced the limitations imposed by a lack of water could be expected to understand the constant difficulties this contributed to already trying conditions. Governments were soon under siege to provide artificial water to hasten closer settlement and heavier rates of stocking. This led to the tapping of the Great Artesian Basin in the mid-1880s. By the early 1900s, artesian water had transformed much of the inland and, together with sub-artesian (non-flowing) bores, earth tanks and hundreds of miles of bore drains, had begun converting the dry waterless plains into some of the best watered regions of the State. It became the era of giant windmills towering above deep sub-artesian bores sunk at intervals along major stock routes to allow the movement of travelling stock. But development of the dry flat interior of the Australian continent was slow and arduous. Hot summer temperatures, evaporation and seepage soon whittled away the meagre surface waters that were always hard to find. In these days of comparative comfort, there is little appreciation of the degree to which distance, loneliness and lack of communication changed the lives of the pioneers as they battled distance, lack of water, recurring droughts and rock-bottom stock markets.

Back in Brisbane again, Dad found the Bollon block (later Thrushton) was still open for selection. It seemed nobody wanted it. As it was the only other block and couldn't possibly be worse than the Cheepie/Adavale block, he took it up in partnership with his younger brother Hugh, who was still at school, their father providing most of the money in the initial stages. As pressure for new grazing lands increased, large company-owned runs were being cut up and reallocated to meet this need. Hence Cypress Downs in the St George district in Queensland resulted from the 1890 subdivision of about 1,000 square miles of country in the name of Forest Downs Holding, first taken up in the early 1860s. As the country was surveyed into portions, each block was given a name or a number, a prescribed accumulation of adjoining blocks forming a pastoral holding. Thus the Thrushton and adjoining blocks resulted from the 1914 subdivision of Cypress Downs, which itself had been a subdivision and re-juggling of blocks from the original Forest Downs Holding.

Leaving Doolie at home this time, Dad got his gear together and went by train to Mitchell. Rather than hang around waiting for the coach to Bollon, he bought a buggy and some horses from a place down the river and headed south-west along the Bollon road. He camped at Homeboin, a big cattle run joining the new blocks and waited a few days for the Crown Land Ranger to arrive with his horse and sulky to help find the boundary corner pegs and finalise occupation. The middle of Dad's block was about thirty miles from the Homeboin homestead with nothing on it but mulga scrub, spinifex and dingos — no hut, no fences, no tracks and not a drop of permanent water on the entire 42,000 acres. Dad later named the place Thrushton after the old family home of that name built on a hill in the Brisbane suburb of Coorparoo.

Homeboin and its Bindibango out-station, with an area of several hundred thousand acres, was a large run for that region. The homestead complex was like a small township. The big old rambling homestead was separated from kitchen, office and station store and the bookkeeper's, jackaroos' and cook's quarters, by a long cypress pine walkway covered all the way along by creepers. Station hands, stockmen, jackaroos, bookkeeper, gardener and cook were under the direction of the manager, while an overseer and head stockman who lived in the homestead when not camped out on the run, were in charge of station work and ran the stock camps. There was a fleet of horse-drawn vehicles and the station ran a mob of brood mares from which the working horses were bred and broken in before being sent out to the stock camps to be bumped into shape by the ringers working the cattle. The bookkeeper also ran the station store which was stocked with common bush groceries and tinned food, dog traps, dog chains, poison, hobbles, ropes, saddlery and harness.

Jack Turner was manager and knew the Thrushton blocks well from all the scrub cattle mustering he'd done in that country. Company station managers those days sometimes ran a few of their own cattle and horses on the place they were managing. Jack, being a bit of a rogue and a good stockman with an eye for a quality yearling, was always on the lookout for a good style of filly coming through the yards at branding time. When one of these was cut out of the horses coming through the yards, he'd drawl: 'By ghost, that's old Maisie's foal. Yer cin always pick 'er foals a mile off. Always throws a good stamp of a foal does old Maisie.'

And with that, he'd grab his brand from Charcoal, the Aborigine over at the fire keeping the brands hot, and slap it on her. Homeboin stockmen always claimed that Jack's 'old Maisie' must have been 'a terrible good breeder' because she always had five or six foals a year!

Jack took Dad several miles north of the Thrushton blocks to an out-station bark hut on the bank of a small waterhole in Neabul Creek, known locally as Pumpkin Bed Hole. It was only about 100 yards long by 30 or 40 feet wide and local blacks and stockmen claimed it had rarely gone dry. The name probably indicates that some old fossicker had grown pumpkins there. One of the first things bushmen did, if they were camped for any length of time somewhere, was plant watermelon and pumpkin seeds. It gave them some rare variety to go with their usual salt meat, damper and black tea. The hut had probably been built about 1860 and bullock teams had scooped up a bank to hold water in a nearby watercourse beside the creek lower down. The bark roof was falling in and the hut was badly knocked about by white ants. In earlier times it had been in constant use by musterers, drovers and bullockies working that end of the run but, with labour shortages during the war, had been neglected and only used on odd occasions since.

Before subdivision for closer settlement during 1914 (the subdivisional survey plans were gazetted in 1915), Cypress Downs was also a big run of about 500 square miles. The original cypress pine and bark homestead was at Cypress Tank, a hole sunk in Cypress Watercourse with bullocks, which later became a watering reserve at the junction of three stock routes about thirty miles east of Thrushton. Pumpkin Bed Hole was an excellent camp site on the only good water for miles around, kept cool by overhanging river red gums while cypress pines and box trees lined the sandy levees higher up. Dad made his permanent camp at this shady watering spot until an artesian bore was sunk a few years later. A new bark hut and horse yards were built after patching up the little horse-paddock fence which had enclosed the original out-station hut. He started work on the Thrushton blocks, carting stores, tools and other essential bits and pieces from Homeboin in a dray he bought from the station.

Though surveyors had pegged out the boundaries the previous year, the line was already getting hard to find as regrowth reduced visibility and pegs fell over. As fencing was not due to start for several months, Dad's first job was blazing a thirty-mile line around the Thrushton boundary along the few remaining surveyor's pegs that hadn't fallen over. This would save time finding the pegged line the following year when the fencing gangs arrived. He also surveyed a north–south line for ten miles, separating the two blocks as well. As new blocks were taken up, the Government set up trusts and a plain-wire and netting dump at the FortyMile stock watering reserve and former Cobb & Co coach change on the Cunnamulla Road midway between St George and Bollon. New settlers carted their wire and netting from this dump to dog-proof the boundaries of each new run as quickly as possible so the dingos could be cleaned out. Fences were to be six feet high, with six plain wires to which rabbit netting was attached on the bottom half and dog netting on the top half. Contract fencing gangs began turning up in 1920, shortly after the teams unloaded at the central wire dump near the site Dad had chosen for the Thrushton homestead.

The red-soil mulga plains in dry conditions present little to excite the imagination. Before clearing and pasture improvement, it was comprised of reds, browns and drab greys in monotonous proportions typifying the country in average seasons. But 1919 and 1920

were above-average seasons with good rain in the South West; it was
nature's lush green garden now. Dad found the dry scrubby plains of
a few months earlier had been transformed into a waving patchwork
of green grass and succulent herbage below a silver-grey canopy of
mulga scrub with emergent shiny-leaved poplar box, grey and white
stemmed forest gum trees and currajong. While the moisture lasted,
it was a land of beauty, with birds singing, bees humming and native
animals everywhere. Water was lying in shallow gilgais surrounded
by sheets of white paper daisies. Dotted about the sandy spinifex and
heath country in slightly higher park-like settings, were angophoras
(rough-barked apple), silver-leaved ironbarks and tall stately cypress
pines rising above their surroundings like dark green church spires.
Spinifex country has a perfume all its own. The multitude of flowering turkeybush shrubs heavily laden with great clumps of rich
yellow buttercup flowers and heath-lands of every imaginable
colour were in full bloom issuing forth a distinctive, heavily laden,
sweet-scented atmosphere which becomes part of you and is never
forgotten. Even now, a lifetime later, one sniff on the evening breeze
brings back childhood memories in a flash. The deep loamy red soils
of this 'soft' mulga country also hosted masses of bluebells, corn-
flowers and yellow everlasting daisies. The beautiful sheeny-pink
parakeelya also was a distinctive splash of colour in amongst patches
of other beautiful ground-hugging flowering plants. Grey-green
nardoo and small yellow waterlilies floated among clumps of silvery
rushes, which rose from sheets of white paper-daisies throughout
the flat sandalwood country and the small sandalwood trees were
festooned with creamy-white bells. There were large spreading
oval-crowned wilga trees that drooped right to the ground, too,
with quandong trees laden with their distinctive bright red fruit
scattered here and there to complete a most pleasing picture. A
carpet of herbage, soft pink daisies, the delicate little dark green
mulga ferns and moss blanketed the lower country after good spring
rains.

Knowing Doolie would be in raptures over the wildflowers, he met her in Mitchell in the buggy when this could be arranged to show off the country soon to become her new home.

Doolie returned to Brisbane to await their marriage later in the year and men started turning up with swags and gear to start building horse and cattle yards, holding paddocks and clearing tracks to various parts of the run. This work well in hand, Dad returned to Brisbane and bought six month's supply of stores, along with several tons of plain fencing wire for internal subdivisions. The wire and netting at the FortyMile dump was government material for boundary fences only. Other items were tents, flies, ropes, axes, crosscut saws and pitsaws, fencing tools, camp ovens and a heap of other essential gear needed to start developing the new run. He arranged for all this stuff to be off-loaded at Mitchell by the agents, who arranged for a wagon to cart the load out to Homeboin, the central depot for wagons coming down from Mitchell and then on to Thrushton.

Meanwhile, Doolie had been busy getting a glory box together, some cooking gear, a sewing machine and material plus a few items of furniture and other bits and pieces. There was no way of getting anything you'd forgotten once you were out in that country. Heavy rain in the South West created difficulties on the boggy roads, which meant the teams could sometimes take weeks to come down from Mitchell. The young couple were married in Brisbane and, after a short honeymoon at Noosa, boarded the train for Mitchell to collect the horses and buggy and start out for Thrushton. The wagon carrying their household supplies, they learned, had only left a couple of days before and was bogged a few miles out of town. There'd been a lot of rain on the Bollon road so tons of off-loaded produce was strewn about on each side of the stranded wagons. Boxes of tea, bags of flour and sugar and a few other perishables were covered by tarps, but the rest lay about in the mud. Dad's unloaded wagon had been dragged several miles past the worst areas of bog where it was reloaded by drays that ferried back and forth with light loads. Teams and horse-drawn vehicles using the Mitchell to Bollon road every week cut the road to pieces after heavy rain. When wagons bogged and bullocks knocked up, the men often camped on top of the load until the rain cleared and roads dried out, often for a week at a time in a wet season. If they were a long way out of town and ran out of tucker, they started opening your stores — it was nothing to find half-empty boxes of tinned stuff and dried fruit with the lids nailed back on.

Waiting in Mitchell for the weather to clear, Dad and Doolie made friends with people from other properties in the district also held up in town. Among these were the Loughnans from Abbieglassie, a cattle run about halfway between Mitchell and Bollon, which became Dad and Doolie's main camp on that trip. The weather fined up, but they hadn't got far before more rain set in and they were holed up at Abbieglassie for a week or so waiting for creeks to go down, and again at Homeboin because Wallam Creek was too deep to cross. Over the creek at last with the small amount of gear they could carry in the light buggy, they headed for Thrushton but were again blocked by a big flood in Neabul Creek, forcing them to camp for several more days. The country was so waterlogged that the horses bogged before they even reached the creek and the thin buggy wheels sank halfway to the axles. It was one of their worst trips. As soon as the country dried out, it was back to Homeboin in the dray for more stores. The Homeboin people were good neighbours, helping all they could. They offered to ride over with word when the wagon arrived, which turned out to be many weeks later.

Doolie returned to Brisbane briefly for the birth of their first child Keith in December 1920. On one of their routine trips to Homeboin shortly afterwards — generally in the dray once every month or six weeks — to replenish stores and collect mail, they had a bad accident. Keith was only a couple of months old. Because there was only a light load to bring back, they took the buggy to make the trip more comfortable. While still inside the Thrushton boundary, the swingle-bar broke and the loose chain tangled round one of the young horse's legs. The horses took fright and bolted, one of the buggy wheels hitting a tree and capsizing the whole outfit. Dad and Keith were thrown clear, Keith landing on a pillow, but Doolie was trapped underneath with the frame of the buggy across her back, badly damaging a vertebra. Dad galloped on one of the horses, with Keith on the pummel in front, to where some of the men were fencing several miles away to get help. As the pole was broken beyond repair, they set up a fibre mattress on the dray and took Doolie the twenty-odd miles to Homeboin — must have been a dreadful trip. They changed over to a Homeboin buggy, made comfortable as possible, for the long haul towards Mitchell. They got word to the Loughnans at Abbieglassie who met them halfway along the road where they had camped and took them the rest of the way to the train in one of the few early cars in the district at that time.

Being a former nurse at Pyrmont Hospital, this was where Doolie was admitted. Thereafter she was always troubled by a bad back. While in Brisbane waiting for her recovery and having seen the advantages of a motor car in those remote areas, Dad bought a second-hand 1917 model single-seater Renault. It was very small but the only thing he could afford. Its clearance was so low it was always getting hooked up on stumps and logs and the engine overheated during summer, boiling the petrol out of the carburettor and fuel lines. It might have been alright poking around the streets of Paris, but it was useless in that country and spent most of its short life bailed up somewhere along the track, to be dragged back to the hut by a draughthorse.

The small hut, with its loose sandy floor covered by bags, was so cramped for space that most of the gear had to be stored outside under a fly. A house could not be built on the waterless Thrushton blocks until the promised artesian bore was sunk. This could take a long time, so cypress pine logs were cut and pit-sawn into slabs to build a twelve by ten addition to one side of the bark hut. This gave them more room and a bit of comfort until the permanent move to Thrushton. In 1921 the steam-driven boring plant and wagon loaded with bore casing, coils of heavy wire rope, stores, camping gear and men turned up to start sinking the Wierbolla bore, accompanied a bit

later by the survey gangs and bullock teams. As the surveyors pegged
out the contour lines the various drains were to follow, the bullockies began slowly following the pegged line with mouldboard plough
and delver.

The daunting business of starting from scratch with few tools and
no materials with which to build a house was partly overcome when
Dad bought the old Dunkeld cypress pine and galvanised iron pub.
Dunkeld was a small settlement and Cobb & Co coach change on
the Mitchell to St George road. As the old pub had been abandoned
and was up for sale for removal, he arranged finance through his
Brisbane agents, the Australian Estates, and bought it. The next job
was to pull it down and have a couple of wagons cart the heavy load
to the house site on Thrushton. Being old brittle cypress pine, many
of the boards split and broke as a bush carpenter and his couple of
offsiders flogged the old building apart for loading on the wagons.
The teams eventually headed off, but within a few days heavy rain set
in and the wagons were abandoned where they bogged. The bullocks
were turned loose until the weather fined up and the country dried
out. They loaded and unloaded from one bog to the next in the following weeks. Dad said nobody ever prayed harder for a drought.
Much of the timber was useless by the time it arrived, but at least the
iron and most of the uprights, rafters and floor joists were sound.
With the teams unyoked and the wagons unloaded on site, the hunt
began for trees straight enough to cut for house posts (three feet in
the ground and seven feet out). They were snigged through the scrub
to the house site with the draughthorses or bullocks.

The pitsaw was used to cut local cypress pine to replace broken
boards. Pitsawing amounted to digging a large trench about six feet
deep, three feet wide and six feet long, across each end of which was
sunk a log, adzed at the top to make it flat and level. The log to be
cut was rolled on top and wedged so it couldn't move. One man
stood on top of the log with one end of the seven-foot long pitsaw
and the other got down the hole underneath with the other end. It
was a terrible job for the bloke down below, especially in hot weather

with no ventilation and half-suffocated in sawdust and sweat all day as well.

While the house was being built with what was left of the old pub, Dad and Doolie sometimes camped at the site during the week to avoid riding back and forth to the hut each day. Water had to be carted from Pumpkin Bed Hole almost every week during hot summer weather to water the horses and fencing camps. Facing the lack of water on Thrushton was one thing, doing something about it, to enable fencing and ringbarking gangs to continue work, was another. But Dad got round the problem by getting a couple of ship's tanks from somewhere. One was mounted on a heavy dray so water could be carted from Pumpkin Bed Hole to the fencing camps through miles of scrub and spinifex. The other tank was left at the main camp where they'd dug a hole four or five feet deep with one sloping side, down which the dray was backed for unloading. The tank, full of water, was levered off the dray on skids and replaced by the empty tank that was carted back to Pumpkin Bed to be refilled. The dray and heavy riveted square ship's tank was lowered down the bank on a corduroy of logs into the waterhole and filled by a small hand pump and buckets, then snigged back up the bank by a Spanish windlass. This was the bushman's winch — a long pole used to hand-wind a wire rope round a post or tree. One end was tied to a tree, the other to the dray. The rope was shortened as it was wound round the post or tree, dragging the dray very slowly to the top. As the number of men and horses at the camps increased and the hotter the weather became, the more often the tank had to be dragged back to the creek for a refill, often at night, if there was a good moon.

The following year, there was great jubilation when the boring plant struck a strong flow of artesian water. As some of the drains close to the bore had already been constructed, it wasn't long before water could be turned into them. In mid-1922, just before the house was finished, Doolie went back to Brisbane and waited until I was born in June. With two children in the family now and the old Renault so small and unreliable, Dad traded it in Mitchell as part-payment on a second-hand 1919 Model T Ford. So Doolie and I, the new baby, came home in style.

Dad bought several hundred head of cows with calves at foot from Mona and Homeboin to stock the place. After the dingos were cleaned out, a woolshed was built along with sheep yards and small holding paddocks in preparation for the change-over from cattle to sheep. Frank, the youngest member of the family, was born at the end of 1923, by which time all the boundary fencing and some of the internal subdivisions had been completed. The house, when finished, was seven feet off the ground with three bedrooms, a kitchen, lounge-dining room and verandah on two sides in the top half and two galvanised iron rooms, a gauzed-in meat house, wash bench and storeroom underneath. My parents having now shifted over to the new Thrushton house, the hut was no longer needed. When Dick Taylor left Isis Downs and bought the adjoining Rutherglen blocks from Sandy Reid in 1924, the hut was loaded on a bullock wagon and became the kitchen of the rough old Rutherglen bush home-stead built with cypress pine slabs and round-backs.

Wierbolla bore was sunk in 1921 on adjoining Rutherglen (at the northern end of Thrushton). Good artesian water pressure was struck at 3,338 feet with a flow volume of 1.169 million gallons a day that was estimated to run around 70 miles of bore drain.

About 15 miles south of Wierbolla bore is the Randwick bore on adjoining Mourilyan (at the southern end of Thrushton). It was sunk in 1900 to a depth of 2,778 feet and flowed 2 million gallons a day which ran about 100 miles of drain. The water in both these bores was of excellent quality.

By the early 1930s, some drains began drying back miles each summer, which meant pulling water during high-evaporation summer months. Before pulling, we shovelled out all the mud and weed, and with one foot on each side of the drain, threw the mud and damp sand up over the bank. Bent double all day in the heat of summer, this was a back-breaking job. Pulling water was done by cutting the leafy top out of box trees and tying them in a big bundle a mile or so past the point where water had dried back to. The bundle was then rolled into the drain and dragged along very slowly with the car. (No tractors out there in those days.) With the drain full of water from bank to bank, we'd get about half a mile with each pull, then go back for another load and start again. The idea was to get the soil wet as far along as possible and leave as much water lying along the drain as well after pulling each day, so that water from further up would hopefully follow along in the cool of evening and at night. It all proved a waste of time. But nobody had any money through those dreadful drought years during the Depression when we cut mulga scrub from daylight till dark every day for years. You just struggled to survive and keep a few head of breeding stock alive at the same time. There was no money for sinking tanks until later. As the situation continued to deteriorate, we had to sink tanks on some drains and hope we could get enough water into them during winter months to keep stock going through the next summer.

Though the deepest artesian bores exceed 6,000 feet, most averaged between 2,500 and 3,500 feet where flows of more than a million gallons a day were common. Depth, flow and water quality varied considerably from district to district and from bore to bore. As holdings were large, each bore could rarely water more than a couple of runs. The man at the end of the longest drain had a mere trickle if all went well, which it rarely did, and he had to rely on those closer to the bore head to keep the water flowing because it often had to run 80 or 100 miles of drain. As water was crucial to survival, bore drain maintenance meant constant riding to check for blockages as storms and whirlwinds blew branches, leaves and dead grass into the drains and weak stock often bogged or fell in when drinking. This could hold water back until it broke over a low part in the bank and formed swamps. Blockages could be anywhere along thirty or forty or more miles of drain and, if not found and repaired quickly enough, the bloke at the end of the drain was in trouble. Water dried back for miles and in very hot weather stock could soon start dying if there were no tanks, and often there weren't, to augment the artesian supply.

Construction of bore drains involved ploughing twin parallel trenches along the surveyor's pegged line, which followed the contours of the land where possible. The channels were opened up by the man steering the long-handled mouldboard plough dragged behind a team of bullocks and later deepened by a delver dragged in the same way until the drain was about eighteen inches to two feet deep (depending on soil type) and properly formed. Though water travelled in drains at a fast walking pace close the to bore head, its pace gradually tapered off with increasing distance. Soakage was enormous, especially in the softer sandy loam country where patches of currajong had previously died or had been cut out to feed stock. Here, the water came to a standstill, often for a week at a time as it siphoned out along the old rotting pithy roots and soaked into the porous sandy loam soil. It was impossible to ride a horse anywhere near these places without bogging to the guts. In the worst areas, where soakage wouldn't take up, the bullockies called it mud-larkin' an' puddlin'. The bullocks were yoked in pairs and driven round, bogged to the guts until the whole area was a squelching mess and all the roots were broken up and the water slowly moved on to the next bad patch. A couple of men with shovels followed the water when it got a go on in the harder country, cleaning out debris and building up banks in low places so water wouldn't break over and form swamps in sandalwood hollows and run-on depressions. These areas of lower country were always pegged round and avoided where possible by the surveyors. Where this wasn't possible, drains were often a problem for many years.

Dad planted melon and pumpkin seeds in the soak of the new drains as the water moved on. The prolific growth of vines in the new damp soils soon draped nearby small mulga trees and shrubs with melons and pumpkins so large the vines couldn't hold their weight, many falling to the ground around the trees and rotting before they were found. We had an old photograph of a huge watermelon three-quarters the width of the old Model T Ford with the cook sitting on top. The meagre nutrients plus the compacting effect of bore water on these infertile phosphorous- and nitrogen-deficient acid soils meant that initial prolific growth was never repeated. After a few years, the only thing that ever grew along the drains, immediately above the water line, was couch grass. Drains had to be delved twice a year to remove mud, weed and debris. In the 1920s and 1930s this was contract work with bullocks. Now it's all tractor work and very much quicker. Water was turned off at the bore head a couple of days before to reduce water level in the drains while delving was in progress. A team of about twenty or more bullocks yoked in pairs, one pair on each side of the drain, pulled the heavy delver. It was shaped like the bow of a boat and kept low in the drain by a heavy log (the tail) with two heavy steel-plated, twelve inch by two inch, hardwood wings attached. These forced the mud and debris outward along the banks of the drain as the delver was dragged along.

Sub-artesian (non-flowing bores) were a great benefit and were widely used in country where sub-artesian waters were shallow enough for pumps to extract the water (perhaps 400 to 650 feet). Sub-artesian bores with aquifers shallow enough to be tapped into by giant windmills were sunk at strategic intervals along the inland stock routes, particularly in Central Queensland and parts of the far South West. This allowed stock movement in all seasons and saved millions of pounds sinking artesian (free-flow bores), because many artesian bores north-west of Birdsville and along the fringe of the Simpson Desert and in parts of Central Queensland ranged in depth from 5,000 feet to 6,000 feet deep and water was often fairly saline. As the number of artesian (free-flowing) bores increased, bore flows began to diminish and divisors needed periodic adjustment by Water Resources engineers in accordance with the changing flow rate. For many years bores were not regulated to compensate for variations of evaporation and seepage between cold winter and hot summer months. This accounted for enormous waste of water during winter when evaporation and seepage were low. Lakes formed at the end of many bore drains as excess water ran to waste.

Recent investigations have shown that up to 95% of bore water is lost in evaporation and seepage at ground level, and that only 3% to 5% or less is actually used by domestic stock and other animals. The enormous waste and diminishing flows were recognised before 1930, but little was done until hundreds of bores ceased flowing. Of course, we didn't have all these figures at our fingertips away back then.

Of the 4,730 free-flowing artesian bores tapping the 1.7 million square kilometre Great Artesian Basin, more than 1,600 have now ceased flowing while the flow volume of the rest has been substantially reduced — to a mere trickle in some districts.

It was the introduction of artesian water to the arid inland that allowed closer settlement to progress. Nor did the competition for this vital resource diminish as bore drains progressively laced the arid plains like spider's webs. The history of early settlement abounds with fights over water. 'Water duffers', rogues that pinched some other bloke's water, used all kinds of cunning devices. We pinched it from the Aborigines, drovers and their mobs pinched it from squatters, and selectors pinched it from their neighbours. It was easiest in bore drain country where divisors spanned the main drain at intervals, splitting it into subsidiaries. The divisor was a five foot by two foot length of three-eights of an inch iron plate with a slot cut in the middle, through which flowed the amount of water estimated by the Water Resources engineer to service each respective drain. Always short of water at the end of a drain, the odd rogue selector had a cunning ruse to help overcome the shortage. He'd ride for miles on a moonlit night to the divisors in the neighbour's property, tie the horse to a tree well away from the drain and remove his boots to leave no tracks as he walked the remaining distance to the divisors up the centre of the drain. He carried with him a narrow length of glass between two sheets of bark rolled in a chaff bag which protected it during the midnight ride. The glass was placed across the neighbour's divisor plate just high enough for the stolen water to run his drain those extra few miles into another paddock. The glass, hard to see when riding past to check, would generally be found weeks later when the neighbour's drain unaccountably dried back. When the fault was discovered and the oaths subsided, the neighbour promptly swapped the glass over to the other cove's divisor to give him a taste of the same medicine. The battle raged back and forth until at last the trap was set and the offender beat a hasty retreat through the scrub with a posterior a bit lopsided with shotgun pellets. Other methods included the odd stick, branch or hard old cow pat across the divisor to collect floating leaves that blocked some of the flow yet looked a natural event. There was never any shortage of ideas.

After a few years, small fish began to appear in the drains. At first they were thought to have come up with the hot bore water. How else could they get there? It was later discovered that fish eggs were brought in on ducks' feet from waterholes in some distant creek and deposited in the bore water as they swam along the drain. As kids, we spent a lot of our spare time catching these tiny fish with a bent pin on a length of string or strong cotton twist with a rolled–up piece of dough or meat on the end. They didn't seem too fussy what they ate — they'd have a go at pretty well anything. They were a greenish-silver colour, growing on average from three to four inches, occasionally up to six or seven. Because they were full of tiny bones, Mum minced them up and made fish fritters out of them. Dad sent some samples to the Brisbane Museum for identification. I have forgotten their scientific name, but their common one was Spangled Grunters. Black ducks and wood ducks lived on the drains, and in odd gilgais too, after heavy rain. We were often startled in the middle of the night by a duck crashing into the tin roof of the house. They made a good meal next day. On moonlit nights, ducks sometimes mistook the shining galvanised iron roof of the house for a sheet of water and plummeted down to land on it.

Large numbers of yabbies also began appearing in the late 1920s and started boring holes in the banks of drains and riddling the ground around culverts and divisor plates. Enormous amounts of water soaked out through the holes, bogging up surrounding areas as it soaked into the soft soil and drying back drains for miles. By the early 1930s, every available man was out there with a shovel trying to fill in thousands of holes along miles of drains. There were so many it was all a waste of time. Scientists from the CSIRO and engineers from the Water Resources Branch came out, stirred into action by the sheer bulk of letters from landholders demanding something done before the hot summer weather started. The problem seemed to subside after some years. Though yabbies are still there, they aren't the major threat they were before the ground became so hard from the chemical effects of bore water that yabbies found difficulty burrowing far outside the banks. Recently, feral pigs have begun to root yabbies out of their holes to eat them. Although they are keeping the yabbies in check, the feral pigs have increased the damage to bore drains, with enormous loss of water.

Two shallow lakes adjacent to Randwick bore, into which water had been turned until the drains were completed, held water for a large part of each year. As water close to the bore head was too hot to drink, mobs of brumbies watered at these nearby swamps and fed out over the country for years before subdivision and settlement of the Cypress Downs blocks. When heavy rain filled gilgais on Thrushton in 1921 and 1922, brumbies and dingos watered at these gilgais instead of the Randwick swamps and became trapped in the Thrushton blocks when the netting boundary was closed at completion of fencing. Years later, when shifting stock from Clonard to Thrushton for scrub-cutting, the Randwick swamps had the only feed for miles around so they became one of our main camp sites. (There was no mulga on Clonard, but the 42,000 acre Thrushton mulga blocks had miles of mulga that we cut for alternative top feed all through those years of drought.)

It was a dreadful job on cold frosty mornings wading knee deep in mud and icy water to hunt hobbled horses out of the swamp where they fed on reeds and swamp grass, and sheer agony trying to unbuckle hard, mud-slimy leather hobble straps with half-frozen purple fingers.

In the 1920s, odd motor vehicles gradually began appearing in western towns, eventually taking over from the horse and bullock transport. But it was back again to the more reliable though much slower bullock teams and horse-drawn coaches during occasional long spells of wet weather when the old lorries couldn't handle the mud and bogs. The first motor lorry to compete with the horse-drawn coaches on the mail run between Bollon and Mitchell was about 1920 or 1921. Soon after, solid-tyred motor lorries of this type started carting produce and materials from rail depots to main centres not serviced by rail, thence to outlying settlements and cattle runs.

At that time, some shires were paying a guinea a scalp for brumbies, but with so many being claimed, the bounty soon dropped to ten shillings, then to five along with wedge-tailed eagles and foxes, and then to nothing. Dingo scalps were always worth money because they killed sheep and young calves and, as sheep gradually took over from cattle, everyone was trying to poison or trap all remaining dingos as a matter of urgency. Before the bounty could be claimed on brumbies in some shires the two ears and tail had to be dropped off as evidence at the shire office or police station. This was later reduced to just the two ears and scalp. A young cousin from Brisbane on school holidays always claimed the first time he'd seen me was walking home along a pad with a .22 rifle over one shoulder and a brumby's tail over the other. The mane and ears were at the end of a long strip of hide trailing along in the dust behind. I'd have been about eight or nine at the time.

Brumbies were a constant problem for many years because stallions broke down fences and crippled working stock horses in fights and damaged bore drains. There were hundreds of wild horses in that country which were only worth a few bob a head because there were so many of them. During wars, when big droving plants everywhere were abandoned and their mob of horses were turned loose as drovers and ringers joined up, many never to return, hundreds of horses roamed the country and bred up with the cattle station mobs to run wild wherever they found water. In 1923, a professional shooter named Daryl Smythe and a couple of his mates from around Dirranbandi cleaned up most of the big mobs of brumbies on Mona Station, which adjoined Cypress Downs before subdivision of the Thrushton blocks. The weather was pretty dry and hot and the mobs had eaten out large areas of country all round the Randwick bore and swamps and tore station horses about in fights. The bore also was a major cattle camp where the station had a big set of yards for handling cattle at that end of the run. The drain between Mona boundary and Randwick bore and around the swamps was fenced off, the brumbies hanging around the fenced-off water half perished from thirst. With help from the station stockmen, the mobs were worked into a dog-netting boundary corner a few miles from the bore. The men positioned themselves at the butts of trees and shot the lot. For thirty or forty years after, the surrounding country was still littered with white bleached bones like a vast cemetery.

Nobody worried much about the small mobs of brumbies left on Thrushton until some of the work horses had been run into corners and torn about by stallions, then the men went out and shot some. There were a few fair horses among them, but most were pretty plain types that just kept on breeding up. I later broke in some, but eventually shot the rest to get them out of the way.

There was an old grave not far from the bore with a bit of crumpled rabbit netting round it. I often wondered who it was as I looked down from the horse when riding past. I found out later that in 1923 a cattle buyer had come out in his sulky to inspect a mob of Mona cattle being held at the bore. As he walked over towards the mob, he fell over dead from a heart attack. The weather was very hot and there was nobody within miles anyhow, so they just dug a shallow hole and put the poor old bloke in, covered the grave and ran a bit of rabbit netting round the hole.

In 1925, Dad's younger brother Hugh, who had left Queensland University in 1918 to enlist in the Australian Imperial Force, came out to take over his section of Thrushton. The property was worked as a single unit comprising two blocks of roughly equivalent size in the name of W & H Gasteen. For the first year or so, he lived in the Thrushton house with Dad and Doolie, along with a couple of jacka-roos and a cook. Two or three station hands, who were housed in a tin shed down the paddock a bit, also had their meals at the home-stead. When Hugh was married in 1926, a new homestead was built on his block about four miles from the Thrushton house. By this time, a branch line from the St George/Bollon telephone line had got out as far as Oaklands, a property about twenty miles to the east, and Homeboin had been linked up with the St George-Bollon-Cunnamulla line. Roads gradually improved too as motor cars and lorries began to appear more frequently. Improved mobility and com-munication was very welcome, especially in times of trouble.

CHAPTER 2

Wild Bush Kids

B<small>Y</small> 1925, prickly pear (*Opuntia stricta*) had taken over millions of acres of farming and grazing land in the 20 to 30 inch (508 to 762 mm) rainfall belt in Queensland and north-west New South Wales. It became Australia's most potentially dangerous introduced pest species bordering on a national disaster. Prickly pear was introduced into Australia from South America by Governor Phillip as host for the cochineal insect, the cultivation of which he hoped would yield the red dye for his soldiers' uniforms. Less favourable soils and climatic conditions in the south discouraged the plant's growth to pest proportions. It wasn't until squatters brought it to northern New South Wales around the 1820s and later to Queensland about 1880 as a possible cheap hedge for enclosing sheep in small paddocks that the trouble started. In these localities, prickly pear seemed to find its perfect niche and exploded in plague proportions both north and south of the border. It was firmly entrenched and spreading throughout large areas in the Burnett by 1912 and had become a worry to farmers in many areas of the Darling Downs and other parts of southern Queensland. With most of the workforce away at the war, prickly pear went wild and spread rapidly everywhere in the heavier soils along the river flats and gilgaied belah and brigalow country. It wasn't long before alarming reports from pastoralists and local authorities began alerting people to the potential catastrophe facing land-holders by the rapid encroachment of pear thickets on some of our best agricultural country.

Pear-cutters, a dozen or so men to a gang, established camps every few miles in the worst affected areas to cut the pear and stack it up for burning. Later, horses with old motor tyres tied round to protect them from the pear thorns were used to drag a cart or dray (poison cart) about through the dense pear. A drum of liquid arsenic was anchored on top of the cart from which it was fed via a rubber hose to a long-handled atomiser gun. When speared into the base of the pear plant, a grooved bayonet attached to the end of the gun delivered pressurised poison to the area immediately above the root system. The pressurised arsenic was injected by squeezing a lever attached to the handle, an ordinary tyre pump being used to maintain a constant pressure in the drum. It was dreadful stuff to use and dangerous too. The old type hoses with inside and outside rubber coatings soon perished and cracked as the hose was dragged about in the pear. The leaking contents saturated trouser legs and shirt sleeves and got down into boots as well, while men fought their way through the pear trying to control the horse. Toe and finger nails dropped off after building up with pus from underneath as infection took over from the poison. Many of the bad cases were a horrible sight, some of the men treating the poison with contempt as if it was just water until it was too late.

But they were wild and woolly mobs from all accounts when they hit the local towns on weekends after collecting their cheque. I was talking to an old retired police sergeant one time about the pear days and how rough things were in some of those western towns on a Saturday night. He was sent out to Thallon in 1924 as a raw young police constable from Brisbane to keep the peace in this one-horse town near the end of the railway line while the sergeant was away on holidays. Along the river country in the Thallon, Nindigully, St George and western Darling Downs districts at that time were among the worst areas of pear infestation and large gangs of men were camped up and down the Balonne, Moonie and Macintyre Rivers west of Goondiwindi cutting and poisoning.

The old sergeant told me —

The Thallon police sergeant gave me a run-down on everything and told me not to go throwing my weight around or getting about by myself after dark on a Saturday night. 'Keep away from that wild mob of pear poisoners when they come into town or you'll be in trouble!' he warned. With that bit of parting wisdom he climbed into the guard's van of the old steam train that pulled up there once or twice a week before heading on its slow haul back to Brisbane, stopping at every bit of a town and siding with mail and rations and stuff for the stations on the way. But I was a big strong raw-boned young cove, fit as a fiddle from sparring with all the others in the police gym every night. Hadn't I been sent out there to uphold the dignity of the Force? I wasn't about to be stood over by a bunch of scrub-hick drunks if they didn't behave themselves. Only had a day or two to have a look around before Saturday night arrived. Long before dark a steady string of horses and carts began trundling in as the place began to fill up with a motley crowd of young coves from the bush camps with braces over sweat-flannel shirts holding up heavy work trousers and feet jammed in hobnail blucher boots. They seemed orderly enough. They'd thrown a couple of tarpaulins under some carbeen trees along the dirt road outside the pub, lit a big fire and were having a feed and scruffing about with one another like young coves generally do in a mob. It all seem pretty harmless, so I kept out of the way as instructed, even though they shouldn't have had their horses hobbled round the police station, in the police paddock and tied up along the fence each side of the pub.

But it didn't last long. By nine o'clock, some were having wrestling bouts under the trees with hurricane lights hanging up in the branches; others were foot-racing up and down the road. Suddenly there was a great din inside the pub. Men could be heard yelling and windows or china or something was smashing on the floor. I pulled on my uniform jacket and helmet and headed for the pub where all the noise was coming from amidst a chorus of catcalls and abuse from the mob under the trees. Elbowing my way through the door, I could see several fights were in full swing inside and everything was upside down. The publican was standing on the bar counter, threatening to close the doors. With all the authority I could muster, I pulled the first two apart and ordered the others to behave themselves or I'd put them where they'd give no more trouble. With that, a great hairy gorilla in sleeveless flannel shirt and enormous tattooed arms, stepped out from along the wall. He reefed off my helmet and put it on his head then jerked off my tunic with a force that lifted me clean off the floor; the polished brass buttons dancing across the boards.

'Where'd this bloody toff of a thing all togged up like a friggin' Christmas tree come from — ain't 'e nice?' he bellowed to the rest of the mob.

The next thing I remember was being draped over his shoulder with an arm like a horse's leg over my back and my right hand held in a grip like a vice as he headed for the door with the mob cheering him on.

'Orr, put th' poor little bugger down an' let 'im go 'ome ter bed,' someone yelled out.

But he kept on in the dark with me belting into him with my left fist, but it was like hitting a stump. I began screwing away at his ear till I could hear the cartilage crackling then reached for his nose to do the same thing, but he nearly bit my finger off. I suddenly realised he was heading for the bore swamp full of black mud and bulrushes down the paddock behind the pub. I could see myself being speared in head first and trampled into the mud, while a dozen or so of his mates followed along behind in a noisy procession with not very polite suggestions as to what the big bloke should do with 'th' little city toff'!

I was saved from the indignity of all the things that seemed likely to happen, when the publican, himself a big man, and a few helpers came running up. Between us we pulled Samson down — he was as strong as a bull and roared nearly as loud too. But we wheeled him back to the lockup where he stayed till well into next day. The others quietened down after that and there was no more trouble for the rest of the night. But no doubt it would be on again when they all came back the following Saturday. I was thankful I only had to see another couple of weekends through before the boss returned and I could escape back to Brisbane again.

About 1924, the Commonwealth Prickly Pear Board was formed to deal with the problem, which by then had reached critical proportions. This was a research body jointly funded by the Commonwealth Government and New South Wales and Queensland State Governments. Block after block had been abandoned as settlers walked off their runs with pear covering practically every inch of their country in a solid wall, feet high, right to the very walls of their huts. By 1925, prickly pear was at its peak and was reported to have over-run a staggering 60 million acres of agricultural land in north-west New South Wales and southern Queensland and was spreading at the rate of three acres an hour.

The prickly pear moth, *Cactoblastis cactorum*, was introduced from South America in the hope of halting the spread. Breeding stations were established at various centres throughout affected districts from which cactoblastis moth eggs were distributed. The eggs were referred to as 'cacto sticks' because the eggs were attached to one another like a central stem with branches or sticks protruding from the sides. Boxes of 'cacto sticks' were regularly made available to farmers and graziers direct from the Central Research and Breeding Laboratory in Brisbane. Cattle and birds, particularly emus, were the main agents responsible for spreading the plant. The prickly pink pear fruit were full of large seeds like a pomegranate which were readily eaten by cattle, as were the fleshy leaves. Stock routes and watering reserves became heavily infested as travelling mobs distributed pear seeds in their dung as they went. Cattle could live on the thick moisture-laden leaves indefinitely and didn't have to come out of the thickets for water. This meant the scrubs soon became alive with unbranded scrub cattle, pigs and dingos which couldn't be got out. After living in the pear and eating it for years, cattle developed hard tongues that stuck out of their mouth like a peg and wouldn't bend because of the thick pad created by deeply embedded pear thorns. Cactoblastis moth eggs were distributed throughout pear-infested districts where the prolific small orange and black striped caterpillars soon hatched and began hollowing out the fleshy pear leaves.

Every leaf that fell to the ground, as the pear began to wilt or when knocked about by grazing cattle, immediately took root and grew into another patch of pear. Though the caterpillars ate only a portion of the plant, it paved the way for fermentation and decomposition to set in and finish off the plant. After its release in 1925, cactoblastis rapidly became firmly established in all heavily infested pear districts and by early 1930s, the worst of the threat was over. Hundreds of square miles of formerly impenetrable pear thickets became a tangle of dead rubble covering the ground in a thick layer of fibrous bone-like bleached stems in every direction. Key men in all pear-affected districts were empowered to act as cactoblastis distributing agents and to report back to governments on the results of the program. One of my father's friends, Ken Cameron ('Cactoblastis Cameron'), whose property was Bullomen Plains on the Moonie River near Thallon, was a key figure in the program. Outlying fringes of pear infestation, which included all our country, were controlled by each property owner and checked on by Crown Land rangers responsible to the Queensland Prickly Pear Board through the Lands Department.

Dingos, which had been closed in on completion of the Thrushton dog-netting boundary, howled round the camps all night. Dad and Doolie dragged nightly trails for miles and laid strychnine baits, but with so much other work to be done, they eventually got a dog poisoner and trapper in to tackle the job. His name was Phil O'Shea (he never knew how it should be spelt). Phil worked on Thrushton until 1927.

Phil was a champion dogger from all accounts and even thought like a dog. When dingos are poisoned a lot, those still remaining get bait-shy and are always hard to get. But Phil had the answer to this and started trapping and had his own methods of doing this.

He turned up to start dogging with a mate, Bill Boyd, in an old Model T Ford ton truck that was held together in places with fencing wire. Everything they owned was tied down on the back under three or four enormous stag hounds that rode and fought on top of the load. I remember being frightened by those huge dogs as they ran down emus and kangaroos in the night paddock and tore them to pieces right in front of the house.

I don't know where these two old scrubbers mated up and decided to work together, but it was likely they were part of the many big droving plants shifting cattle from the Gulf and Territory stations to southern railheads and markets. He and Bill were middle-aged. Both had beards and were big wild-looking old bushmen, or at least they seemed terribly old in my young sketchy memory of them before they left. Phil was a big powerfully built man over six feet tall and very strong. In his prime he would have weighed fifteen or sixteen stone. He was a noted overproof rum drinker too, generally with a dash of bore water to soften the bite and was known far and wide as a great pub and dance-hall fighter after the rum started to work and he got cranky and picked fights. Phil didn't drink when working out in the bush, but when he was cashed up and hit the western towns, look out.

He'd studied a dingo's every movement and knew that sooner or later a dog always comes onto a netting fence, a road or a pad and follows it. So he waited until the station bitches came on heat, then collected their urine in tomato sauce bottles. He rode about the scrub and along cattle pads and fences for miles until he found fresh dingo tracks. Knowing that dogs mark their territory by cocking their leg against trees and stumps as they trot about, he'd sprinkle a few drops of the bitch's brew on these as he rode along. He set his traps where he knew the passing dog was sure to stop in excitement and start sniffing.

To make sure it stepped on the trap plate, he'd arrange sticks in a way that broke its tread so the dog stepped over the stick and stood on the plate, setting off the trap. Trapping is terribly cruel, but so is a dingo partly eating a sheep and leaving it to be covered with ants and have its eyes picked out by crows. It wasn't a place for the faint-hearted when, out of kindness, you knocked it on the head or cut its throat to put it out of its misery. Trappers tied paper round the trap jaws to avoid the trap breaking the dingo's leg when the trap was sprung and the dog jerked at the trap trying to escape. If the bone was badly broken, most dingos chewed their leg off at the trap jaws and escaped — three-legged dingos were not that uncommon. This is why traps were generally tied to a light log the dog can drag about with less chance of broken legs than making it a fixture to a tree. Phil's dingo talents were so successful that after a year or so he'd cleaned up the last of the dogs and was on fencing work until he left in about 1927.

What he did in the following years is a bit of a mystery. He simply disappeared without trace until he turned up one day at Clonard, another property we'd got in the meantime and stayed with us until he died in 1943 in sad and tragic circumstances — but more about that later. When I was a boy, drovers and men around the country couldn't hear Phil's name without recounting some notable fight they'd seen or heard talked of around the pubs. Phil's wilder moments at the end of a bottle or two of overproof rum had elevated him to champion pub and dance-hall 'bare-knuckle' status — a legend in the art of flattening other drunks, opal scratchers and drovers' cooks. This was in the days when fighters were looked up to in the bush like gods. It was a time when toughness and fighting skills were very worthy and gallant attributes in a man. It put the other bloke in his place and enhanced a man's stature to a leading position in his group. Anyway, of all the wild back-country fights I was told about, the one in the old Goodooga pub stands out in my memory, for it must really have been something out of the box.

It took place in the Goodooga pub just over the border in New South Wales from Dirranbandi in 1928, not long after Phil had left Thrushton. Phil's opponent was a little sawn-off opal miner from Lightning Ridge called Jubilee Bob. He was as wide as he was long, with enormous arms and shoulders, and tough as greenhide from all the pick and shovel gouging down the holes at 'The Ridge'. The big bout was described to me originally by drover Tom Duffy. He was part of the mob of onlookers. About forty years later I was talking about this to a mate of mine, Bill Neilly, who grew up on a big Company station between Heble and Dirranbandi his father was managing at the time. To my surprise, he said he remembered this fight well because people were still talking about it for years after, all round the district!

It had been raining for days and the black cracking clay plains had turned into a sticky waterlogged mess. The old pub was jammed full of trapped drovers, miners, station hands and cattle buyers, none of whom could get out of town because the country was all under water. Things came to a head when everyone in the packed bar had been drinking solidly for days and tempers began to deteriorate.

Jubilee was built like a gorilla, short and thick with hair all over him and, like many short little blokes, was full of cheek and swagger too. He was sitting on the bar counter giving lip as usual but those who knew him didn't answer back, for Jubilee was 'King of The Ridge'. Jubilee and Phil had never rubbed shoulders before and Phil, being new to the area and the toey sort of customer he was when he'd been into the rum, well, it was only natural that the inevitable had to happen.

A few feet along the bar from Phil, Jubilee was giving cheek to everyone in a loud voice. He nudged his mate and, pointing to Phil, said: 'When ole Long John 'ere falls down d'reckly an' goes ter sleep, I'm gunner snuck up an' hack that bloody mouldy lookin' beard orf of th' ole bastard's hugly dial with me daggin' shears an' stuff me piller with the bits.'

Phil roared like a scrub bull: 'Bastard's a fightin' word insultin' ter me mother. I'm gunna play "'Ome Sweet 'Ome" up yer bloody ribs fer that, yer 'airy little barboon an' yer'll be 'angin' be th' bloody ears to the dorg nettin' fence fer th' crows ter turn yer into a Chinese lantern be th' time I'm finished with yer.'

So, amidst the roars, a hole was cleared in the mob in the bar and into it they hooked. After the first five or six rounds, there was nothing left standing in the pub and the ferocious battle now shifted to the lean-to in the mud outside the door. At a time when most of

Phil's other opponents would have long since been stretched out on the ground, Jubilee Bob hardly had a sweat up.

Years later Phil told me: 'Hell th' little bugger could fight, an' tough as a 'orse's 'oof too. Kep' chargin' in all doubled up about three foot orf th' ground. I couldn't git a good hit at 'im, jist brushin' the back of 'is 'ead all th' time as 'e bucked around th' bar. Every time 'e come in, it felt like someone was throwin' bloody rocks at me. Me guts 'ad gone ter jelly an' me belly button was shakin' 'ands with me kidneys, so I thought, there's only one thing fer this. So next time 'e come in, I leaned over 'im and grabbed 'olt er the cheeks of 'is arse an' fell down on me back, draggin' 'im with me. I got both feet under 'im an' kicked as 'ard as I could. They call it th' flyin' mare, boy, an' Jubilee took orf like a stone outa a shanghai an' landed in th' water table with is 'ead buried to 'is shoulders in the black mud. He came up clawin' mud an' blue burr outer 'is eyes an' I was on me way over ter finish 'im orf while 'is eyes was full er mud. But th' rum was at me, boy, an' I put too much weight inter th' swing that was supposed to lay 'im out cold. I missed 'an slipped arse over 'ed at 'is feet instead. They drug us apart after that an' wouldn't let us fight no more — called it a draw.'

After a long silence I asked, 'What did you do then, Phil?'

'Orrr, we jist went back inside, boy, an' got full — we was good mates after that!'

Phil had a bark hut down the bore drain a mile or so from the house and a couple of times we were allowed to camp with him overnight. He was a great old cove with kids and used to fill us up on brownie made with emu eggs, washed down with black tea drunk from enormous pannikins with the enamel chipped off them.

He'd be telling us, 'Yer know, boy, they buggered all that "beauteeful" back country when they brought in yeast bread an' six-wire fences.'

How true, but, at that tender age, none of us had any idea what he was talking about. I've always remembered it and have thought a lot about it since. It was a pretty wise statement coming from an old scrubber like Phil. I'm sure he saw those things as the beginning of modern technology, which has changed the very face of the country. He didn't like the way it was going, even then.

Like Phil's stories, other things I hadn't thought of for years came to mind as I wrote. One was running out all excited to see the first old hard-tyred motor lorry lumbering along the track leading to the Thrushton homestead. It was the middle of summer. The ground was like the top of a hot stove. I fell over yelling as the ground burnt into my bare feet and someone carried me back into the shade under the house. I was probably about three at the time. Another was when Dad was bogged in a gilgai somewhere after a heavy storm. I don't know who else was there or where it was, but somebody obviously was holding me so I didn't take a header over the side from my standing position looking down from the back seat of the old Model T Ford. The beautifully coloured circles made by oil dripping from the hot sump into the water have lingered in the memory. As each drop fell, it made a tiny rainbow ripple on the surface as it slowly moved out across the water to the outer bank of the gilgai.

Another one, probably about 1926 or 1927, was kneeling on the back seat hanging to the side of Cactoblastis Cameron's Model T Ford while he and Dad bounced in and out of gilgais and over logs as they bashed their way between thick patches of prickly pear. They kept telling me to get back inside in case the pear that constantly thumped the side of the car belted me across the face. They were probably checking the hatched-out cactoblastis eggs Mr Cameron had distributed in the pear thickets. Most early memories seemed to be of cars and hard-tyred lorries in bogs on station tracks some-where after heavy rain. Motor vehicles were such oddities in those days, especially if they were bogged down with chains on the back wheels throwing mud high in the air. We threw branches and sticks under the thrashing chains on the spinning back wheels as men pushed from the back. What exciting times they were as the engine roared and spluttered with steam and smoke billowing up from a red hot exhaust and boiling radiator — and us covered with mud from head to foot.

We were fortunate to have been brought up as carefree, wild bush kids at a time when there were few other people and the country was still being cut up and settled. With no telephone, wireless or up-to-date newspapers, life was so simple and the small things that brought such pleasure and excitement cost nothing, yet filled our life with interest so there was never a dull moment. Communication with other parts of the country, let alone with the rest of the world was non-existent. The world for us went no further than the boundaries of the adjoining runs. As we got older, our only worries in life were how to shift the latest governess without getting into too much trouble; when the quandongs would be ripe and how long before the next rain — in about that order.

The kind of make-believe stuff some kids were brought up with passed us by. There were no fairies in our lives that came in the dead of night to leave letters predicting future exciting events. Even the mysteries of Santa Claus didn't last long. One Christmas, Santa Claus erected a little Tom Mix tent beside the house with Indians in head-dress painted on the sides. 'Wasn't Santa good to know just the kind of thing we wanted?' But Santa had left tracks. From the tent he'd put up during the night, we tracked him over to the wire heap and from the wire heap back to the front steps. His tracks hadn't come down again, so he must still be in the house somewhere! A bit of detective work on Dad's boots and the wire at the wire heap soon unravelled the mystery of Santa.

The old Model T Fords were tantalising contraptions to most men brought up with horses who didn't understand their many mysteries. They were periodically found beside roads and station tracks with bonnet up and a man's head peering inside. The pile of ash at the fire alongside and the depth of dust under countless boot tracks at each side told the story of a long and fruitless battle to get it started. A long narrow box of coils, wires and things attached to dry-cell batteries connected to the magneto that nobody knew much about hung down on a tin bracket under the open dashboard and was always giving trouble from dirty or loose connections. Incorrect spark settings, too, often broke arms or wrists from kickbacks while cranking and a rear wheel was generally jacked up so the wheel spun instead of the outfit chasing you when it started from a 'grabbing' clutch.

A ride in the old Tin Lizzie was a rare treat as we rattled along through spinifex, box and mulga scrub, stopping every few dusty miles to open and close wire gates. But excitement knew no bounds when we saw the first railway line. For weeks before the long dusty trip to meet someone coming by train all the way from Brisbane, there was a great hollow feeling inside. In vivid nightly dreams the vision of two railway lines shimmered in the mirage across the plain. Standing on the little railway gravel platform we actually lived the dream. For indeed, there was the train away up the line, a mere dot in the distance whistle-blowing and belching black smoke as it slowly approached the siding and stopped beside us. We watched the steam blowing from pipes as the engine panted and sung and felt the hot wheels and caught drips of oil in tin matchboxes. We nearly died when they blew the whistle to see us jump. The engine driver lifted us into the cabin while he shunted the engine over to big square water tanks on high stands to top-up the boiler.

Back at the siding again, a continuous click, click clicking came from the station master's little sweat-box office. Inside, the station master sat hunched over a bench beside a bright light with green cardboard eye shade out in front, held in place by a white elastic band round his head. Sweat streamed down his cheeks as his hand worked away at a small metal contraption Dad said was the morse code machine. Then he scribbled down some message as it click, clicked back. Alongside was a big black typewriter surrounded by piles of important-looking letters. And there were big brown envelopes lying about the table with OHMS printed in the top left corner. Dad said this was important mail because OHMS meant it was 'On His Majesty's Service'. I couldn't work out why King George away over there in England needed a mail run in this little remote railway siding hundreds of miles out in the scrub in Western Queensland, but he evidently did. Hanging from nails hammered in the walls were bundles of old dog-eared dusty government forms and weighbills with flies walking over them. Outside, another man weighed parcels and boxes on platform scales like those that weighed our wool bales. When finished, he weighed us, too. Dad eventually dragged us away to begin the long trip home. But the excitement wasn't over yet, for we were to stay the night in the Commercial Hotel. It was an old wooden building on high stumps with wide verandahs festooned by creepers loaded with little prickly red fruit like miniature porcupines. They covered the nearby high tank stands, too, sheltering swallow's mud nests underneath — and Mum had promised sausages and eggs for tea. How could Christmas ever be better than this?

It was in this same old Commercial Hotel, years later, that a little baby Austin car was found on the front verandah. A mob of us young coves were in town for a buckjump rodeo and were always looking for a bit of fun. We noticed a baby Austin car parked under a pepperina tree at the back of the pub. A long set of wooden steps ran up to wide verandahs that were about ten feet above the ground, right round the building. We lugged the little car up the stairs and pushed it round the verandah where we left it with a chock behind the wheels, and waited to see the look on the bloke's face when he came out to drive away after he'd finished dinner. Quite a crowd gathered to see the fun. The bloke took it all in good spirit, so we lugged the little car down the steps again and gave it back to him.

Trains have always been a source of bewilderment and great excitement for all bush children living on runs a long way out from railways. Many only saw a train perhaps once a year, if they were lucky. I never lost my child-like excitement about trains. When camping out in the bush or travelling to distant land investigations, I always camp the night as close as possible to the railway line in the hope of seeing or hearing the train rattle past. Just after Moodgie and I were married and returning from our honeymoon, I'm sure she thought I was mad, because I rolled out our swag about six feet from the Dirranbandi railway line. I kept getting up through the night and putting my ear on the line to hear if the train was coming. I heard the ring through my ear on the line long before its light could be seen. What excitement! Our swag was gradually bathed in the engine's bright light as it approached. We watched from our cosy swag a few feet away as each wheel slowly clattered over the gap in the line alongside our pillow, until, what seemed an age later, the red light of the old swaying guard's van slowly disappeared away up the line. It was the goods train dragging a string of empty cattle trucks for load-ing at the Dirranbandi railway yards.

I still remember parts of my first train ride, aged about four. Sleep was impossible once we were in the carriage, in case something was missed. Exciting things were happening out there: kangaroos and emus; big mobs of sheep and cattle being driven; bullock wagons loaded with logs; and all the different country never seen before. Mum put down the window for a better look and, though coal cinders blown back from the engine brought tears for a while, the musical clackety-clack of wheels over gaps in the line soon over-came discomfort. When daylight came, we were rattling and swaying through virgin scrub and forest — no houses and no people. Further on were miles of stark dead ringbarked trees like skeletons growing out of white sheets of early morning mist hanging a few feet above the ground. Canvas tents were strung out along the line at intervals. These belonged to the news-starved railway fettlers who maintained the line. As the train slowed down as it went past, they yelled out *paper, paper, paper*, their calls tapering off to a whisper as they were left behind.

The country gradually changed and Mum, explaining everything as we went along, said it was the Darling Downs. The scrub had given way to more open cleared country with big paddocks of green crops and horses were pulling ploughs driven by men sitting up on top holding the reins. How wonderful when it began to rain! Cows were being milked and were bogging away from yards full of mud while men in big boots carried buckets to feed pigs and calves in slab yards. Horses harnessed in drays and sulkies, their wheels clogged with black mud, stood rigid with heads down, ears laid back and rumps facing the driving rain. The train stopped a long time at a station and another stopped alongside. Every deck was full of squealing pigs and bellowing young calves. I hadn't seen or smelt pigs before and the calves never stopped bellowing. My first train trip was something right out of this world.

I still laugh at Dad going to look at a mob of sheep out along the Nockatunga stockroute somewhere and pulling up for lunch at the old Thargomindah pub. As he ran the T Ford under a big shady bottle tree beside the fence, he wondered why a couple of other drivers had left their cars out in the scalding sun instead of in the cool shade under the tree — 'Some people never look after anything!'

Entering the dining room, he sat down at a table, whereupon he was approached by an outsized sweaty lady with a chaff bag apron tied round a fair swag of gut by a length of rope and a pretty strong whiff about her. She handed him a piece of paper with 'MUTTON: HOGGET: LAMB' written on it. He belted away at the hordes of flies while deciding which of the three sounded the best, but the lady wasn't one for deliberation. Leaning over his shoulder she rasped, 'Say MUTTON, yer bloody fool, it's all orf the one piece!'

Returning to the car to hit the road again, he was confronted by a big long-horned black and tan billy goat, bogged to the guts with all four legs poking through the canvas hood. So this was the reason cars were baking out in the sun instead of in the shade under the trees! There were goats everywhere around the western towns, and every time a car pulled up under a tree the goats used it as a ladder. The first jump was on to the running board, then the mudguard, then the bonnet, then on top of the hood to eat the leaves they tried to reach by standing on their hind legs. In this case, all four went straight through the sun-perished canvas hood, where the old billy stayed, helpless, until Dad came and dragged him out, and half the hood with him.

The Depression years of the late 1920s and early 1930s saw

many swagmen walking the roads. Some turned up on pushbikes or
worn-out old motorbikes, often with tyres stuffed full of dry grass
or spinifex. Tie-wire was wound round and round the tyres and
rims because the tubes had gone to pieces with punctures or blow-
outs. Others rode up on a bony old horse or arrived on foot. Most
carried little more than a quartpot or a fire-blackened seven-pound
treacle-tin billy, a sugar bag with nothing much inside and a dusty old
blanket. Life on the road was pretty tough-going and all of them were
dog poor from not enough to eat because they hardly ever stopped
walking.

All these swagmen relied on the kindness of the stations along the
track to give them a bit of tea and sugar and some flour and baking
powder to make a damper and a bit of salt mutton or beef to go with
it. All were looking for work, any kind of work as long as it was something to show they weren't bludging on the generosity of the station
folk while they were camped nearby regaining a bit more energy to
attack the next dry stretch. The motto was 'Yer never know, somethin'
might turn up d'reckly'. But things were nearly as tough on the
stations. Nobody had any money and there was practically no work
anywhere for the walking wounded of the Depression years. There
were metho-pickled opal miners and men from railway gangs whose
contract had folded or from sheds where shearing had cut out. Others
were from the cities, just walking the roads looking for work to feed
the family they'd left behind. They could be anyone, you didn't ask
questions. But all were 'down on their luck'. They camped along the
bore drain for a bit of a blow before moving on. Some stayed longer
if Dad had a few days' work.

A Frenchman, a Mr Turbain, was one of these — a one-time bank
manager, someone said — probably on the road after a stretch inside
for raiding the bank vault. They called him Turby-th'-hair because he
had a big handlebar moustache. He turned up leading a lame horse
and had on a waistcoat and tie with heavy watch chain draped across
the front. He was a tall, distinguished, well-educated gentleman, a rare
sight indeed in that country in those days. Pappy must have been

starved for a bit of culture, because Turby-th'-hair moved into our room while we three boys had to camp out on the verandah. I don't remember him ever doing much on the place, but he made a great fuss of us. He was always producing pennies and ha'pennies that he put in a tin matchbox he called our treasure chest. He put it high up on a ledge above the door to keep this wealth in a safe place. He'd take the matchbox down every now and then to show us the treasure within. When he eventually left, the first thing we did was get a chair and climb up for the matchbox to distribute the fortune, only to find that the matchbox and pennies had gone with him.

In about 1927 we had a jackaroo named Jack Wilkinson on Thrushton. He came out raw from Gatton College and, having been involved with pasture trials at the college, brought a variety of seeds with him in tobacco tins. Among these was a small quantity of lucerne seeds, the variety the college had been experimenting with for grazing pastures and commercial seed lots on the Darling Downs. He planted some of the lucerne seeds in a small netting enclosure in the house paddock where we kept poddy lambs and calves whose mothers had died in droughts. Later, when kangaroo shooting, we often reared young joeys in there too. A channel was dug from the bore drain to the enclosure to water the animals and also kept the surrounding soil damp for all the grape vines Dad had on trellises covered with rabbit netting to keep birds away. Jack planted paspalum (*Paspalum dilatatum*) seed in the moist soil along the bore water channel and sprinkled lucerne seeds with it. The paspalum flourished everywhere he planted it outside in the orchard and inside the enclosure too and quickly became the dominant plant. The lucerne also flourished, though it took many years before it began to thicken up and eventually choke the paspalum. When the animals were shifted out after they'd grown, the lucerne, now the dominant species, grew two feet tall and flowered prolifically. Some lucerne was still growing with the paspalum at the time Thrushton was sold in 1947, even after the enclosure was abandoned and the water was cut off. A few plants lingered on until 1975, finally dying for good in dry times shortly afterwards. It surprised me that lucerne could persist in that dry country without assistance from fertilisers and without water for the last thirty years of its life. From all accounts Jack was the legendary absent-minded professor. He'd be halfway through a job and suddenly think of something that anchored him to the spot staring into space for half an hour at a time until Dad prodded him in the ribs with the shovel handle and told him to wake up.

One day he announced he'd have to knock off and go to the toilet, which was the family one-holer thunderbox between the wood heap and the dog kennels about a hundred yards from the house.

'Take this kangaroo leg down as you go and cut it up for the dogs — it'll save me having to do it later,' said Dad.

Jack walked down to the old dunny, opened the door, lifted the lid and dropped the kangaroo leg down the hole and continued on to the dog yard empty-handed. He just stood there for a good while scratching his head and wondering what he'd gone there for. His mother claimed he'd been 'born on a wet and windy night an been wet and windy ever since'!

CHAPTER 3

The Wool Game

THE reason for the in-built animosity between graziers and shearers was that both were looking at different ends of the same equation. When wool prices slumped and overhead costs kept rising, the shearer was often much better off than some of the small, almost bankrupt growers in poor country, who were just about to walk off their runs. These small land-holders and their families often were forced to live in the most appalling conditions of hardship, often with inferior amenities to those being demanded by the Australian Workers' Union for the shearers. Small land-holders, therefore, felt it wasn't a fair go that the shearers, who only had to put up with the conditions for a few weeks each year, sometimes had better amenities in the shearers' quarters than the land-holder could afford for his wife and family in the homestead. Farmers and their families couldn't get away to a new town with money in their pockets like the shearers could every few weeks. They were anchored to their block, the servants of banks and wool brokers, with the size of their overdraft escalating by the day.

Though conditions on the land gradually improved as the country was opened up for closer settlement, there was still trouble and occasional shearers' strikes and bad feelings when I was a boy.

One cranky old cook didn't like the stove, though it was the same as the one we had at the house. To make sure it wasn't there for the next shearing, he got a red-hot fire going in it with ironbark slabs and when the shed cut out and the gang was about to leave, he threw a bucket of cold bore water over the top, so that fixed that.

In 1928, we had just started shearing when a horseman galloped up saying a couple of loads of union shearers were on their way out to close the shed and cart the men away. There must have been some non-union shearers amongst our gang. Anyway, everyone armed themselves with rifles and saplings as the shearers were reported to be armed and on their way out from St George. Suddenly the St George and Bollon police arrived on the scene with .303 rifles and fixed bayonets. Some took up guard at both boundary gates and one stayed at the shed. The big fat sergeant gave me nightmares for a week after, when he rushed at me with his .303 rifle held out in front and pulled up with the bayonet an inch from my stomach, yelling, 'Ow'd yer like that run through yer belly, sonny?'

We always looked forward to shearing time when the contractor and all the shearing gang turned up. We hardly ever saw anyone apart from family, so all the new faces and games every night and roo shooting every weekend provided a welcome change. After tea at night, they hung hurricane lamps in trees and had foot races and wrestling matches. Another good game was one they called skitters. The cook saved up all the condensed milk tins, each of which was punched with a different number of holes. About twenty tins were lined up in the shape of a 'V' twenty yards away from the throwing line. Each man made a throwing stick to his own design, but no more than a foot long. Everyone had one throw, the winner being whoever ended up with the greatest number of holes in the tins he knocked over the boundary lines drawn round the original group of tins.

Our Tin Lizzie, as the old spluttering Model T Fords were called, lasted right through until 1928, when Dad cashed his insurance policy and bought a little four-cylinder Whippet car. By then, vehicles were becoming fairly common and some of the young coves had old beat-up wrecks to get them from shed to shed instead of the usual pushbike. Nobody knew much about cars but a group of 'experts' always seemed to be huddled about the open bonnet tinkering with the engine and offering advice on how to get it started. Power was the important thing most talked about: which were the best makes and how well did they pull in top gear.

The wool presser, Barney, had an old Morris Cowley with long iron spokes in high thin wheels and one of the shearers, Jackie, had an old Dodge tourer with no hood and a mudguard missing.

Barney claimed: 'They make terrible good cars in England — buggers never wear out — that's why me Morris Cowley's the best puller ever I seen.'

Jackie, with America's old Dodge, reckoned: 'Bullshit, th' bellowin' bloody ole thing wouldn't pull a greasy stick outa a pig's arse.'

It looked like a fight was brewing, because cars were things of great personal pride: to insult the car was to insult the owner.

Someone suggested, 'Why don't we scratch a line on the ground an' hook the buggers together with a wire rope an' see which one gits dragged over the line first — that'll settle the argument.'

The old Morris Cowley snuffed out after one bit of a jerk and refused to start, so Jackie claimed victory.

The cookhouse was the favoured place we kids always managed to turn up at around smoko or dinnertime. Most of the cooks took pity on us after a while and nearly always opened a tin of peaches or pears for us. Sometimes they mixed in a few left-overs too, if there was anything left after the rouseabouts had finished gorging themselves stiff at the last feed. Most of the shearers, and especially their cooks, were pretty solid drinkers of anything they could get hold of — metho included, if there was nothing else. Within minutes of letting the last sheep go, they'd be in whatever means of conveyance was handy, heading for the nearest pub. In town there'd be a dance or a buckjump show or something on every Saturday night, often following a race meeting or cricket match during the day.

George Ashwin was our shearing contractor and Pelican was the old bearded cook who followed the plant around from shed to shed — when he wasn't on the grog, that is. At the end of the first week's shearing, everyone raced off into Bollon because Lance Skuthorp's buckjump show had hit the town and there was a dance that night as well. Halfway through the night when everything was just warming up properly, the Pelican, who'd started to hit the rum pretty early, had reached the rowdy stage. The shearers didn't want their good cook wheeled out to the lock-up pen for being drunk and disorderly. So some of the them manhandled him across the road and shoved him under a big heavy ship's tank with the top cut out that they'd noticed lying upside down on the creek bank.

When they'd all slept off the big binge, they headed back to the Thrushton shed again. At smoko time when they'd finished the first run and went to the cookhouse for morning tea, there was nothing there, no fire going, and, of course, no Pelican. Someone suddenly remembered ramming him under the tank so they raced back hoping he'd still be alive. When they lifted up the tank, there was Pelican curled alongside a huge python with a big lump in the middle, both sound asleep. The old python had swallowed a possum or something and, like Pelican, was sleeping it off.

It was about this time that Jack Turner from Homeboin came over to Thrushton in a brand new 1928 Model A Ford the station had just bought. He was still learning to drive it and had already demolished several gates. The only things he'd ever pulled up in his life were horses. A gate loomed on the track ahead but by the time Jack had groped around looking for the reins in this thing, the wire gate was already draped over the bonnet. He'd come over to tell us that poor old Mr Wells, the station bookkeeper, had been killed while they were loading wool. He was at the side of the lorry counting the bales and entering the numbers in his book when the last bale they were juggling around on top of the load overbalanced and fell on top of him, breaking his neck. Mr Wells was a kind old man who was highly regarded by everyone. If we called in at the station, he'd always give Mum something out of the big vegetable garden and had a few boiled lollies for we three boys that he'd delve out of a big glass jar from a shelf in the store.

★ ★ ★

Dad began designing a new automatic drenching machine around 1927–28 to overcome the slow dusty work of drenching thousands of sheep by the standard method used at that time. Until the end of the 1920s, sheep were drenched with measured quantities of bluestone and arsenic and bluestone and nicotine mixed with water and administered by bottles rammed down the sheep's throat. Mixing the drench was a horrible job that brought tears streaming down your cheeks from the powerful mixture as it was stirred in a petrol tin. When thoroughly mixed, generally in hot water heated over a log fire alongside, it was allowed to cool, then poured into tomato sauce bottles. (Everyone had plenty of them.) You couldn't leave the drench standing in the tin for too many days or the bluestone would eat the bottom out — what it did to a sheep's gut, I hate to think. The bottles were stood upright in a timber frame made from six by one cypress pine board with holes cut in it. Each bottle went into a separate hole so it couldn't fall out of the crate, which was fastened to on the top rail of the drenching race. Sheep were packed tightly in the race so they couldn't move about. Each man caught and straddled a sheep while forcing the neck of the bottle down its throat where the contents of the bottle slowly glug-glugged away until the dose was gone. As kids, one of us handed out the bottles as required and collected the empty ones for refilling. The dust was blinding and stuck to tears running down your cheeks. It was a slow and filthy business. Care and a lot of patience, which soon became a pretty scarce commodity with sharp hooves trampling painful corns, was needed to get this horrible mixture down the unwilling sheep's throat as it bucked about with the drencher on top. During the struggle, a portion of the drench ran back out of the corners of the sheep's mouth and down the legs of dungarees and into the drencher's boots before the race was half finished.

When Phenothozine became the standard new drench, less efficient ones were phased out. It was a dark green powder mixed with water, making a green drench that turned into a potent and penetrating red dye when exposed to the atmosphere for a day or two. Any portion of the fleece contaminated by the drench changed to bright red, the colour soaking deep into the wool, impossible to remove. The sheep's urine also turned red, with the same effect on any saturated part of the fleece. As sheep will often urinate while lying down camped and then rub against one another when confined to yards, these discoloured portions had to be discarded during wool classing. The loss in wasted wool and fragmented fleeces would have been prohibitive.

After drenching the old way for years, it was a welcome relief when Dad's automatic drencher came on the market — at a cost, I think, of five guineas. The U-shaped container holding two gallons of drench neatly fitted the curve of your back like today's knapsack sprays. From this position the drench gravitated down a length of hose to the one or two ounce measured nickel-coated brass barrels of the drencher, which were screwed in as required. The barrel containing one ounce of drench was for lambs and weaners, and the two-ounce one was for grown stock. Attached to this was a slightly curved outlet nozzle for delivering the drench down the sheep's throat, a hole drilled in the side of the nozzle so sheep couldn't put their tongue over the outlet to block the drench. The double click-click of the shut-off valve in the barrel told when the automatically measured dose had been taken, whereupon the applicator bar was released and the barrel refilled again in a couple of seconds, ready for the next sheep. It was clean and easy, one person being able to drench a whole race full of sheep by simply working backwards and forwards across the race, keeping the un-drenched sheep in front and pushing the others as they were drenched back behind. This revolutionary invention was soon pounced on by the city sharks who were always waiting to make a kill.

When the Thrushton Automatic Drencher was patented and reviewed in agricultural journals at the start of the 1930s, it caused quite a stir and was widely advertised by stock and station agents everywhere. The drencher went to New Guinea, New Zealand, inter-state and all over the place. Dad should have made a fortune out of this device, which largely did away with one of the worst yard jobs. But he had no business skills or sales experience either, of course. He thought, and everyone else thought, the Brisbane manufacturing engineers, Preston and Dalby, would have difficulty keeping ahead of inquiries and sales. But, as time went on, the initial brisk sales practically came to a standstill. The mystery was solved when the Australian Estates pastoral inspector came round trying to sell Dad his own drencher under a different name.

The manufacturers changed the original design to a 'drenching gun' instead of Dad's bar applicator and patented it in their own name. In this way they were able to withhold Dad's drencher while promoting their slightly improved model throughout the Australian and overseas wool industries. By the time Dad discovered what was happening more than a year later, it was too late to do anything. But it was all quite legal, probably because the change to a gun instead of an applicator bar certainly made it easier to use.

Years later, Dad explained that the idea for the invention came from the old Model T Ford gravity-feed fuel system. The petrol tank was anchored high above the engine in front of, but just below, the windscreen and fed petrol by gravity to the carburettor down below. Most of the early cars of that vintage were fitted with vacuum tanks that were connected by pipe to the inlet manifold. The vacuum thus created by suction siphoned petrol from the tank at the rear of the vehicle to the carburettor in front. Vacuum tanks often gave trouble in hot weather from vaporising or dirty petrol or if a slight air-leak developed in a gasket or fuel line connection joint. The slightest leak meant no vacuum and no petrol. In contrast, the Ford gravity system was completely trouble-free because the petrol just ran down from the tank to the carburettor by gravity.

Dad took it all very philosophically when he found his invention had been pinched, without enough from sales to anywhere near cover the costs or even buy a tin of tobacco. He simply accepted it as just another bit of a setback of no great importance and got on with work on the place that he could never get on top of. I don't remember him speaking about it again, and it was only by asking a few questions years later that I can say much about it at all. I'm pleased I've kept the old 1932 *Queensland Agricultural Journal* all these years. This was typical of Dad. I've often thought since he died, that he was the kindest, most honest man I've known. If he was selling a mob of cattle or sheep, he'd always throw in an extra few head for nothing. As long as the buyer went away happy, knowing he'd been done a good turn, that was all that really mattered.

Dad was a good sheepman, always keen to improve the quality of sheep and wool through breeding. He was also a competent surveyor, inventive and good with figures. In many ways he was more cut out for clerical work than he was for the land. He became involved with the CSIRO in various early experiments with drenches, dips, mineralised salt licks and molasses. He had live-weight gain experiments underway from a combination of these in conjunction with available alternative paddock feed (mulga and wiregrasses, spinifex, cut mulga scrub, etc.). This meant we were often weighing sheep by using a corn bag to cradle them while they hung from a set of meat scales as we recorded their weights. He also corresponded with wildlife authorities who at that time were investigating western bowerbirds and their playgrounds. Dad claimed the bowers all ran north–south but this wasn't always the case. Like the northern 'magnetic' termite mounds, though, they did have a tendency to face north where the prevailing winds were from the west, which they largely were in our area.

Law and order was always important to Dad and he felt threatened and uneasy with anyone who had ideas of rocking the boat or causing unpleasantness. He avoided argument, too. When his mind was made up about something, you couldn't shift him. Exasperating as he could be to work with at times, he was a wonderful father and I miss him still.

Doolie also was a very kind person and went to great lengths to provide some comfort for men working on the place over the years, especially those camped away out the back by themselves. She always seemed to be cooking cakes and biscuits and other little goodies to go with their weekly stores when we distributed these round the camps on weekends. Other times during sickness or axe cuts to feet or legs, they'd be brought back to the homestead to be fed up and nursed back to health again. The homely atmosphere and family kindness was greatly appreciated by the men, one of whom gave her a red coloured rock about two inches long and more than an inch wide, like a piece of mottled red marble. It gleamed with beautiful flashing opal in rich reds, greens and blues. He'd dug it out of a hole when mining at Lightning Ridge and gave it to Doolie when he was leaving. Others sent back pieces or sets of china from the first town they came to after leaving, as a thankyou present. She loved all the birds, too, and fed large numbers of jackasses, butcherbirds and magpies every morning to encourage them to stay and nest around the house, while mobs of lousy-jacks and bowerbirds were fed with the fowls and ducks down in the fowl yard.

CHAPTER 4

Bullockies and Old Timers

Bullocky Smith (Alf Smith) was the same age as my father. They'd both been fighting over the other side in the same world war and were now working in the same district as returned soldiers. Alf had been given the first contract issued for delving the seventy-odd miles of bore drains from the recently sunk Wierbolla artesian bore a few miles north of Dad's block. Alf also had delving contracts tied up for a number of other artesian bores with several hundred miles of bore drains in the Bollon/St George districts. These kept him going all year, broken perhaps for a week or two snigging wagon loads of logs to sawmills or for yard building. He was known through all that western country as 'a top bullocky'. Always on foot, he walked up and down beside the team all day from the 'leaders' in front to the 'polers' at the back, talking to the bullocks all the time as if talking to his mate back at camp cooking the damper.

He'd be drawling away quietly, 'Gee orf Pilot, come 'ere Tidy.' A bit later, you'd hear, 'Git over Piker, *git over.*' Occasionally, after a hard prod in the ribs with the whip handle a bit further down the team, he'd call: 'Git up 'ere Spindle. *Up*, yer bludgin' bastard. Yer been bludgin' on Brindle there — *git up 'ere* — *inter* that bloody bow — *now*, an' pull yer weight.' Then another prod.

Spindle would spring to attention, jump into life and obey, ramming the great bulk of his shoulders in behind the bow and leaning into it. You could almost hear him apologise to old Bullocky: 'Sorry mate — muster dozed off — she's been a long hot thirsty day, you know!'

When the pull was steady and uniform, so was Bullocky's voice. Each of the older bullocks in the team understood Bullocky's lingo and knew his own name, responding to whatever instruction was given immediately his name was called. And he knew, by the tone and volume of the order being delivered, whether things were going well or not. The younger bullocks, not so long in the team, took time to learn their own name and Bullocky's soothing team lingo during early breaking-in stages. The degrees of urgency in the commands were identified by sound. Bullocks soon understood that loud roaring commands, accompanied by long bursts of rugged swearing with whip held high in the air, meant there was trouble ahead. The wagon was bogging or the delver was digging in too deep and pushing too heavy a load in front, so they had to lean into those bows and give their all.

Emergencies called for maximum effort from the whole team. If the leaders were pulling and the polers were bludging, you only had half a team, so Bullocky danced in great bounds up and down the string of bullocks swinging that huge ten- or twelve-foot whip. The whip was attached to the five- or six-foot long whip handle, straight as a die and stripped of its bark, it was like whalebone. Bullocky had hold of it with both hands, each hand a foot apart for extra purchase and to guide the heavy whip high above his head. And every time he swung and cracked that whip, it was like a .303 rifle going off. The whole team became alert and leaned hard into yokes and bows, pulling as hard as they could — some even down on their knees.

The only time I saw Bullocky Smith in a cold rage and nearly in tears was when his wagon was bogged in the bore drain alongside the Neabul Downs homestead when the travelling parson was holding a service there. Nobody was taking any notice of the parson, because all eyes were on poor old Bullocky and his bogged wagon. Being so close to the homestead with all the district's ladies dressed up in their best church gear, Bullocky couldn't swear. And of course, the bullocks soon picked this up. It was a new kind of language he was talking and the bullocks couldn't work out what he wanted them to do. No good getting stirred up any longer, so Bullocky boiled up and had a feed until the show was over and all the ladies had gone home. By that time Bullocky was back to normal again, as the bullocks soon found out. The great whip started cracking like a rapid firing .303 rifle, accompanied by the Bullocky's catechism yelled in loud bursts, guaranteed to make the toughest parson's hair stand on end. The team leaned into those yokes and bows and dragged that wagon out as though it had been a toy and old Bullocky was his happy self again.

Alf was a good man with cattle and, like most bushmen, could turn his hand to any kind of bush work. He'd been right through the 1914–18 World War, and had been gassed and suffered from shell shock. Dad and Alf were always recounting amusing war episodes when they were working together on some job.

Although most Australian bushmen had been practically born on a horse, riding instruction was still considered necessary as part of their pre-war training on arrival in England. A big fat illiterate Irish corporal had them all lined up with their allotted horses early on the first morning.

'Right, now place the reins over th' 'orse's 'ead an' put the toe of th' left boot in th' near-side stirrup an' rise inter th' saddle,' he instructed. 'Now yez is mounted, pick up the horf-side stirrup without th' haid of the 'and or hye.'

Most of these wild young coves thought it all a great joke — some just flew over the horse's rump and landed in the saddle. Others raced around the barracks back to front and some galloped round and round the old corporal, two or three on the same horse, while he bellowed threats of court martial!

When all the men got together on some job or other, the conversation was always about exploding shells on the front lines in France, of trenches and the endless mud. The only way they had been able to cope with the daily slaughter all round them and the stink of rotting death, had been to make jokes about it in an effort to boost their confidence and take their mind off the daily slaughter. Alf described how diggers had put a tin of bully beef on a stiff hand in one of the bombed-out trenches in France and had hung a pannikin on one of the rigid fingers.

In occasional fits of deep depression, Alf turned up in town and got on the grog and just kept on drinking until he passed out somewhere. Generally he was found in a shed or under a bush somewhere around the town before he was too far gone. The time came when he wasn't found until it was too late and he died of pneumonia in the St George hospital. All the old diggers felt they'd lost a good friend. Dad and I were repairing a gate down the run when Charlie Deshon from neighbouring Belgaum rode over with the sad news. I remember how much it affected Dad. Alf had worked for many years on Thrushton and surrounding properties building yards and sinking tanks. Most of his working bullocks had been run out of the scrub on these properties. He used the standard method to break them in. Wild young clean-skin bulls, occasionally bullocks, some that had never seen a yard or branding iron, were coupled round the neck and horns with a length of chain to a big powerful old working bullock. It was very hard on the working bullock until he'd dragged the younger one round for a day or two and it had started to settle down. The bullocks had to be found every day in case they got tangled round a tree or a log.

Dick Taylor used to tell a yarn about Bullocky Smith and Colin Cameron from Oaklands. Bullocky had been yard-building there and, as was the standard practice during cool winter months, each station took turns killing a bullock every couple of weeks for meat. It was divided equally among the neighbours and those working there, everyone taking turns for the best cuts — oxtail, tongue, sweetbread (pancreas), steak, roasts, etc. Frequency of killing was in accordance with the number of people working on each place. Early one frosty morning, they were cutting up the carcass that had been left hanging on the gallows overnight to set the meat. After dry-salting all the worst cuts and putting some in tins of brine, they began sorting out and dividing up all the favourite pieces. Both Bullocky and Colin claimed it was their turn to have the tongue, which had been thrown over a log until the argument had been settled. But Bullocky's blue cattle dog, whose eyes had been fastened on the tongue ever since it had been draped over the log, sneaked up and dragged it down the paddock under a bush and ate it while they were still arguing. Until the day they died, each blamed the other for pinching it!

When delving drains, the bullockies always camped close to the homestead for a bit of company. They yoked and unyoked the bullocks alongside the night paddock or horse paddock fence. Each yoke and bow was laid out on the ground beside each bullock as it was unyoked each afternoon ready for yoking again in the morning, each bullock always keeping to their own position in the team. Enormous Condamine bells nearly as big as your head were strapped round the neck of several bullocks in the team so they could be found easily. The bullocks often wandered miles at night looking for feed and would be scattered all over the place. In the clear winter air on cold frosty mornings the bells could be plainly heard eight or ten miles away — must have nearly driven the bullocks mad flogging away wherever they walked and fed.

We always seemed to be over at the camp yarning with Alf and his mate, Bricky Sting, while they filled us up with damper and treacle and pannikins of black tea. Our eyes would be sticking out of their sockets while old Bullocky told us the most outlandish wild yarns. (I realise they were now, but not then!)

'I 'ad a big white bullick called Snowflake and I'd trained 'im to tell me when the damper was cooked. Snowflake always camped beside the wagon wheel at night and when I lifted the lid off the camp oven with the wire hook, he'd get up and walk over to tap the top of the damper with his right hoof. If she wasn't cooked, he'd shake his head and walk back and lie down again. When it was cooked properly, he'd nod his head and stamp his left hoof and wouldn't leave till I gave 'im a bit.'

Old Bullocky, very serious, would be telling us all this stuff without a smile on his face and his mate Bricky Sting would be nodding in agreement and saying: 'Yeh, an' 'e wez a terrible clean bullick around the camp too. If 'e 'ad a shit, 'e'd hold a piece of bark in 'is mouth wile 'e scraped the turd on to it with 'is hoof, then cart 'er down th' paddick an' drop 'er behind a tree and go over to the bore drain an' 'ave a wash!'

'Yeh, that's right,' Bricky continued. 'An' 'ow about that flash little French sheila you was tellin' me about in Armentières that 'ad two tailor-made cigarettes stickin' out of her mouth, two out of 'er her nostrils an' two out of 'er ears and one stickin' out of 'er arse an' could blow smoke rings with all of them at the same time; 'ad to pay to look at 'er, didn't yer say? Gees, she muster been good.'

We'd be listening pop-eyed to all this stuff and could never quite work out whether it was all fair dinkum or not! Most of the old bush blokes liked kids around them — we, no doubt, formed a good audience for the yarns. Bricky was always rolling cigarettes for us out of his tin of Welcome Nugget or Wild Woodbine tobacco. They were very kind too. Alf gave each of the three of us a pocketknife out of his big tuckerbox one time. This was really something, because the old bushmen had very few possessions and practically no money — everything they owned in life was on top of the wagon amongst rough bush tools and spare yokes and chains and stuff. As there were gangs of ringbarkers in all that country, we formed our gangs too and our axes were Alf's pocketknives. We'd find a thick scrub of emu bush, peg out our lines like the ringbarkers did and ringbark the thin stems.

The only time I ever saw Alf get wild was when he was in the yard trying to couple a young bullock he'd run out of the scrub, wild as a hawk, to one of the old workers. They had to run the youngster along the rails behind the old worker and try to keep him there long enough while Alf leaned over the neck of the big bullock to get the chain round the youngster's neck without getting horned. We kids must have been like fleas on a dog — you couldn't get rid of us. We'd be outside the yard behind a tree with our heads sticking out so we didn't miss anything and, of course, frightening the youngster every time old Bullocky was just about to hook the chain. In a very loud and not very polite voice, the things he was going to do to us when he ran us down, would have made any parson's hair stand on end — in fact, drop clean out!

Tough, adventurous young people from many diverse backgrounds selected the scrubby mulga blocks as the big undeveloped stations taken up in the 1850s and 1860s were cut up. Most of these new blocks were out in Queensland's South West, all undeveloped wild virgin mulga and box scrub and water was always scarce. They had practically no possessions — a buggy, a dray, a few draught horses and stockhorses their only means of transport. But they didn't need much more because there were few roads, few other people and only isolated struggling settlements miles apart at intervals along dusty roads and stockroutes as the country was opened up. They cut a track into their new block and stripped bark off some of the largest box trees that had survived the big 1902 drought. Cypress pine trees were cut down too, and the logs pit-sawed into slabs for huts and sheds which became the homestead. New settlers accepted drudgery and hard work as their lot to survive in the bush. They rarely left the place and, when they did, it was generally to meet the wagons from the railhead loaded with stores and gear as the new blocks were taken up. Lack of money was not a great bother because there was nowhere to spend it anyway.

Greenhide Liz was the wild and woolly daughter of one of these settlers, tough as nails and brought up to handle every kind of bush labouring work, just the same as the men. She cut her teeth on gouging clean-skin cattle out of mulga scrub so thick a dog couldn't bark in it. They reckon she could down a mickey full flying gallop through the scrub and knock the agates out of him before you had time to get off your horse.

Bullocky Smith's mate Bricky Sting reckoned:

She could teach a bullick to know 'is name and remember it quicker than anyone ever I seen. She'd gouged this snorty lookin' cock-horned steer out of the mulga scrub to break him in for the team and decided to call 'im Jack. She had him in the crush, and every time she called out Jack, she striped 'im across the arse with a shovel. It wasn't long before he'd nearly fly out the end of the crush every time someone said Jack.

When 'e was properly broken in to the team and they'd put a young lad on to help with work around the place, they had to change the lad's name, because it was Jack too. When somebody yelled out, 'Jack, give us a bit of a hand here for a bit, will yer?' the steer started bellowing and went berserk — ripping backward and forward in the bow and frightening the rest of the team. So they changed young Jack's name to Toby.

But Toby reckoned: 'Bugger that bloody Greenhide. Why couldn't she 'ave changed th' bloody bullick's name — done like bloody Toby — sooner 'ave Jack.'

The bullock bellowed again an' charged inter th' bow.

'Look, fer Christ sake,' Greenhide says, just arriving on the scene, 'don't say Jack in front of that bullick.'

But it was too late — she'd jist done it. Aaaaaa. Soon as Greenhide mentioned Jack — 'e wez down on 'is knees an' bellowin' agin.

As horses bred up, they were run out of the scrub, wild as hawks, and broken in for dray and buggy work or as saddle horses for stock work.

The boss was up in the buggy breaking in a toey young colt early one morning. Greenhide Liz from the shade of a mulga tree, was shrieking Father, Father — as chips of shattered pine dashboard started whistling all round the boss's head from flying hooves as this wild scrubber colt kicked up and farted. It had just about demolished the dashboard while nearly turning itself inside out trying to dislodge the crupper jammed under its tail and leave the harness and rig behind. Impatient to be part of the action, Greenhide bounded up among the flying bits of dashboard and reefed the reins out of the boss's hands. She shouldered him overboard and brought the kicking farting colt back into line with a few stripes of the whip and a volley of bush lingo not meant for the ears of respectable delicate ladies.

When we were young, most stations had Aboriginals working on the place. Dad always paid our Aboriginal station hands proper award wages, but other places often paid very low wages or none at all, just keeping them in cheap working clothes and tucker. Sometimes, perhaps as a special treat, they were given a few shillings if the hawker turned up, and, on rare occasions, perhaps a trip to town if someone from the station was going in.

A well-known drover with a couple of places not far from us used to bring mobs of cattle down from the big Gulf stations. When he was in that remote country, he and the men used to round up a few likely looking young blacks and bring them back with the cattle to work on one of his runs. He chained them to the wagonette wheels with the dogs at night so they couldn't get away. His exploits were well known, but nothing was ever done about it.

The Aborigines I remember were quiet, decent old people, certainly very lonely if there was only one on the place. There was a blacks' camp on Wallum Creek near Bollon when I was a boy and others were camped along the Culgoa and Balonne Minor rivers, both sides of Dirranbandi, and along the Balonne River around St George. Other small groups had camps at permanent holes along all the western rivers, generally close to local towns.

The Dirranbandi publican was well liked by the local Aborigines because he always treated the kids with kindness and helped the old people in times of sickness. In hot weather he made a practice of having an afternoon swim in a waterhole in the creek. The kids from the camp went in too. They were all eyes, of course, and never missed a trick. They noticed he wore a wide leather belt low down to hold in place a hernia, which had sagged down and formed a large lump in one testicle.

When he wouldn't hand out any more drinks and tobacco to the mob that gradually began hanging around the old pub, they'd wait until he went to bed upstairs, then start chanting from down under the verandah: 'Ole boss pubman got a big ball, ole missus pubman got none at all, Dirranbandi.'

They'd keep it up until the poor old pair came down in their nightshirts with some lollies and hunted them away so they could get some sleep.

Most of the scattered small groups of Aborigines gradually moved in to the fringes of western towns where they built a collection of rough bush shanties out of flattened petrol tins and old bags on the banks of permanent holes bordering the towns. The shanties were like rubbish dumps full of dogs, naked dirty children and often drunk unemployed parents lying around in the dust. (Cheap plonk mixed with metho was common drinking gear in those days.) A few white people felt sorry for them, but most didn't bother to analyse why this formerly proud race had reached such levels of depravity or why something wasn't done to help these poor lost people get out of the hopeless mess they were in. Their country had been taken from them and their culture destroyed as the tribes became fragmented. They were constantly raided by police and often belted up for being drunk and dirty. At no time was the provision of any form of amenities contemplated. Eventually they were rounded up and shifted away to distant government reserves and church mission stations like Cherbourg and Woorabinda to get them out of sight. Some on cattle stations where they were part of the stock camps were taken away, often against the wishes of the owners or managers.

Many of the Aboriginal stockmen had a wonderful, refreshing sense of dry humour. The trouble was, it often came at a most inopportune moment that was something of a crisis in the eyes of the white boss, but one hell of a big joke to them. The Crown Land ranger responsible for our area was a huge fat man nearly 20 stone. His main job was plotting scattered prickly pear that had escaped the cactoblastis and checking boundary fences and areas of ringbarking and suckering. The property he was inspecting at the time had to supply him with quiet horses, all of which ended up with sore backs in a day or two and out of operation for weeks. He'd have to find a log or a stump to climb on before flopping into the saddle with a bit of a squelch, whereupon the horse staggered away with a bowed back under the load. Dick Taylor on adjoining Rutherglen always maintained he had 'teeth in his arse', because everything he rode had a sore back after a day or two and a patch of hide missing. Of course this wasn't wasted on Harry, the tall thin Aboriginal Stockman we had on Thrushton off and on for years. He was about six feet three long and poor as a crow — you could nearly see through him.

The day arrived when Thrushton was due for inspection. Dad gave the big ranger a couple of quiet horses and hoped for the best. Sure enough, the first horse was out of action halfway through the first week, so he started with the second horse. A few days later he came back with it puddling along sideways, its back bent down in the shape of a pothook under the load. He climbed off the horse and, being a very hot day, made straight for the waterbag. While he was away, Dad removed the saddle and as he lifted it, a big patch of hair and hide as big and round as the top of a tobacco tin came away, stuck with blood and hair to the saddle cloth.

'Holy Moses, what's a man to do,' Pappy snorted. 'We'll all be walking soon. There'll be no horses left if this keeps up much longer. Wish he'd finish and get off the bloody place while there's still a few horses left.'

Harry, meanwhile, was leaning up against a nearby mulga tree, sizing up the situation and, of course, still chewing over the bit about 'teeth in his arse' — really top stuff that amused Harry no end. He was a very funny old cove who started every sentence with 'I finkt, boss, yer know, boss'.

As Dad inspected the damage, Harry left the tree in peace for a bit and came a couple of steps closer to be nearer the scene of disaster. 'I finkt, boss, yer know, boss, tat ole Range man got big set of little tooth belong 'im tat bloody arse'ole, yer know, boss. I finkt tat ole arse'ole 'ave little feed of 'orse wile ole Range man poke about a scrubs lookin' for a pears plant [prickly pear], yer know, boss.'

'Yes, yes, Harry, all right, all right,' said Pappy. 'Get me the Stockholm tar out of the shed.' Under his breath he muttered, 'Bloody old fool.'

Harry had a bit of a limp from a fight with a spike-horned mickey. While mustering he was trying to shoulder this young scrub bull back into the mob, but his horse was too light and the bull too strong.

There was only one tree on the plain and the horse, not being strong enough to turn the bull, they were heading straight for it. Harry dragged the horse sideways to miss the tree but, as he came round the other side, the bull met him and drove a horn clean through the calf of his leg and reefed him off the horse. He hit the ground with the bull's horn still through his leg as he was dragged and thrown about in the burrs.

For thousands of years, Aboriginal tribes had worked the country hunting and gathering while surface water remained, but, as the country dried out, they shifted their main camps to more permanent holes. They generously passed on information about water, its location and the type of surrounding country in friendly fashion and child-like trust. This was their custom. Many a sick or lost white man had been led to the safety of a shady waterhole, given food and treated with kindness. But, as settlement spread, stockroutes followed major streams for the water and the best permanent holes were soon confiscated for homesteads and out-stations. It wasn't long before competition for water and the best country surrounding it led to confrontation between the original tribal owners and the new settlers. The old people watched with alarm as the white man's destructive animals ate out the best hunting grounds and bogged and muddied up the waterholes.

Cattle seem to have no brains at all where water is concerned. You'll often see them wade through the mud of a drying waterhole and as they reach the water and lower their head to drink, their tail goes in the air and they start to defecate and urinate in the water. It's no time before the last remaining water is a thick mixture of mud reeking of ammonia and green with cattle dung that nothing can drink.

As the country was eaten out, game moved further from water and the hungry local tribes began spearing an occasional beast for food. Relationships, though friendly at first, deteriorated as natives strived to maintain a foothold in their own country in order to survive and the settlers wanted them gone. These wandering hunter-gatherers were no match for the white man's introduced diseases, police and guns.

Indigenous peoples had been here so long that they'd become an important balancing force in the local environment. One of the first signs of a breakdown in the natural control system was the increasing kangaroo population. Kangaroos had been a major part of the Aboriginal peoples' diet, which kept their numbers low. The eastern scrubby mulga country has always favoured grey kangaroos, with reds occupying areas of heavier soils and the open western plains. As the local Aborigines were wiped out, their hunting routine died with them and kangaroo populations exploded, later increasing dramatically as country was opened up and developed for grazing animals and watered by artesian bores and tanks.

When Edmond Kennedy left Sydney en route to central Queensland in 1847, his expedition rode through the bush for hundreds of miles before sighting the first kangaroo on a tributary of the Warrego River, near where the Queensland–New South Wales border is today. Twenty-two years later, the then *Brisbane Courier* gave a graphic account of the explosion of kangaroo numbers:

> *Surely no man can believe, with such numbers of kangaroos staring him in the face that preserving the dingo will eradicate the kangaroo. No Sir . . . the cause of the great increase in these animals is due to the destruction of the Aborigines. I have often seen as many as 300 of these daring muscular hunters and any number of hungry looking dogs all fed on the spoils of the day's hunt, mainly kangaroos.*

With the Aborigines gone, hundreds of kangaroos bred up where few existed before. Kangaroos plus introduced animals like pigs, goats, donkeys, camels, dingos, foxes, cats, rabbits and domestic stock increasingly threatened the land and the smaller marsupials and other native wildlife. The former healthy biological balance disappeared with settlement. Provision of artificial water and land clearing for agriculture also played a major role, as did the absence of tribal hunting and their constant seasonal burning that kept the country open and well grassed. All these factors, superimposed on continuous heavy grazing with insufficient spelling, has led to the woody weed (shrub regrowth) invasion of arid grazing lands and has provided protective cover for native and feral animals while reducing its viable use for pastoralism. Lack of sensitivity and disregard for the rights of the original owners whose livelihood depended on free access to land and water has been a shameful episode in our early history with which many sensitive people still have difficulty coping.

Growing up in that country in those days was a peaceful, carefree existence surrounded on all sides by nature. At that time families stayed together and everything was shared. Nobody had any money and only the barest of possessions, while home and the close-knit family unit was life itself and we needed nothing more. It was a time before technology and the advertising and media barons began to pull it all apart. It was a time before cooperation had been replaced by ruthless competition and almost hourly 'news' bulletins became sensational serials.

Even the toys that gave most pleasure were made by us — out of herring and tomato sauce tins with a piece of wire through a hole at one end. Our tin lorries, loaded with currajong seedpods we called 'mousies' and bits of coloured glass for money, were dragged along 'roads' between grass tussocks to hollow stumps that became our towns and trading posts. From our towns, we traded kangaroo pills and shiny coloured beetles and bought and sold mousies. When proper mice got into the drums of fowl feed, we'd kill and skin them and, after salting down the skins to stop them going bad, we'd peg them out with pins to dry. We'd load up with mouse skins and currajong-pod mousies and drag our herring and tomato sauce tin lorries along dusty roads to our trading centres to start a booming fur trade. It kept us busy and was good clean fun.

We always had plenty of pets too; mostly bowerbirds, magpies, butcherbirds, jackasses, lousy jacks and a white-faced heron that couldn't stop eating. We'd keep passing him bits we cut off an emu's leg until he was so full the last bit was jammed just behind his tongue and couldn't go any further down — but he still kept trying! Old Wizzbang, the bowerbird, was the daddy of all rogues and always took the prize when it came to skilful manoeuvring. Often pushed about and bullied by the bigger birds at feeding time, he'd get right up high on the top perch of the big bird enclosure and loudly mimic hawks and crows until all his terrified mates feeding down below scurried away for cover. Then he'd drop down in a flash and have a great blow-out of all the tucker by himself. The strange thing was that the other birds never woke up to old Wizzbang's crafty antics, which suited Wizzbang because he soon started shining like a corn-fed horse on all this free tucker.

And, of course, we always had stacks of fowls and chickens and ducks as well. Some of these also were pets. They became our horses and cattle as we worked them about the chookyard and in and out of boxes. And we put bells on them too (quandong seeds) and hobbled out the roosters by tying string round their spurs and had great fun watching them trying to mount the old clucky hens or chase the young flappers. They'd fall head over turkey and kick about in the dust every time they tried to get on top. The old hens just lay there in the dust wondering what the hell had gone wrong with these normally virile strutting gentlemen.

But our very special favourite was Tuckey Crotchety who became part of the family.

Our neighbour's governess kindly approached we three red-eyed boys after poor Tuckey Crotchety's sad accident —

'So why the minute's silence,' she softly asked. 'This surely must have been some personage of note?'

Well yes, I suppose she *was* a personage of note to bush kids like us, you know. It's all so long ago now but it's how it was with us then — her unique qualities and tragic death, I mean, and the effect it had on us.

Memories become fuzzy with time, don't they? I can't even

remember how she got that name now, yet I do remember she was the runt in a family of eight — small, delicate and prone to tripping over long crooked toes on tiny feet that ran east–west. You see, Tuckey Crotchety was a White Leghorn and Black Orpington cross and, being so odd and runty, so to speak, she was picked at by every passing fowl. So my younger brother Frank in his kindness saved her from further distress.

'Poor wee mite,' he said. 'She's not quite the full quid, you know, as he carefully slid her under his bed in a discarded David Jones' shoe box.

Revelling in such kindness, Tuckey Crotchety soon outgrew the shoe box and graduated to a colourful Arnott's Biscuit tin from which she made excursions, along with Allawichis, our liquorice-all-sorts cat, to pick up scraps we *accidentally* dropped at meal-time.

And she grew and grew like Jack and the Bean Stalk until one morning the strangest thing happened that startled Allawichis. Numerous black spots, leopard fashion, if you get my meaning, like extra eyes peered out from her snow-white gown of new-spun silky feathers. Armed with the newly acquired status of dainty princess she began helping herself to food on the dining-room table. Often bogged in gravy and custard, she left tell-tale crooked tracks on the white table-cloth so numerous they couldn't all be covered with salt and pepper shakers or by tomato sauce bottle and chutney jar. Pappy demanded her removal forthwith — from house to chookyard where fowls belong. This sudden decision had a marked effect on Frank, who sensed the imminence of tragedy, being as he was, spiritually connected to Tuckey Crotchety's soul which flashed visions of future worldly events before him like a magic lantern show.

It all started in the night paddock. Tuckey's glittering spotted appearance and dignified upright stance attracted the big rooster's strutting attention. Quite overcome, he sidled up to her with one wing hanging down rigid and clicking beside a frantically kicking leg as he shouldered her about the yard and under bushes. These feather-rattling antics embarrassed poor bashful Tuckey, as you'd expect with one so young and innocent. She became ruffled and bedraggled and

lost considerable weight from his constant advances, which left her no
opportunity to develop a personality of her own.

She was in the paddock scratching around grass tussocks one
morning when the big boss rooster, bewitched by Tuckey's reserve
and carriage, decided to run her down and demand his perceived
conjugal rights. He took off, head stretched out in front, stirring up
little puffs of dust as he gathered speed, flashing spurs of enormous
proportion so alluring to the lower classes but terrifying and insult-
ing to one of Tuckey's station. She took one look over her shoulder
and bolted with wildly flapping wings for extra speed on those long
east–west crooked toes. The boss rooster was closing fast when the
fence loomed ahead and Tuckey speared straight under the bottom
wire. But the rooster, his mind full of male-conquering intrigue,
didn't see it. His long glistening neck with bight red comb and black
beak attached (the ultimate sex symbol to the irresponsible) spun twice
round the wire. The rest of him continued on, hanging momentarily
in space with the odd departing feather, until the stretched wire,
shanghai fashion, shot him back to earth with a thump. Brave Tuckey
kept going and didn't look back. My two brothers and I watched in
dismay at this stirring display of Tuckey's resolve and turn of speed,
but, alas, the rooster was past resuscitation. So we plucked and cleaned
him and Doolie roasted him for dinner along with beautiful big
brown potatoes, pumpkin, onions and gravy. He was just lovely, — so
sweet and tender, Pappy said, and we all agreed.

Approaching poor Tuckey Crotchety to offer our condolence, for
she was quite deranged by her ordeal, we found she had lost one of
her eyes, torn out on the barbed wire fence. As Frank observed, 'Poor
Tuckey has only one lamp now.' Thereafter she ambled along sideways, leaning against the fence on her blind side as if about to climb
the netting, her head bent a bit to one side and bobbing yoyo-
fashion. Just then our Sunday's mail lorry came rumbling along the
track following the fence, its engine noise and rattles startling poor
Tuckey Crotchety, bless the tiny soul. She took fright and shied sideways straight under the back wheel with a muffled little squawk,

leaving a slightly out-of-shape yet neat little bundle of black and white spotted feathers on the track behind.

Tears of mourning for poor Tuckey fell like a shower of rain. She'd become 'one of us' and hence sorely missed, you see. Frank was adamant she receive a proper Christian burial commensurate with the dignity and royalty of such a fowl. On our way to the cemetery, a hole dug at the butt of a box tree near the bore drain in front of the homestead, we were a small solemn procession. Keith, Frank and I lead the way, followed by Allawichis, our two dogs, Spare-Ribs and Bootlace, our pet galah Gibbit and pet bowerbird Whizzbang. Tuckey, bundled up in a white pillow-slip, was reverently nursed between us. With closed eyes and bowed heads in respect for the recently deceased, we said a prayer and covered her up.

Frank made a little white cross for the grave at which, on more than one occasion, I found him silently standing with head bowed. The sun had gone and the bush birds were silent as the evening stars began to appear. Poor Tuckey Crotchety, soul now at peace with her maker, had been lain to rest.

I hope this adequately expresses the sorrow felt by three bush kids in their great loss all those years ago.

We called ourselves 'Spirits of the Night' because of our nightly raids on the mobs of sleeping lousy jacks. There were always mobs of lousy jacks (happy families or apostle birds) around every homestead. These medium-sized friendly little brownish grey birds are common to inland areas. The noisy little blighters scurry up into the nearest tree with a loud rasping chorus of nasal squawks at the least sign of any unexpected movement. They make good pets and love being bunched together in a heap while chattering away building their mud and grass nest. Packed tightly together along the top rails of yards and gates or balanced along the top wire of fences, they never miss a feed with the fowls and ducks, which they seem to accept as their natural right. We carefully noted the mulga trees the lousies camped in at night. No modern things like torches for us, of course. Such gear belonged to the more privileged classes, so we made our own by anchoring a candle in the bottom of a shiny new four-gallon petrol tin. Made quite a good light, too, that worked pretty well when there was no wind, though the range was a bit on the short side. We boys camped out on the verandah and pretended to be asleep until everyone had gone to bed, then up we'd get, light our beacon and start out nightly prowling. We'd climb up to the rows of lousies, one with the beacon and the other with a sugar bag.

The old lousies would all be tightly jammed together along mulga limbs with heads tucked under wings snoring away, probably dreaming about bran and pollard in the chookyard. We'd reach up and jerk them down into the bag one at a time and climb down. On the ground again at the butt of the tree we'd pull out their tail feathers and let them go in the tree again. There'd be all sorts of chattering going on as they asked each other what had happened so suddenly. Pappy and Doolie used to go crook, but we told them the lousies got caught in a whirlygig (whirlwind) that blew their tails off. They'd be all bottom-heavy for a day or two as they peddled about the sky with their butt ends facing the ground. They used to line the chookpen fence like lumps of horse dung. A passing cattle buyer wanted to know what kind of birds they were — hadn't seen that kind before!

When Frank was about six years old, he had a very close shave. We were always burning off and clearing the scrub around the homestead so you could see out a few hundred yards and to make it easier to handle stock. We all worked together but Dad sometimes was away on the run and it was only Doolie and we three boys.

We had started in the night paddock and had fires burning everywhere in the dead ringbarked box trees. We loved fires, just as the old Aborigines did, but they can be very dangerous if you don't know what you're doing and haven't learnt to read the signs. The Aborigines never stopped lighting grass fires while ever grass would burn, and stopped only when dry times made it dangerous. It made the country easier to walk through and easier to see game in when the bush animals followed the fires to get the green pick sprouting around burnt tussocks. Also it got rid of the burrs and sharp sticks.

Frank went in to stoke up a big box tree that had been stoving for days down in the roots below the ground. It was on the point of falling but we didn't notice that. When he'd almost reached the place where the smoke was coming out, there was a loud crack and the tree began to fall. We all yelled out, but it was too late. As he ran to get away, one of the small top branches hit him on top of the head and knocked him flat. He didn't move. We raced in, but he was limp as a rag and wasn't breathing. Terror-stricken, we thought he was dead. Doolie carried him back to the house and, after what seemed hours, he started to breathe again and began to cry, so we knew he was going to be all right.

As there were no schools at all out in the bush in the early days, many of the old timers couldn't read or write and their speech was often a collection of bush phrases, strung together without any precise meaning. But they always seemed to be understood, particularly by those of their own age and circumstances. They all had a certain dignity about them. Most were kind old people with hearts of gold who could always be relied on. Some were closed-up types who'd been poked away in camps for so long they'd forgotten how to converse. They always camped away from other people and seemed a bit strange somehow, only talking to themselves or their dogs. If anyone looked like turning up at their camp for some reason or other, they wouldn't be there — they'd have planted out in the scrub, just far enough away to keep an eye on the caller without being seen. They couldn't face going through the embarrassing ordeal of trying to hold a conversation. As kids, we were as wild as hawks and tough as nails from living with all these old whiskery, pipe-smoking scrubbers, who treated us no differently from all the other men. Some would carve a knob of black plug tobacco off the cake and stoke up their pipe, others would chew it instead and, as often as not, pass it over to us to have a go at too. The things we used to get up to make my hair stand on end now but were perfectly natural then. How we ever grew up without someone knocking us on the head before we had time to change our ways has always remained a mystery.

We had an old draught-mare called Leaner, because that's what she did. When the woodpile got down a bit, Alf White, a typical good old cove, would harness Leaner and back her into the dray, then away we'd go to find a good hollow log that was easy to split. It could be a mile or two down the run. Very slowly poking along to the plop-plop, scrape-scrape of Leaner's hooves as she dragged them through the dust, it got hotter and hotter as we went along. Alf was perched up on a kerosene case in the centre of the dray, holding the reins, giving Leaner a stripe across the butt end with them every now and then to stop her going to sleep. Frank and I sat on the crossbar in front just behind Leaner's tail, with legs dangling down underneath.

As the painfully slow swinging motion continued, old Alf, with cinders and smoke funnelling out of his pipe, began to snore-off as things got slower and slower. Every few minutes Leaner's tail rose up gradually, inch by inch, till it was nearly standing on end, then a great shining black arse, like the snout of one of those old sliding Kodak cameras, just as slowly came further and further out, glistening as it grew. We were fascinated by this spectacle in slow motion, for everything about Leaner and old Alf was in slow motion. Then came a ferocious, slow motion and long drawn-out fart that seemed to come from the very depths of the earth and go on for about a minute. Alf gave a grunt or two and stirred slowly in his sleep on the box while Frank and I, directly in the firing line, sat suffocated in the foul hot blast.

This went on with monotonous regularity until we could stand it no longer. We looked at each other and then at all the chips from previous loads on the floor of the dray. We got one each about six inches long and waited. Up went the tail again and out grew the shining black monster as it protruded with approaching action. At the crucial moment, in went the chips, and all hell broke loose. Waking with a startled snort, Leaner's tail slammed down like a meat-house door, driving the chips home, to be blown out of this black cannon a second later as the farts began to explode like thunder and she headed for the scrub. We and the dray parted company with Leaner in her headlong flight as she cleared a big log and the dray stayed behind. Alf went up in the air with his hat and pipe a bit higher and carved a furrow through a patch of rolypoly and burrs as he hit the ground, probably still dreaming about some old barmaid in a back-country pub somewhere. He got half up a couple of times and fell down again.

Not knowing which way he was facing as he raked at the burrs and bits of grass hooked up in hair and beard, he started to bellow, 'I'm gunner tell your fuckin' father on yous. Bushrangin' pair er little buggers. Bloody well git a man kilt before yez is through.'

Fearing the worst, we'd already gone, not far behind Leaner's dust as she gathered speed with the harness and trace-chains stretched out behind like a flag. All was forgiven when we turned up a bit later leading Leaner and, with bits of wire, helped Alf put the harness together again.

Our cook was a rough and tough old girl. Dolly had been cooking in camps around the back country for years with ringbarkers, shearers and droving outfits.

There was no humbug with Dolly — a spade was never a spade, it was 'a friggin' shovel'. The twenty-stone Crown Land ranger had just left and the jackaroo, hearing Dolly flog the brake drum, came over for smoko. As he came through the kitchen door, he asked Dolly what she thought of the big old ranger.

With sweat dripping off her brow, Dolly was halfway between the galley and the kitchen table with a camp oven half full of spluttering fat with a mob of puftaloons galloping about on top. Propping in her tracks to consider such a searching question, she put the camp oven on the floor as a puzzled look came over her sweaty face. She struggled for the right answer, and found it: 'Well, 'e 'ad a nice harse for driving a lazy prick!'

Dolly was no lady and wasn't one for chitchat. That summed up the situation as far as she was concerned with a bare minimum of effort!

Times changed with closer settlement and better roads, and the

Queensland Correspondence School was established to bring education to bush youngsters on the new runs. Packets of lessons were sent
out from headquarters in Brisbane to all outlying properties where
there was no school, which meant everywhere away from the occasional towns. Up until about 1930, lessons came out on the mail lorry
every second week and went back for marking, meanwhile being
replaced with a new batch. As conditions and road access improved,
mail services increased to once a week. These days it's two or three
times a week. Doolie began giving us lessons as best she could, but
with all the other work in and around the house, she had to put on
a governess to belt a bit of gumption into her wild bush kids. When
we weren't trading salted mouse skins we devoted out efforts to
devising new and terrible methods of getting rid of the latest governess. To us she was just another obstacle to be overcome. Most of
them poked off back to the city after a bit, but we had to stuff a frill-
necked lizard or two under their blankets on a cold winter night to
shift some of the more stubborn ones.

Cars and motor lorries eventually replaced the bullock wagons
and horse and cart. Before pneumatic tyres, the heavy, lumbering,
solid-tyred lorries bellowed their way through the dust, often with a
column of steam belching forth from a gaping hole where the radiator cap should have been. It was impossible to cool the old heavy
engines, which never stopped boiling in the summer time. Tins of
water had to be carried on the back to keep topping up the radiator
before it boiled dry every few miles. Afghan and Indian hawkers too,
with their horses and covered wagonettes, worked their way round
the western stations for many years. Most moved out rather than try
to compete with the new breed of European hawkers who took over
with motor trucks and cars.

Old Fuzzel Dean, the Indian hawker who did the three-monthly
rounds of that country when I was a boy, was always cause for great
excitement. He trundled out of the scrub in his covered wagon and
horses to a chorus of barking dogs and pulled up in the shade beside
the homestead. With a 'Woah now 'orses and 'dit away tinkin blooda

dorgs', he'd climb down off the load sporting an enormous grey beard with a little brown hole in the middle, singed bare from lighting cigarette bumpers and a set of well worn fangs gone rusty from chewing puftaloons and treacle. He had everything on that wagon from mouth organs and carbide to spurs and chamber pots — the white enamel ones with black handles and pink roses round the side. 'Look 'ere, missus, nice beauteeful calico,' he'd say, 'only ninepence 'apenny a yard I gibbit.'

As there was never any money and labour was always short during mustering time, we sometimes became part of the mustering camp away out in the back paddocks miles from home to give a hand with the stock work, much to the annoyance of the governess. Our job was to drive the mob of sheep from each day's muster along fences to the woolshed and yards seven or eight miles away. Also we were to have wood at the fire and fill nosebags to feed the horses when the men came back to camp about dark.

We sat looking into the fire for a while after tea, listening to the hair-raising tales told by the old blokes round the fire. They picked their teeth and blew the loose bits into the coals with a bit of a sizzle and we'd eventually go to sleep to the music of card talk over in the tent.

This is how it went:

'Oos knocked me bloody pannikin er tea arse over 'ead? Bet 'e put 'is stinkin' great 'oof in it too.'

His mate alongside would reply, 'Orrr stop belly-achin', yer coulden a wanted th' bloody stuff any'ow or yer woulder drunk 'er a bloody hour ago.'

'Fifteen two, fifteen four an' a pairs six — aaaa, 'ang on a bit, wot about 'is bloody knob, yer git a hextra couple for that bastard too, yer know.'

From over at the poker game would come: 'Jesus Crise, 'e's th' luckiest bugger ever I seen. That's 'is second full 'and in 'alf a hour. More harse than the bloody ole cart mare an' 'ers is four foot wide — shit, jist as well I didn't went, aaaaaa?'

Sunday tennis parties at neighbouring properties became the general entertainment on weekends and many good times were had. There was very little other entertainment for adults, few motor cars and poor roads. Every property had a tennis court and there was a tennis party on somewhere every Sunday. But the men were often too knocked-up from ringbarking, fencing and scrub-cutting to be bothered opening and closing all the paddock gates while travelling miles through endless dust in churned-up dusty stockroutes on bad roads to a party if it was too far away.

While the older people were on the court, all we kids would be out in the scrub roo shooting or climbing trees after birds' nests and collecting the eggs. Every bush kid spent a lot of time bird nesting and each had a collection of all the different kinds of birds' eggs in their district. Many of the eggs were beautifully marked. Some were in delicate pastel shades of blues, greens and buff, overlain with different coloured spots or squiggles. We punched a hole in each end of the egg and blew out the contents, and, after drying, put them in boxes lined with cotton wool.

We all were proud of our collections and were always swapping eggs with other kids to increase our range. Everybody who came to the place was treated to an inspection of the prize collection and gave the expected praise for presentation. Of course, there was always a bit of roguery attached to it too. We often got the common white eggs like those from crows, egrets and jackasses and painted them with mulberry juice, red and blue ink and paint. We couldn't fool each other, though, because we'd all had a go at the same thing. The pretty 'doctored' eggs were reserved for the inexperienced only, where they generally met with success.

Many of the Aborigines were expert at carving emu eggs too, with all kinds of designs in the different coloured shell layers. Others carved bullock horns, bones and wood. Like many white people, they were artistic, clever with their hands, and could sit all day scraping away at whatever they were working on at the time.

CHAPTER 5

The School of Life

CITY people had no conception of pastoralism or the living conditions of those working inland runs. They thought graziers lived the free and easy lifestyle of the wealthy squatter, who presided over vast stretches of land from his rambling colonial homestead. Most governesses probably came out to the bush with the aim of trying to snare one of these tall, bronzed tycoons. Then they planned to settle down to play the boss's lady, dressing up for tea that was prepared by the cook in the kitchen and brought to the long polished dining room table in style by a maid and a wing of jackaroos dressed up in collar and tie.

They probably nearly passed out when they found that most of their 'wealthy squatters' were uninteresting hide-bound bush labourers who knew very little of anything but hard work from daylight till dark and who had just enough energy left to crawl into their swags after a feed at night. It was mostly hard axe work cutting scrub, ring-barking, suckering and cutting rails, humped long distances on your shoulder for yard building. A surgical operation would have been needed to carve the axe from their leathery claw-like hands, all cracks and corns. Maybe it was this let-down feeling that made some of our governesses as cranky as old barren cart mares. Miss Brady was one. Always slimming, she only ever had a cup of warm water for breakfast — probably full of worms too. It was never safe to say 'good morning' to her till about three o'clock in the afternoon.

I don't remember any of the governesses teaching us much. In fact, looking back now, they themselves didn't know much. There were so many interesting things happening into which our 'bush' ears were tuned all the time: a bull bellowing away out in the scrub somewhere, a dog barking, horse bells ringing, bird calls we knew by heart and kept a tab on, an emu drumming out in the spinifex.

One sound that always brought giggles, accompanied by a stripe across the butt end with a mulga switch, was the high-pitched, sing-song sounds made by nest-building hornets. They were different sizes and colours and built mud nests on pretty well anything they could find. They even started building behind grandfather's ear while he was asleep on the verandah one hot afternoon. We used to watch these fascinating hard-working little hornets for hours, as they scurried back and forth building their nests with rolled-up balls of mud, each compartment carefully moulded to the correct shape. Their nearest mud supply was only few yards away beneath the leaking waterbag which made a tiny puddle of mud on the dirt floor alongside our schoolroom door. As they rolled up each mud ball with their front legs, their eyes glistened and feelers waved while they hummed and wined like a bogged lorry. The sound gradually tapered off to a low drone as the operation was near completion, exactly the same as a vehicle labouring under a heavy load. It was a constant source of mirth to us, but really stirred up the cranky old governesses to fever point because they had no sense of humour at all.

The hornets built a series of mud compartments, one beside the other, along rafters or walls and under the house. As each cabin was completed, the hornet buzzed off to find a spider out sunning itself, swooped in and stung it behind the head to paralyse it, then labori-ously lugged it, often twice its own weight, in reverse gear up the tree trunk or wall to the nest. Here, the spider was unceremoniously bun-dled inside and an egg was laid on its big fat tummy so the young hornet would lead a life of luxury at the spider's expense until the time to leave home. Each compartment in turn was then sealed off with a mud door, one at a time, until every compartment supposedly

Hillsborough, not far from Thrushton, out in the Maranoa country in south-west Queensland, was one of the first runs taken up in that country by the pioneering Marsh family. The homestead was built in early 1860.

The St George—Yeulba coach-change at Burgorah.

A family picnic on the new Thrushton block in 1919. Left to right: Dad's sister May, younger brother Hugh, Doolie (Mum), Grandmother Gasteen, Grandfather (John), Dad's eldest sister Elsie and her husband Len Byth. Dad took the photo.

Left to right: Auntie May and her daughter Mary, Jim, Doolie, Keith and Frank on the edge of the spinifex in front of Grandfather's seat where he sat while handing out jelly beans and peanuts to we children.

Wrixon and Lorna (Dad and Doolie) on their wedding day in 1920.

On the running board of Dad's old Model T Ford in 1925. Left to right: Keith, Ena (Hugh's wife), John Gasteen (Grandfather) with me on his knee, and Dolly the cook.

Me with two of the old saddle horses in 1925.

The old 'Tin Lizzies' (Model T Fords) and horses were never far apart in the 1920s when heavy rain turned the station tracks into muddy swamps.

Dense prickly pear infestation for hundreds of square miles on each side of the Dirranbandi/St George road before the release of cactoblastis in 1925.

Me with a pet kangaroo in 1936.

Keith and me pretending to be Fuzzle Dean — the old hawker of all manner of things — who did the six-monthly rounds of that country in his horse and cart in the 1920s.

Doolie with we three boys: me with glasses, Keith and Frank, in the Thrushton garden about 1926. The netting enclosure, to stop birds from eating all the grapes, had just been erected.

Dad and Doolie's Thrushton garden, watered by carrying four-gallon kerosene tins of bore water from a 'dip-hole' in the Wierbolla bore drain.

Tank sinking with the bullocks, mouldboard plough and scoop on Thrushton in 1938. The ground was so hard the plough would hardly mark it, which accounted for the many shallow tanks in that country before the arrival of powerful heavy bulldozers.

Keith's friend Ida with me and Moodgie in front of the Sixty-fiveMile bore in 1939, with Tom Duffy's old bark hut in the background.

housed a fresh spider, at which point the hornet called it a day and faded away.

We found an old 1892 model American 32.40 Winchester rifle at a camp some men had just left down the back of Thrushton. It had no front sight and its rusty octagonal barrel was full of hornets' nests and dirt. We poked out the dirt with wire and filled the barrel with vinegar and let it soak there for about a week, then cleaned it out and fired a few shots that blew a great hole in the ground. It was a big heavy rifle, with an enormous bullet and a kick like a draughthorse. No smokeless gun powder in those days, of course. Every time you fired, a cloud of black smoke and flame followed the bullet and then a shattering explosion. The black gunpowder came in tin cans with a screw-top lid to keep out the moisture. Most stations had their own reloading gear with calibrated measure for the correct amount of gunpowder for each cartridge before the lead bullet was pressed home. If nobody was watching we put in a bit more powder to give her that extra boot.

We were in the schoolroom under the house just before lessons were about to start. I was showing Keith and Frank how to uncock the old Winchester without opening the breech from underneath. The trick was to hold the hammer with the thumb of your right hand while squeezing the trigger with the index finger of the same hand while letting the hammer in slowly so it didn't strike the firing pin and fire the bullet. But I'd been oiling the breech mechanism and it was slippery.

'Quick, here comes old Daydie [Miss Brady],' warned Frank.

Hearing the rapid jerky tock, tock, tock of her boots on the dirt floor under the house as she made for the schoolroom, I tried to hurry things up. My thumb slipped off the hammer and the bullet went off just as she put her foot on the corn bag mat in the doorway. A tongue of flame flew out the end of the barrel followed by a thunderous roar and black acid smoke filled the room. The bullet blew a crater-like hole surrounded by a big black circle of gunpowder soot about an inch from her big toe as she stood on the mat. She let out a blood-curdling shriek and reared straight over backwards on the ground with a thump, her eyes turned back to front and her eyelashes battered like the wings of a butterfly. Stunned and pretty alarmed by the sight, we just looked her over for a bit, stretched out there — didn't know what to do. Suddenly we thought, *water*, that's supposed to bring them round when they faint or whatever. So we grabbed the four-gallon kerosene tin that caught the drips from the rusty rain-water tank and threw the cold water all over her. Strike, there was some action then. She flew in the air with a half-throttled scream and fell down again. We panicked, dropped the tin and bolted for the scrub and stayed out there all day, not game to come home until after dark.

Hunger got the best of us. We gingerly sneaked into the kitchen to see if any tucker had been left lying around. We were much relieved to find Daydie had gone to bed early with a 'bad headache' and we only had kind-hearted old Pappy and Doolie to contend with. A long lecture followed with promises to be more considerate in future and Pappy announced that we wouldn't be allowed to shoot again for a whole week. But we knew that wouldn't last long because all the dogs had to be fed and it was our job to keep the roos and emus up to them. It wasn't too bad though. Most of our governesses didn't stay long and, after our jobs were done, we were soon able to get back to our hide and fur industry, fed by mice trapped in the fowl feed bins.

Frank and I walked miles along bore drains roo shooting. In dry times (the norm out there in the 1920s and '30s) roos came into the drains to feed on the couch grass that grew in the moisture along the water-line. As all the ringbarkers' camps were on the drains for water, we always managed to turn up at one of them right on dinner time on a Sunday when they were cooking their one big feed of the week. We stood around talking with our mouth watering as the beautiful scents of roast mutton, potatoes, pumpkin, onions and gravy wafted up from the camp oven down the hole with coals and ash covering the lid — couldn't take our eyes off it. Eventually acknowledging defeat, the old blokes would ask us if we'd like to stay and have a bit of dinner with them. We never put up much resistance to such an invitation. I'll never forget those beautiful meals. Some of the old coves were wonderful bush cooks and would always have a big fresh damper to go with the roast and as many pannikins of black tea as you could drink. We'd head back home, miles away, so blown up with tucker and black tea we could hardly walk.

Most bushmen who camped about the runs made beautiful dampers in the camp oven, which was the standard method of cooking. In many ways, they resembled the Aborigines, in that they tended to use whatever seasonal fruit was plentiful and easily gathered from bush plants at the time. In the quandong season, generally September/October, they nearly lived on quandong pies. The red quandongs (*Santalum accuminatum*) are small spreading trees with fleshy green leaves that, depending on the season, provide a heavy crop of round red fruit like large marbles. The fleshy outside skin is the part you eat. We used to eat them raw but the fruit makes delicious pies or stews with a good amount of sugar to counter the acidity. Most people on the properties collected quandongs when they ripened, took out the seed and threaded the two halves of fruit on wire to dry in the sun and be used during the off-seasons.

In the emu nesting season too, when birds started laying, they were tracked back to their nest and eggs collected, always leaving a couple behind to keep things going. Camps were stocked up with eggs for puddings and all kinds of dishes — one emu egg being equal to about ten ordinary fowl's eggs. They mixed an emu egg with flour, then stirred in raisins or sultanas, sometimes quandongs — in fact, whatever happened to be on hand at the time and cooked the most wonderful brownies. You couldn't beat them with a pannikin of black tea when you were hungry — they were a feed in themselves.

Tom Duffy from the Sixty-fiveMile and his droving plant were shifting a big mob of fats from Bulloo Downs on the border south from Thargomindah to the railhead at Cunnamulla. They used the Queensland/New South Wales dog-netting border fence as a wing on one side of the mob until they hit the Paroo River at Hungerford, then followed the Paroo up to Eulo and then the main stockroute to Cunnamulla. At Hungerford the mob met up with Crongy Green, an Aborigine who was camped under a tree on the creek. Crongy pointed to the cattle and then to one of the horses, signifying he wanted a job. As Tom was a man short, he gave Crongy a horse and put him on the tail behind the mob where he couldn't go wrong, indicating that this was to be his position. Crongy was a man of few words and everyone just accepted he was dumb because he only pointed and didn't speak. Things went along fine until a couple of days before the mob arrived at the Eulo watering reserve. Tom reckoned Crongy must have got a whiff of grog wafting on the breeze blowing off the old pub, because he suddenly started to get excited. They were all sitting around the fire after tea that night. Nobody had much to say, just staring into the fire as drovers often do with a full gut while they think their own thoughts.

The usual silence was abruptly broken by Crongy saying, ''Ad a 'orse.'

The whole plant sprang to attention and everyone gaped at one another — hell, he wasn't dumb after all. So they waited for about ten minutes but nothing more came out.

Tom came to the rescue with 'Well, I'll go to buggery — you had a horse one time, Crongy?'

Nothing more happened for about another ten minutes, then Crongy, busy digging a stick in and out of the dirt, 'Yeh' — and about five minutes later — 'Good 'orse.'

They all looked at each other round the fire and waited for the rest of the yarn, but it had already finished! Half an hour later, Crongy got up and crawled into his swag. Next morning there was nothing there — just a few tracks in the dust where his swag had been. He'd walked out sometime during the night. The pull of the grog had been too strong, as it so often was when these old bush hermits got close to a town. When the mob strung into the Eulo watering reserve a day or two later, Crongy was as full as a boot, stretched out under a tree asleep with a couple of dogs and Tom was left to pay the bill, which had been booked up on his account.

We had an old ginger dog that had a terrible snout on wild cats — there were plenty of wild bush cats around. Mustering one day, we heard a 'whoof' away in the distance and rode over to see what he had bailed up this time. Sure enough, there was a big old black and grey striped tom cat perched up on a stump with tail all fluffed out. Ginger, bristles up, was stalking round and round at the base of the stump looking very cocky. As we rode up, the cat flew off the stump and fastened on to Ginger's nose, with its front legs in a bear-hug round his neck and his back legs furiously raking back and forth along Ginger's stomach with tufts of hair hitting the ground with every outward stroke. Trying desperately to shake him off, then trying to ignore him as if he wasn't there, was all to no avail. By the time we belted off the old tom, Ginger's undercarriage was all red stripes and not much hair. But it didn't stop him. In a few days he was at it again.

Dad was always interested in wirelesses and bought his first set in about 1927 — a long black box a couple of feet long with a row of dials and other gadgets in front and a big horn speaker. He corresponded with other enthusiasts all over the place and constantly experimented with new bits and pieces that came on the mail lorry from time to time and were soldered to the rest of the apparatus. One of the accessories was a shiny tin box with a big black dial in front that he was always fiddling with and placed great faith in. He said it was designed to cut out static produced by thunderstorms and dust particles in the atmosphere. If the roars of static and frightening squeals that came out of the speaker were anything to judge by, it wasn't a great success.

To improve reception, he got Bullocky Smith to drag in two tall cypress pine poles and erected them with the aid of winches and several helpers. They were in deep holes he dug close to the house, about fifty yards apart. Twisted copper wire was threaded through pulleys attached to the top of the posts and, when the posts were standing erect and had been properly rammed, the wires were joined to the wireless in the house. But the wire aerial, swinging about in the wind, soon became the favourite perch for mobs of galahs that frequented all that country and, being playful birds, they put on a circus every day. As they clustered close together, their weight bowed the wire down in the middle and stretched it so Dad had to keep re-straining it.

Sometimes, after a dry summer storm, when about a dozen or so enormous raindrops splattered into the dust leaving little saucer-like craters a few feet apart and then blew away, the galahs put on a most hilarious display of gymnastics. Holding the wire in their beak and with wings wildly flapping they'd spin round and round the wire like beautiful pink and grey catherine-wheels, often cutting through the soft copper wire in the process. As birds constantly flew off and circled, others took their place in noisy relays. Everyone enjoyed this entertaining and amusing display and even old Pappy got a smile up and couldn't help seeing the funny side of things until the sheer weight of birds broke the aerial with their wild flapping antics. Then out would come the shotgun to hunt them away for a while.

Dozens of young galahs in nests in the hollow box trees along the bore-drain kept up a continuous monotonous chorus that only changed key from a nasal squawk to a half-choked watery cackle as food was rammed into their mouth. It was a bit like the dripping water of the old Chinese torture and didn't let up till dark, someone racing out every now and then during the day to flog the trees with an axe to break the monotony for a few minutes. Peace and quiet while the axe was at work but, when it stopped, straight back to the squawking again as if nothing had happened.

Australia can proudly boast a very wide range of bush birds, many of them brightly coloured parrots including the common galah, which if not so common would be better appreciated for the beautiful bird it is — the most delicate rose-coloured breast and head and smoky grey back and wings. To see hundreds of them lining the branches of large dead trees as the sun goes down and highlights their colours is a sight of great beauty. Hundreds of them arrive in noisy array to drink at a tiny waterhole in the still of evening. The ground disappears beneath a stunning pink and grey garden as the great pack of birds is compressed around the water. On quiet hot days across the vast yellow Mitchell grass plains of the arid inland, great flocks, perhaps ten thousand strong, rise like a fog to twist and twine. A mass of pink one second, a smudge of grey smoke the next as they wheel like a single programmed bird above the plain, so closely packed together yet never quite touching the one alongside.

Masses of little pink and orange-cheeked grey quarrions or green and yellow bush budgerigars in some inland areas darken the sky as they rise with a roar of wings from the grass in front. They dart and twist as a smudge on the still air across the plains like whisps of coloured smoke, gone one minute, a stationary cloud of greenish grey mist the next as the pack wheels above the early morning mist. Acres of white cockatoos, and the little white corellas too, blanket the red sandhills, spinifex corridors and floodplains of the Channel Country like a heavy snowfall as they feed in their thousands on little bush melons.

In the nesting season, heads appear from every hollow in the coolibahs and river redgums lining the banks of western streams. The competition is keen, for few other hollow trees adorn the western plains. Among my many favourites are the Major Mitchell parrot, a more solitary bird in twos and threes and occasionally in small flocks. It is a faded light pastel pink with large erect orange/pink crest and darker pink underwings. The crimson or red winged parrot too is another favourite, but, of course, they're all favourites, as are the beautiful mulga parrots and Mallee-ringnecks or bullenbulls. So many of these wonderful birds paint our bushlands in striking colour in good seasons — they become your feathered friends, as much a part of the landscape as the trees and grasses.

Among the many interesting birds is the common bronze-winged pigeon. Coming into water just before dark, it travels at high speed — some say at eighty miles an hour — between eight and twelve feet above the ground. I don't know how they miss all the tree branches and shrubs at such speed and have on more than one occasion had them whistle past my head when riding home late, nearly knocking my hat off. Following a pad along a fence with telephone line draped between taller posts above, I was on my way home late from roo shooting when there was a loud thud followed by the ringing and swinging about of the telephone line. At the same instant the air in front was suddenly filled with feathers and bits of bird — a leg here, a wing there, and even a piece of rib cage and neck with part of its gizzard still attached. It was a bronze-winged pigeon and the bird had simply disintegrated as it hit the line at I don't know what speed.

Wedge-tailed eagles are wonderful graceful birds too — incredibly efficient hunters with amazing powers of sight and flight. Their wingspan of between six and seven feet (up to nearly nine feet has been recorded, I believe) means they need a fair bit of space to become airborne, which, of course, wasn't wasted on us. We'd shoot a roo or emu and drag the carcass into a patch of thick whip-stick mulga scrub and wait a few days until the eagles got used to it being there and began feeding. Then we'd sneak up and race at them belting kerosene tins while they all had full guts and were fighting one another on top of the carcass. It certainly was funny to see perhaps four or five eagles at a time trying to get airborne, but not able to spread their wings because the closely packed mulga stems were only a couple of feet apart. All they could do was just hop about like big black and tan bullfrogs, clucking and croaking with neck feathers all fluffed out. With such intellectual activities, we needed nobody to entertain us because our days were always full and there was so much variety!

We had a Saturday night ritual for years with our neighbours, the Taylor family from Rutherglen, that alternated between nights of music or cards at one or other of the two places. Everyone came for tea — the Taylor family and their governess, cook and jackaroo and Dad's brother Hugh, his wife Ena and their governess from the other Thrushton house four miles away. Often the travelling Bush Brotherhood parson, if in the area, would turn up too. As soon as tea was over the concert started. Doolie played the piano while the men sang songs. Auntie Ena was a good pianist and often played the piano while Doolie accompanied on her violin and Hugh played a tin whistle while Dad and the parson sang — it became a real party. Other times it was Saturday night tea at either place followed by a game of bridge that went on until midnight.

Gib and Joy (Possum) Taylor were about our age and we raced around all night playing games if there was a good moon. Gib was highly strung and used to go a bit wild when he got excited. He and Keith were good mates and Gib talked flat out all the time as he ambled about with a jerky gait, often clucking like a fowl and propping every now and then to furiously rub his feet together like a cricket. Frank, always on for a bit of fun, washed up and the rest of us wiped up and put away. Gib, all excited, would be talking non-stop as he wiped a pudding dish and put it behind him on the table. Frank picked it straight up and washed it again and Gib, still talking non-stop, wiped it and put it down in the same place. This went on for a quarter of an hour or more one time, until Gib, having wiped the same dish sixteen times and with everyone in fits, suddenly remembered wiping it up before! The excitement of actually being with someone his own age was a bit much for him at times.

Miss Robinson (Old Robbie) was the Rutherglen cook for as long as I can remember and went to Brisbane with the Taylors when they finally left the land to live in the city. She was a meek, thin, little old Scottish lady with a very broad accent you could hardly understand. She was like a little bird just ruffled up a bit in a whirlwind with a tiny pie melon head with undershot chin and a tuft of straight grey hair on top. Numerous two-inch-long curly grey hairs grew out at right angles from her pointy little chin and from the side of her cheeks. They always fascinated us and we wondered if we could hook onto them with a pair of pliers while she slept and drag them out. She was a great old stick and everyone liked her, but what a woeful cook. The meat always had blood running out of it and all her cakes had mud springs in the middle, while her scones were so hard they'd break a fang off quick and lively if you didn't treat them with proper respect.

Old Robbie and the governess acted as fairy godmothers to the Taylor children, writing endless nightly letters from fairies, singed on the edges with candles to make them look more authentic and put them under the pillow beneath each sleeping head. With great excitement we'd be shown the fairy's letters which were sometimes collected from postboxes down the paddock in a suitably marked hollow stump with postage stamp drawn and decorated for the occasion. It brought them such excitement, but, alas, only knowing giggles from we non-believers.

Emus were our favourite entertainment — they're such stupid clumsy things, we had fun with them for hours. When we knew where they were, all we had to do to attract them was lie down on the open ground and wave a bag or a shiny powdered milk tin or condensed milk tin about on the end of a long stick for a while. They'd come right up with the odd throaty grunt and slowly saunter round, getting closer all the time until they were almost on top of us. With much gaping with those enormous bulging eyes sticking out of a little dishmop head that was all beak and feathers, and nothing much inside, they'd goggle down at us with much curiosity. We'd wait until they were peering down from a few feet away, then suddenly fly in the air waving a bag. Look out! Feathers flying and legs pedalling in mid-air while a shower of shit and quandong seeds sprayed the ground from the exhaust end. They cannoned into one another as they bolted, leaving that ridiculous little head behind at the end of a long skinny neck to catch up later like a yoyo on a piece of string. We told ourselves they enjoyed it all just as much as we did.

It was a real circus to watch their evening antics after a brief summer storm. A small mob aimlessly stalking across a patch of cleared country suddenly went mad. The leader stretched his neck out in front like a fluffed-up mop handle a foot above the ground and took off flat out with a great knob of tail feathers bouncing about all bunched up and trailing behind. Lumbering away with noisy long strides as he gathered speed, he'd suddenly collapse in mid-air and bounce as he hit the ground with the odd feather dropping out. He'd lie motionless as if dead while the others tore past, circled and jumped over him. As the 'dead' one jumped to his feet again, another fell down to take his place as the others tore round jumping over him too. The scent of fresh wet earth, though, from only a few raindrops on the dry dust in a drought seemed to send everything into a wild frenzy.

Nearly everyone had a pet emu or two poking round the homesteads. They'd swallow anything left lying around, especially if it shone or rattled. They'd think nothing of swallowing half a box of .22 bullets, one at a time, if you left the box open for five minutes and went away to get something. We were changing a tyre one time — the old split rims were held on by six big nuts, but one was missing. We looked everywhere, then noticed the pet emu stalking slowly round and round the car looking very suspicious. So we ran him down and while one sat on top of him the other got a stranglehold low down on his long neck and working upwards, gave his head a good rattle, and, sure enough, out flew the nut!

Pet emus were a real menace if you were breaking in young horses. They'd be planted in the shade somewhere and suddenly race out and charge under the horse's neck as you rode past — of course, the horse would go stone mad and take off with some fancy footwork.

We had a bit of a contract going with the old Indian hawker. He was always after quandong seeds — said he'd give us two big bars of chocolate each if we collected a half-sugarbag of quandong seeds for him. This generous offer was most exciting until we realised how many quandong seeds fit in half a sugarbag! But, too late, the deal was done. Nobody knew what he wanted the seeds for until years later when all the sets of Chinese Checkers started coming on the market, done up in gift-wrapping and sold as Christmas presents. All the markers, about six or eight in each box, were quandong seeds, painted a different colour for each player. We knew every quandong tree on the place, of course, and on Rutherglen too. We'd be on our horses and gone before daylight so we'd be back in time for school, otherwise old Daydie would be up our ribs for being late.

We could go round all the trees closest to the house during the week, but all the others, some eight or ten miles away, would have to wait for the weekend when we had plenty of time. We gathered up all the old seeds around the quandong trees and collected all the dry emu dung lying about the paddocks which was often full of seeds and carted them home for washing. The constant vision of that big feed of chocolate at the end of the job kept us going flat out.

It wasn't long before we realised that, no matter how early we started, the emus had always beaten us to it. They'd have worked over all the good trees and eaten all the ripe fruit that was easy to get at or that had dropped to the ground during the night. Most of the trees were small and the emus could easily reach everything about six feet off the ground and even higher by jumping and picking off the fruit. This was knocking the cream off our contract. So we thought things out for a bit and decided the best way to get round this catastrophe was to harvest the emus instead of the trees.

All animals make for water after a big feed and we knew emus did the same. So we found all the pads along fences where most of the tracks were, the number of tracks increasing as emus got close to water and others joined the main pad from other directions. Armed with a chaff bag tied to a long stick, we planted ourselves a few feet off the main pad behind trees or clumps of turkeybush, about a hundred yards apart. Covered with ants and flies, we waited, wondering whether it was such a good idea after all. But, at last, they came, all with a gut full of quandongs — a whole string of emus slowly sauntering along dragging the odd big toe through the dust, with heads low and beaks open as they panted in the hot sun. A few feet off the pad, hardly game to breathe now in case the slightest movement gave us away, we waited till the mob was between us. We charged out and striped them down the brisket with the bags and made as much noise as we could at the same time. They got such a fright, a tangle of dust and feathers filled the air as a wall of emus hit the fence. They went end for end as they cannoned off one another and fell down. All the time, the exhaust end blew out a steady stream of shit and quandong seeds that danced and rolled about the hard ground. Every time we striped them with the chaff bag we got another jam tin of quandong seeds out of them. It was all over within seconds, but what a harvest! For the next half an hour we scraped this potent brew into our bags and took it all to the nearest bore-drain for washing. When the seeds were all nice and clean we rode home with them for drying in the sun. By working other areas in the same way, it was no time before we had well over one sugarbag full of seeds and eagerly awaited old Fuzzel Dean's return with his horses and covered wagonette so we could claim those long-awaited bars of chocolate. We began to wonder if he'd ever come back but eventually he turned up, and, as good as his word, handed each of us a big bar of chocolate — and threw in some jellybeans as well when he saw how many seeds we had for him in the bag. We headed for a good shady tree down the bore-drain, well away from anyone who might want to share the spoils of our labours and started our mouth-watering chocolate feed. But the weather was so hot the chocolate started melting as we walked along. We had to drink it from the packet then lick out the bit still lining the tinsel paper wrapping. That beautiful taste stayed in our memory for years.

Old Fuzzle was a kind, quiet old bearded Indian hawker who always wore a dirty length of cloth wound round and round his head. Not long after he'd left Thrushton one time, the horses took fright and bolted while he was opening a gate. He was knocked down and the wagonette wheels ran over him, breaking his neck, poor old bloke.

CHAPTER 6

Growing Up Fast

Bush kids, generally, were used to fairly hard work from an early age and were much older in their ways, tougher and had a more highly developed sense of responsibility than city youngsters of the same age. There were so many jobs that had to be done in the early morning before breakfast so the men weren't held up to start the main work out in distant paddocks. Keith, the eldest, milked the two or three cows, I got the mob of horses in, and Frank fed all the fowls and ducks and filled the wood box. The men did the heavier work of cutting the wood and carrying four-gallon petrol tin buckets of water dipped from a hole in the bore-drain to water the large flower and vegetable garden and had the horses saddled ready to go as soon as breakfast was finished.

Getting the horses out of the three or four hundred acre scrubby horse and spell-horse paddocks meant you had to be up at daylight or well before daylight at mustering and shearing time while the horses were still feeding and the bells were still ringing. When they finished feeding at sunrise, the bells stopped ringing and they were hard to find because you never knew where to start looking. On windy mornings you couldn't tell in what direction the sound was coming from because wind seemed to blow the sound of bells all over the place. When I couldn't hear the bells at all or find the horses, I put my ear against the side of a big ringbarked hollow tree as these acted like an aerial or loudspeaker. It was exasperating to hear the sound of bells coming so clearly down the hollow tree, yet have no idea what direction to head off in. Even though winter mornings were so cold and frosty that you felt like getting a good fire going, I always loved the bush at this time. Everything was so fresh and clean and damp from heavy dews and such a variety of scents coming from all the bush plants while birds were out sunning themselves and performing their early morning chortling chorus. The strange variety of calls from a distant fox, and an answering call from another close by, intertwined with the hoarse throaty bark of the old grey bucks as they sparred with one another in the frost. All the different sounds were so exciting while ice hung like magical earrings from every leaf and blade of grass and herbage during winter.

Some of the flat circular ground-hugging plants like purple milkweed (*Euphorbia drummondii*), which never rises more than an inch or so above the ground yet covers an area as round as a dinner plate, are breath-takingly beautiful. Every minute cluster of silver leaves attached to thread-like red stems holds a single tiny dewdrop of crystal-clear water that reflects the early morning sun's rays until the whole plant sparkles like a circular diamond-studded dressing table doily. The bore-drain, too, had its special charm as it gurgled along through the bush and heath with a slender line of white mist just above the banks marking its course. There is great beauty and never-ending fascination in the Australian bush, particularly in that very special light of early morning and late afternoon.

The McDougals of Neabul Downs, about twelve miles from Thrushton, were our best friends, mainly because the four children were about our age. We often went to one another's place for weekends to play cricket and tennis. Although their property was only half the size of Thrushton, they always seemed to be much better off than we were. Bob McDougal's father had a farm on the Darling Downs, where all the family had been brought up. When the old people died, the farm was sold, and Bob, the eldest son, got money from the sale that enabled him to spend up big on all sorts of things that we were unable to afford. But we were all roo shooters, which was an important talking point among bush kids. There was always rivalry between the eldest son Bill and me over the size of the roos we'd shot. Some of those big old bucks ended up about two or three feet across the chest and about eight feet tall by the time we'd finished!

The boys were always trapping rabbits in warrens on a cypress pine sandhill not far from the Neabul house. Len, the second boy, taught us all about trapping. When a rabbit is caught, it makes a loud piercing high-pitched squeal that can be heard a long way. Any fox within hearing distance comes at full gallop to eat it while it's still in the trap. So we made whistles out of the top of tobacco tins by folding the thin metal over and punching a hole in the upper side. With some practice, we could blow the same high-pitched whistling sound the trapped rabbit made. Foxes would come charging up flat out to grab the rabbit, where we'd be waiting with our rifles and skittle them. One day when we were out of bullets we started blowing our homemade whistles and, sure enough, up came a fox full tilt to eat the rabbit. Ears cocked, he looked very alert as he picked up our scent. Len poked his head out from behind the dead tree we were hiding behind and said, 'Good morning, Mr Fox.' Strike, there was some action then!

Keith was the more studious and docile of the three of us and always seemed remote from Frank's and my bushranging activities. While we were down the paddock sneaking up on emus having a snore-off under a bush or, for a bit of variety, chasing the odd wild cat or lousy jack, Keith was up in the house making model aeroplanes and boats or reading. He was solitary and artistic and liked working on pastel and black and white drawings and landscape scenes in watercolours and oils. No minute detail in his boats and aeroplanes was overlooked when being painted in the standard Air Force colours or camouflaged for battle. A travelling piano tuner turned up one time in a little 1925 model Austin 7 single-seater aluminium car shaped like a cigar that came to a point at the rear end and with a tiny little dicky-seat under a lid on top. Dad gave him the job of overhauling and tuning Doolie's piano, which she played every evening. The family had regular singsongs round the piano at night and at parties now and then. If anyone else could play the piano, Doolie accompanied on the violin and Dad always did a lot of singing. So the piano was always an important part of their lives.

The piano tuner was an interesting chap, good at his trade and quite an artist in his own right. He stayed with us for a few weeks while going right through the old piano and making new bits to replace those buckled by summer heat and fitting new strings. Being an artist himself, he was able to teach Keith a lot about the use of oil paints and blending to get a range of colour effects.

In 1933, the Queensland Correspondence School organised their first big inland competition. It was a surprisingly big affair open to all correspondence school kids of all ages. Months beforehand, all bush pupils were instructed on every aspect of the competition. Lists of all the things you could enter came with the packet of new lessons. They were cooking, needlework, knitting, poetry, composition, painting, pastel-work, black and white drawing, woodwork, plaiting, metalwork, leatherwork and a host of others. A hall was rented in St George for the competition, where the judges walked backward and forward along the rows inspecting entries laid out on long tables that went right round the hall and up the middle in two or three rows as well. Keith got a number of first and second prizes with his black and white drawings, pastel-work and painted model aeroplanes and boats.

The only item on the list that appealed to me was the 'Collection of Queensland Timbers', which I won both years the competition was held. Frank was younger and didn't put anything in. But I do remember the beautiful work many of the students submitted. I think the quality and quantity of entries surprised everyone, including the judges.

★ ★ ★

Mail day was always the most important day of the week on the land. 'Goodies', like that long-awaited letter or something ordered by catalogue weeks before, turned up. There was generally a big load on the truck — bags of horse and fowl feed, coarse salt, bags of pumpkins, potatoes, sugar, tins of oil and cases of petrol and kerosene. There was nearly always a man or two in front and sometimes a couple on the back with dogs and swags jammed in between other stuff, heading out to some property on the way. The load got lighter as the distance increased and produce was off-loaded at properties along the road. The mailman carried gossip throughout the districts: where the best storms had fallen and who was bogged where; who'd had a fight with somebody; where all the ringbarking and fencing camps were on the different runs. The results of the latest picnic race meeting or air race were always high priority news.

Bill Fein, then the Boolba mailman, with a twinkle in his eye, asked Dad if he knew that Amy Johnson had just 'pinched Bert Hinkler's root'! (Amy Johnson was trying to beat Hinkler's record flight to somewhere or other at the time and was taking the same route as Bert Hinkler.)

The mailman had to call in at every property on his run and, of course, didn't have to pump the station people for news and gossip that constantly flowed out of them. Everyone talked over the top of the other in haste to inform the mailman, who was the naturally appointed courier to spread the news wherever he went. If you wanted something put around, you just had to tell the mailman and the whole district would know within a couple of days. The tale was often so embroidered by the end of the run that it was difficult to know how much to believe. This was always to be expected, so everyone just allowed for that extra bit of embroidering and, with a bit of skill that took time to develop, the facts could generally be sifted out. Everyone was starved for news, especially about local happenings. News travelled fast — especially all the juicy bits like what so and so's new governess was like; who was thinking of getting married or screwing what; who was in trouble with the banks; who had cleared out before the woolbrokers arrived. Nothing was left to chance and, if facts were a bit light on, it was no trouble for a skilled mailman to fill in the extra bits. The mail was contracted to leave the St George Post Office, rain, hail or shine on the Saturday afternoon. It didn't matter if there'd been so much rain that horses were bogging on the main road and it was still pouring. The mail had to leave on time just the same, even though, as sometimes happened, the lorry bogged to the chassis on a road turned to swamp a mile out of town.

Frank and I sometimes turned up for Sunday lunch at Rutherglen to meet the mail lorry during our weekend bore-drain kangaroo shooting. There was often somebody new on the back with their swag and a dog or two, who'd come out to work on one of these places. We were always interested to meet any newcomers and to size them up while having a yarn.

Lewis Bell was the Rutherglen cowboy — a thickset little prize fighter type with muscles sticking out all over him. In the tin hut where the men camped down the paddock behind the old slab house, all we young coves and anyone else who turned up had weekend wrestling bouts where the battle went on half the night beneath a hurricane lamp tied to the rafters. Lewis, always the very cocky little undefeated champion, impatiently awaited mail day. If there was somebody new on the back, the lorry hardly had time to stop before he was alongside inviting the new bloke to take him on.

The day arrived when a tall, rangy looking young Canadian deserter from the navy climbed down from the load. After preliminary introductions to the rest of us in the shade under a wilga tree, Lewis asked him if he could 'rastle'. The new bloke said he didn't know much about it but he didn't mind having a go. So he dragged his swag off the lorry while we threw a few bags on the ground under the wilga tree where all the dogs were tied up and let them off the chains. The bout got under way with a flurry of twisted arms and legs until Lewis latched on to a big toe that was sticking up in the air and began trying to screw it off. The bloke's red and purple face went into contortions. Suddenly, with a movement too fast for our eyes to follow, the navy cove had Lewis in a headlock. Bones or something began making funny noises while Lewis's eyes stuck out like crab's feelers. He was lifted clean off the ground as the Canadian gave a shuffle backwards and fell down on his back dragging Lewis with him. He got his foot under Lewis's stomach, gave a mighty kick as he turned a back somersault, and Lewis went flying through the air like an umbrella caught in a storm. An assortment of discarded bones and old rams' heads from many a dog's feed were lying scattered around the wilga tree. Lewis landed on one of them with a yell as he hit the ground. The bout was abruptly terminated while we extracted a rib chop bone that had buried itself a couple of inches into his posterior. Suddenly, we had a new champion and a very deflated Rutherglen cowboy.

Alarming things were always happening to Lewis. One day he rode home looking a bit white around the gills and told us: 'I was out the back there lookin' for them bullicks an' run inter a terrible bad storm — muster been me lucky day. There was a terrific big clap of thunder and I reefed th' 'orse up when I seen this big blue bolt of lightning comin' straight at me. Jist 'ad time to duck me head sideways as she flew over me shoulder and hit a tree on th' other side an' blew 'er ter bloody pieces!'

As there were no schools anywhere in that country and lessons from the Queensland Correspondence School only came out on the mail coach every fortnight in the 1920s and early '30s, the bit of schooling we got at that time was at home under the house. Later, some of the adjoining station people got together and decided to build a small one-roomed school at Tow Towri, Jack Taylor's small sheep property twenty odd miles from Thrushton. Our elder brother Keith boarded with relatives in Brisbane from an early age while attending the Brisbane Grammar School and, as we rarely saw him from then on, we grew up not knowing one another as well as if he'd been at home. Mum and Dad thought Frank and I would benefit from boarding with the large Taylor family and attending this new school where we'd be with other children of roughly similar age, which would provide a degree of competition. A private schoolteacher answered their advertisement and was given the job. The students' parents paid his salary in proportion to the number each had in attendance.

The teacher's name was Mr Narracott, although we called him Single-bed. He was a good teacher. The poor bloke had to be to cope with the kind of raw material suddenly inflicted on him. He was about twenty-five and of slight build, a kind sensitive person and a real gentleman. He fitted in well with any company and was liked by all the station people as well as by us. Being a keen tennis player, he soon had us all playing for a couple of hours each day and on weekends too, when this was possible. We'd all be roped into scraping down the courts at some place or other and watering the surface to lay the dust if water could be found handy in a bore-drain or stock-watering tank.

Marking the court was a job not to be slummed — it was almost a science with Mr Narracott. His motto was, 'If a job is worth doing, it's worth doing properly, and don't you ever forget it.' We didn't either. The best white ash for marking the lines was from burnt gidgee (*Acacia cambagii*), which was a little better than brigalow (*Acacia harpophylla*). But as gidgee didn't grow in that area, we occasionally talked old Rubin Southey, who had the mail run and store at the FortyMile, into picking up a few logs from along the road somewhere and dropping them off alongside the court. Both these species left an almost white ash when burnt. The ash was mixed with bore water in a four-gallon petrol tin and poured into a big shearers' teapot with a long spout to distribute the mixture as you followed a tightly pulled length of string showing the direction of the line.

Attendance at the school comprised four Jamiesons from Cynthia Downs, four Beardmores from Rose Hill, three Taylors from Tow Towri (most of the Taylor family had grown up before the school was built) and two of us from Thrushton. Mr Narracott boarded with the Jamiesons four miles away and brought the children to school in an old 1923 model Overland car each morning, opening and closing numerous gates on the way.

We all got on well together and had set jobs to do each morning before school. Some got the horses in, some milked the cows, others fed the fowls and turkeys and cut the firewood. One job we took turns at. When old Jack Taylor's cows went dry, we took turns to walk over to Rose Hill, Eddie Beardmore's place about a mile away every morning with a two-gallon bucket to bring back the milk. Eddie Beardmore had a full-blood Aborigine, Roger (Beardmore), whose job it was to milk a mob of cows, separate the milk and make the butter. Between Eddie's house and the cow yard was the pigsty and inside was the snortiest wild pig imaginable. The men had run down this big black and tan spotted wild sow with a litter of six or seven young ones. They'd installed them in a small slab yard, and every time we went past the sow let out a startling variety of loud snorts. Many of them were cut short and chewed up by a frantic gnashing and chewing of teeth and tusks as she hit the rails halfway up trying to get at us. I've seen thousands of wild pigs since then, but nothing more ferocious than this thing. Eddie reckoned it could be as flash and snorty as it bloody well liked. He only visualised it sitting up in a tub on the dining room table surrounded by roast potatoes and pumpkin for Christmas dinner.

We'd get the two-gallon bucket of milk and head back the mile home, two of us carrying it between us because it got pretty heavy after a while. Hot and thirsty when we hit the halfway bore-drain, we'd sit down in the shade of a tree and get stuck into the milk while we had a smoke of somebody's pinched tobacco, topping up the bucket with bore water out of the drain. Old Jack used to go crook about Eddie's mongrel scrubber cows because there was never any cream on the milk. How could there have been when it was sometimes half bore water if we were extra thirsty? But rogues never prosper, or so they say. Jack was pouring some of this watery stuff on his porridge one morning and snorting about its colour when out of the jug came a couple of big shiny black bore-drain beetles with the 'milk' and started galloping about on top of his steaming hot porridge. Jack had seen plenty of these blokes and knew exactly where they'd come from. So the game was up, and from then on we were carefully watched.

It was very hot in the poky little schoolroom during summer — nothing to see some of the students having a snore-off after lunch as attention waned. Mr Narracott was always blaming us for draining his red inkwell and, though he kept refilling it every day, next morning it would be almost dry again until there was hardly any left in the big bottle. We didn't like being blamed for something we didn't do. The mystery was solved when one of us happened to be looking at the roof where the rafters were in bright sunlight. Scurrying back and forth along the top of a beam was a continuous string of common little black ants, all with enormously distended abdomens that shone bright red in the direct sunlight. The string was traced all the way down the rafters to Mr Narracott's red inkwell over in the desk in a dark corner, where the ants formed a black ring round the inkwell like stock drinking round a waterhole.

How could we have known that the happy relationship with our friendly teacher was about to be shattered? When Mr Narracott had severe pains in his side for some days, he was taken to the St George hospital and immediately operated on for a burst appendix. He came back home for a week or so but looked absolutely dreadful and could hardly walk. We were all terribly worried when he was rushed back to hospital, painfully thin and looking like a ghost. Two days later he was dead from peritonitis. The whole district went into a state of shock. I remember the parson coming out and giving a very emotional service under the currajong and box trees near his little schoolroom at Tow Towri. Everyone in the district came, even some who hadn't met him. They'd simply heard kind things said of him somewhere along the road and that was good enough for them to come all that way to pay their respects to a very special man. There wasn't a soul who didn't feel they'd lost a member of their own family.

The Taylors seemed dogged by accidents. The eldest boy, Billy, was killed when his horse galloped into a mulga tree and a pointed stake speared deep into his temple. Arthur had a drinking problem and died early in life. Keith, the youngest boy of my age at school with us, was killed near Boolba in a head-on collision with another car when passing a wool lorry in its trailing dust. He was to be married next day and was on his way into town to make final arrangements with the church. Like so many other small land-holders, life was a constant struggle for the Taylor family. The old story — the family was too large and the place too small. To help make ends meet, Jack Taylor took on wool classing jobs at local sheds.

Towri was one of a number of properties in that area which were so small (13,000 acres) they were constantly eaten out as people tried to gouge a starvation living from this poor sandy loam country. Thousands of acres of dead ringbarked trees stood erect like grey ghosts above a dense three-foot high blanket of yellow wiregrass, very largely the product of continuous over-stocking and ringbarking. The dense growth of wiregrass full of barbed seeds ruined wool and clothes. After walking through it for a couple of hours roo shooting, it was much easier to throw your clothes in the fire than spend the rest of the day trying to pick out the barbed seeds that wound right through the fabric and into the skin as well.

Wiregrass (*Aristida species*) was to become the curse of the eastern mulga country in the 1930s and '40s. With below average seasons and constant over-stocking, the whole region became choked with a dense three-foot high wall of this extremely poor grass. It could be waist high and as thick as the hairs on a cat's back and stock would nearly die on it. When mustering, stock had to be literally flogged through the stuff. On cleared fence lines where it was thicker still, it was impossible to drive sheep at all, particularly if it was into the sun. People tried burning it by filling old motor tyres with lighted sump oil and dragging them about with a horse, but it only burnt for a while and went out.

Our weekly mail day was always Sunday. The mailman camped the night at Thrushton and dropped Frank and me off at the Tow Towri school late on the Monday morning. Sometimes we'd be much later if a load of wool had to be picked up at some shed on the way. Rubin

Southey had the mail contract and wool carting on that run at the time. He and his wife ran the FortyMile store (later Boolba) from which they supplied the district with groceries, horse feed and other sundry goods. Later they had a fuel dump and bowser there as well. It was a pretty dirty, untidy old place full of kids and dogs and about thirty head of cats of every colour of the rainbow. Mrs Southey was once carrying a huge shearers' baking dish full of junket to the long table around which we all sat in the centre of the room when she got her toe hooked up on a nail sticking out of the floor, stumbled and dropped the lot. There was a hell of a commotion at all corners of the room, from under piled-up bags of horse feed, kerosene tins and old corn bags. A mob of half-starved cats and dogs all hit the spot at the same time, nearly knocking the table over in the process. By the time she kicked them all off, there was only a slightly damp but clean patch on the cypress pine boards where the junket had landed a split second before, surrounded by a thick coating of dust and litter that covered the rest.

Old Rubin Southey (we called him Rhubarb) was a very big, stooped man, aged about fifty, with enormous shoulders and arms. He smoked a huge bent-stemmed pipe and dribbled all the time. The thick nicotine-stained brew soaked out the corners of his mouth and formed long shiny drops that hung and swung about from under the bowl of his pipe, which only came out of his mouth when he was having a feed or was going to bed. Frank and I sat out on the front of the lorry deck on the trip to school, one at each side, opposite Rubin as he fought with the steering wheel of the old Willys truck. It had about half a turn play in the steering wheel, which meant he had to be swinging his enormous hands and arms backwards and forwards all the time to keep the nose of the truck somewhere near the centre of the dusty corrugated road. After rain when roads were boggy we had fun dodging great dollops of mud thrown up from the front wheels. We watched the heavy chains on the back wheels chewing away at the sticky black mud as we bellowed along sideways from one watertable to the other with old Rhubarb swinging on to the steering wheel like a prize fighter. He had a startling vocabulary of swear words, none of which were new to us, of course, but they constantly roared out of him while he chewed the stem of his old battered pipe with dribble flying everywhere. We'd watch each shining drop hanging from the bowl as it slowly grew in size, swinging about in the wind, and try to work out which way it was likely to fly when it got too heavy and let go. You nearly needed an umbrella.

When Frank and I went to board at Tow Towri for a year or so and went to school there, Bullocky Smith told Jack Taylor he'd have to 'put chimneys in all the WCs when them two wild little buggers go there'. We'd been smoking since we were about six, and were always pinching old Pappy's tobacco. He used to get a cheap South African black twist tobacco in bulk with the six-monthly load of stores from Brisbane. It came in big square twelve-pound tins and could be dragged out in long continuous thin strips like kangaroo hide ready for plaiting. We'd cart a handful down the paddock under a tree and sit and smoke this terrible stuff in pipes we'd made out of the ends of pine petrol cases. We'd cut out a square block with the hacksaw and bore a large hole in the top and a smaller one in the side at the bottom into which we screwed a Rutherglen turkey's quill for the mouthpiece. The tobacco was as black as the ace of spades and as strong as blazes. We got giddy as our head spun round and round and we got so crook we thought we were dying. But we were hogs for punishment and kept at it until we could smoke it just as well as the old blokes in the finish. Pappy knew we were pinching it but he could never catch us. We were too cunning — we'd picked it up from the roos and emus, you know.

We'd be just starting out on the horses roo shooting or raiding quandong trees or something and out would come old Pap. 'Righto, off your horses and stand over there against the fence.'

'Righto, Dad.'

'Right, now turn out your pockets.' No, nothing there. 'Stay where you are, you must have it planted on your saddles.'

So up would come the saddle flaps. He'd feel round the girth and surcingle, look in the quartpots and in the saddle bags. No, nothing there, ah, under the pummel or along the saddle channel. But no.

'Where is it then? I know you've got it. Where's it hidden? Down the paddock behind a tree, I'll bet.'

'No, Dad,' we'd say, like angels. 'We're only going down to check the bore drains.'

At last old Pap would give in with 'All right then, away you go.'

So we'd get out fast, terrified the old mare would do something rude while he was still searching. The only place he hadn't looked was in the old mare's arse, and that's where she was planted, rolled up in a page of the *Bulletin*.

The biggest get-together of station people was at the annual picnic race meeting held at Boolba. The races always finished with a woolshed dance in the big Miltonise woolshed several miles from the racetrack. Everyone turned up, and a boozer was set up under a large fly stretched between trees and a bough shed. The bookmakers, with sweat streaming down their faces, would be yelling the odds from under the shade of a tree, while the Country Women's Association members, who'd been furiously cooking for weeks, fed the hungry mob. The bar under the fly was the most popular spot as usual and the same old crowd of boozers got more and more turpsed up as the afternoon wore on. By the time the meeting finished just before dark, they'd be stretched out like goannas under any tree they could find with a bit of shade to have a sleep. The blacks would be huddled together under trees a couple of hundred yards away, just staring like a mob of camped kangaroos. Nobody seemed to take any notice of the poor blighters until someone took them something to eat and drink. I've often wondered since what they thought of it all because in those days they weren't supposed to become involved in the crowd of whites and their activities. This strict division began to be watered down somewhat as time went on — not before time either.

The girls would be fixing their hair with those old long-handled curling tongs they heated up in the fire and making dresses for weeks before the big event. Just before the dance started, they'd be down at the homestead half a mile away, getting all togged-up so as to look just so at the dance of the year. All we young bucks would have a mud bath in the bore drain and get all spruced up with silk shirt and tie and hair plastered down flat with Californian Poppy, a sickly-smelling pink hair oil that was all the go with young people in those days. When we got heated up from racing about, the thin oil ran down our face in little pink rivulets, coated with red dust. The very thought of being looked at by a girl was enough to make most of us want to bolt for the scrub and not come back.

In the woolshed, the dance was underway, with old Bert Knights perched up on a petrol case on top of the wool bales that acted as the stage, going boommmmmmmmm-ting-ting, boommmmmmmmmm-ting-ting on his two drums. His mate on a kerosene tin alongside pumped furiously at the squeezebox producing noises like a couple of cats with their tails jammed in the door. A mob of us wild young scrubbers would be huddled round outside the door. Every now and then, we'd pluck up enough courage to peep inside to see what was going on. A row of girls were parked round the walls on forms like a string of lousy jacks having a camp on the top wire of a fence. Half a dozen flash young coves from the town who were used to dancing and didn't suffer from stage-fright like us were flying round the board shoving some back-to-front girl before them doing about twenty mile an hour in reverse gear.

Years later, Moodgie and I had a go there too. I don't know what went wrong — I think the toe of my riding boot got hooked up on a nail or something and we finished up down the chute among the sheep pills and stinging nettles on the ground floor. I was never cut out for that caper, though I think Moodgie would like to have learnt to dance properly.

★ ★ ★

After twelve months or so, we left Tow Towri. Frank joined Keith in Brisbane and attended the Central Technical College as a day student. After leaving the Brisbane Grammar School, Keith went into the Queensland National Bank in Brisbane then out to Laidley, a small town on the Darling Downs and became the teller. When Frank finished school at the College, he worked with Crystal and Maguire's firm of Brisbane solicitors as trainee articled clerk. When Keith and Frank came home on holidays from Brisbane at every opportunity, we'd meet them on the train at Thallon, about 120 miles away in the little light bouncing Whippet car and bring them home amidst much excitement. There were no good roads like there are now, so it was a long dusty trip, generally broken by camping the night in the old Commercial Hotel in St George.

I left Tow Towri at the same time as Frank at the age of 14 and started straight into scrub-cutting on Thrushton, with men in camps scattered about the run for three years with very few breaks. On one break the Bush Brother, Mr Winslow, invited me on a two-week holiday to Sydney. Mr Winslow was about thirty and for some years had stayed the night at Thrushton during his rounds. He was musical and I think was drawn to Dad and Doolie because they were too. Feeling sorry for me camped away out miles from home scrub-cutting at the age of 15, he arranged to take me to Sydney to stay with his parents when he joined them on his annual holiday.

Mr Winslow was born in the inner Sydney suburb of Redfern. His parents were old people and very poor. The little attached house they rented wasn't very far from the Redfern railway station. I had not seen a slum before and hadn't realised people lived in such cramped-up squalor. The street was littered with rubbish, paper and stuff blowing along the streets. The front door of these narrow little houses was only a few paces from the footpath. Most had just the one step up, a sandstone slab, which, from the wear of thousands of feet since the beginning of last century, was worn right down in the middle. Barking dogs raced up and down as they followed the early morning

milkman in his horse and cart while he filled the two or three bottles or jugs left at the doorway from a pint container with flap-top
lid. Papers delivered earlier lay beside the bottles in a great pool of
stinking dog urine that dribbled down the walls and bottles as every
passing dog cocked its leg on the pile.

The western train we arrived on reached Sydney very early and
few people were about. Mr Winslow knocked and his mother, obviously just out of bed and still in pyjamas, opened the door. The rush
of putrid hot air from inside, stinking of mildew, leaking stale gas and
aged bodies, fairly took your breath away. The door was immediately
closed again. It seemed no fresh air ever got into this damp little place
and, having lived inside for most of their lives, they seemed not to
even notice the foul air they were breathing.

Mr Winslow had worked in Redfern, Erskineville and Surry Hills
after he left the Christian Training College. His work was with all the
little neglected slum kids who played about in the streets and spent
most of their lives in and out of alleyways with other ragged kids and
dogs. He later joined the Queensland Bush Brotherhood at their
headquarters in Charleville and later again, began travelling round all
the western stations and giving Sunday services, that were generally
followed by tennis parties or cricket matches as soon as the service
was over. He took me all round these depressing suburbs to see how
these people lived. Many were still drunk at breakfast time and bore
the very obvious signs of recent fights. I hadn't before realised how
fortunate I was to be living away out in the western country surrounded by clean, sweet-scented air and animals while birds called
from the scrub on all sides.

We stayed for several days at Hill End at the invitation of Mr
Winslow's friend who had the local parish, Hill End being an old
almost deserted mining township on the fringe of the Blue
Mountains. In his parish Ford car, he took us on daily trips through
rugged sandstone country, all new to me, before delivering us back
to Sydney. After doing the rounds of Luna Park, the Zoo, and nearly
wearing out the harbour ferries, we headed back home again; he back

to his rounds of western properties and me back to my camp to sharpen axes and start scrub-cutting again. In no time it felt almost as though I hadn't been away at all, the extremes were so great.

CHAPTER 7

Working the Land

BECAUSE of the rapid deterioration of the over-stocked mulga country and the succession of below-average rainfall years in the latter part of the 1920s and through the 1930s, the Thrushton partnership had no possibility of succeeding. The place couldn't keep two families and their infrastructure going and remain viable at the same time. Low wool prices and high overhead costs, with gangs of scrub-cutters employed most of the year, were financially crippling and precluded any opportunity of reducing escalating overdrafts. As the plight of small land-holders, especially those in the lighter carrying red soil mulga country became better understood by governments, pressure mounted to make available 'additional areas' from the sub-division of large Company-owned stations. In cases of difficulty, these extra blocks were allocated to the nearest property deemed eligible under the 'special hardship clause'.

The aim was to establish the economic viability and stability of the original heavily indebted blocks by increasing their size and carrying capacity. Thrushton met all these requirements, so when the adjoining large Company-owned Mona Station was broken up in 1933–34, Thrushton was allotted one of these additional areas. It was a 32,000 acre block of unimproved virgin country with nothing on it at all — no fences or yards, not even a hut. The only water was in a short length of muddy bore drain at the northern end of the block.

Dad named the new block Clonard after the old Gasteen estate of that name in County Meath in Northern Ireland. Clonard was mostly poplar box and belah country and was much better land with heavier soils than the red soil, light mulga country on Thrushton. After struggling for so long on Thrushton, we were all eager to start developing this new block. So work had to start all over again, with an infusion of thousands of pounds of borrowed money to begin belting the place into some sort of economic shape as quickly as possible. Tents sprang up along the two miles of bore drain, which was the only water on the place, and contract fencing, yard building, ring-barking and tank-sinking gangs began work. All this country was part of a big flat scrubby plain with no hills for hundreds of miles, so the only surface water before bore drains was in occasional shallow gilgais. Most of these lasted only a short time after heavy rain. To help overcome this shortage, two thousand-yard tanks were sunk about five miles apart in Piper's Watercourse which bisected the block. This flat drainage line, which was barely noticeable, may have been the remains of an old in-filled stream from the wetter Tertiary period, but as it ran a little shallow water after heavy rain, it provided good sites for earth tanks.

As there was no house on the Mona block, my uncle's house, the newer and more substantial of the two Thrushton homesteads, was cut into sections and carted down for re-erection at the end of the only bore drain, two miles in from the main St George-Cunnamulla road. A woolshed, sheep yards and small holding paddocks had to be built on the bore drain halfway between house and main road, which was the only water for the woolshed, cook-house and men's quarters. A large family comprising old George Coveny and his four or five big strong sons from around Charleville and Cunnamulla and several other axemen and a cook formed the best ringbarking and fencing gang we ever had on Clonard or Thrushton. They were all great axemen and hard workers — nothing was ever slummed. The fence lines were all skyline-cleared and you virtually only saw the first post when sighting along the fence line, straight as a die, with every post the exact same height as the first. I've never seen better fencing. But you had to watch them. They were rogues and would thieve the corn out of a blind parrot's cage if given half a chance.

The Indian hawker and his mate who worked the Bollon/ Cunnamulla districts always focused their attention on the young excitement-starved toilers buried out in the bush for months at a time. They could be talked into buying anything that looked a bit flash or rattled or shone. The hawker turned up one time at Clonard and camped on the drain a couple of hundred yards from the Coveny's camp and hobbled his horses out. They were tough old salesmen, these Indian and Afghan hawkers — they had to be to survive in amongst all the rough and tumble axemen they came up against in bush camps. The men were completely isolated and never left the camp while they were on a contract job, so were always pleased to see the hawker turn up — it was better than a picture show.

The hawker's aim was to sell all these young bushmen anything they could talk them into buying from their big covered horse-drawn wagonette, which was done-up inside like a miniature bush store. Also there was never any worry about not getting paid because Dad had to take the money out of their cheques. Shelves full of bushmen's clothes, hats and boots lined both sides from floor to roof. Boxes full of toothbrushes, combs, soap, enamel mugs and pannikins, tin or enamel eating irons, tobacco, ashtrays, matches, pipes and a host of other things in all manner of different sized boxes were jammed to the roof on racks and shelves in between. Other things hanging from hooks and nails filled up every available space — hobbles, billycans, quartpots, spurs, leggings, dog chains, whips and light harness gear. They carried everything imaginable for a bushman's outfit — hurricane lamps and globes, carbide lamps and bags of carbide, axes and odd bushman's tools. These were the big outfits, generally drawn by four horses. The smaller two-horse outfits did more regular calls round the station homesteads with fruit and vegetables and the better class men's and women's clothing. Later when cars took over from horses, they changed to lorries along with other travellers like Rawleys port-salesmen.

Some big hawkers' outfits were fitted with large doors on both sides. These were hinged top and bottom in two sections; the top half swung upwards with props underneath, and the bottom section swung outwards, held at right angles by a chain at each end. This formed a bench at both sides of the wagonette as a display counter where things were put out for inspection. Being the rogues they were and working long hours, the Covenys arranged to do their buying and inspecting at night after tea. They had it all worked out that someone would 'accidentally' knock the carbide light over and, while all the others milled around offering to get it going again, one was to grab the nearest box and race out into the scrub and plant it behind a tree. After the hawker had harnessed up and gone next day, they knocked off work and raced back to inspect the box they were sure was full of beautiful chocolates. But, alas, when the lid was reefed off, it was full of kid's cheap mouth organs — dozens of them and everyone in the district was blowing one for months after.

The phase of land use that ran into the 1920s and '30s in the mulga lands of South West Queensland, of which Thrushton was a part, was a disaster period as well as one of great achievement. Artesian bores and hundreds of miles of bore drains, earth tanks and sub-artesian bores now artificially watered most of the western country. Wireless sets, telephones and early model motor cars with pneumatic tyres were breaking new ground in communication, while formed roads and extension of rail services provided better access. One of the neighbouring properties had the first proper wireless set (as opposed to the little cat's whisker sets) in our district that I can remember. It was a long narrow box about twelve inches high over two feet long with numerous dials in front and a big curly horn speaker on top. Some of the dials didn't seem to make any difference whichever way they were turned. Men rode for miles from distant properties to hear the cricket broadcast, especially when the young Don Bradman began making his name as a batsman, often amidst loud squeals and blurts of static.

One day when the cricket commentator announced that play was abandoned because of heavy rain, everybody had a long face. Climbing off his horse, one old local, when told of the disaster, said: 'Yeh, I thought they mighter 'ad a drop of rain down there — muster been them big clouds I seen down that way about daylight this mornin'.' That the cricket match was being played on the Melbourne oval, more than a thousand miles away, hadn't sunk in. He'd probably never seen a map.

In the air things were happening too. In 1926 QANTAS set up a workshop and inland terminal at Longreach and began assembling aircraft. Clearing started on the small airstrip at St George. Tiger moths had landed there occasionally but it was enlarged to take a bigger plane. This was all voluntary work where property owners and their families up to one hundred miles away began turning up to tackle the job. We kids camped out there with our parents while trees were cut down and stacked up for burning, stumps grubbed out and depressions filled in. At last the job was finished and the big day arrived when a QANTAS plane on a goodwill flight arrived from Longreach. Everyone had an invitation to the great occasion. It was the very first aeroplane we'd ever seen and the first big plane to land anywhere in our part of the country. It was a monoplane with twin engines and finned cylinders in a circle behind each propeller and metal struts holding each engine to the wings. The body was made out of ripple aluminium sheeting like the small corrugated iron we used to build sheds with. I remember the deafening noise it made when they started it up.

People began talking about 'a flash new meat safe that made its own ice' and wool brokers began sending out travelling salesmen in motor cars who were agents for the particular brand of vehicle they were trying to sell. In 1927 and 1928, I think it was, the wool firm Primary Producers Ltd were pushing the Essex touring car. Other salesmen began working from run to run trying to talk the broke station owners into buying hand-pumping washing machines. Later, the first of the early Silent Knight refrigerators became talking points in many station homestead kitchens. There were battery-driven gramophones too, demonstrating a new brand of reed needles (that you sharpened like a lead pencil) to replace the previous metal ones that ruined records as they scratched their way through the ever-present dust. Technology was on the move.

This was a time of great activity never to be seen again in the west. Hundreds of ringbarkers, fencers, tank sinkers, yard builders, horse breakers, bullockies, scrub cutters, shearers, drovers, kangaroo shooters and travelling skin and hide buyers and hawkers of every imaginable thing were fully engaged all year. But hard work and worry were soon to dampen the spirit of initial enthusiasm, for these were below average rainfall years coinciding with the onset of the Great Depression where wool prices fell below production costs. As drought followed drought and lambing failures were the norm, almost continuous scrub-cutting to keep breeding stock alive became the accepted routine. As banks and wool brokers applied pressure to reduce overdrafts, stock numbers were often increased in an effort to meet these demands.

The phase of devastating droughts and dust storms that so marred the late 1920s and 1930s and part of the 1940s, made newspaper headlines in many countries. Cars drove the southern city streets during the day with headlights on as thick dust made murky twilight and houses and factories, with lights ablaze, hardly knew night from day. It all made high priority news and people began asking: 'What's happening to the land out there? Something bad must be going on or there wouldn't be all this dense chocking dust everywhere.'

Captain Mathews, his aging tramp with half a load of Australian wheat and wool was bound for Argentina to top up with frozen beef and had left New Zealand far behind. Well out in mid Pacific now, he wallowed along in a heavy trailing swell with propellers thrashing as the bow dug deep into the trough in front. But he was uneasy this morning for something was very wrong. A peculiar coloured dense

murky fog enveloped the early morning sky as the sun rose out of the
sea like a gigantic very faint orange balloon and a strong westerly
wind continued blowing with a force of five on the Beaufort Scale.
He thought of typhoons but was too far south for this, so went back
into the wheel house again to check the glass and noted the baro-
metric pressure was high with no sign of bad weather ahead. It was
most disturbing to say the least.

The glass top of the chart table was an unusual colour too. His finger left a clear mark as he dragged it across to check and there was a
slightly gritty feel. On inspecting the tip of his finger, he noticed it
was a reddish brown colour. It was a fine powdery dust and unbe-
lievable as it may have been, there was no mistaking this. It was only
then that he remembered all the talk around the docks in Melbourne
and Sydney while loading up. It was all about droughts and dust
storms, of hundreds of thousands of dead and dying stock, of farmers
rolling their swags and walking off their runs surrounded by half an
acre of idle rusting machinery. With the strong winds blowing steadily
from the west for a week, the dust must be coming all the way from
Australia.

He thought —

*Incredible — the whole continent must be blowing clean away. If this fine
powdery red dust has travelled half way across the Pacific, all the heavier
particles would have fallen in the wake of this tub a thousand miles behind.
Strike, what kind of mess must the country be in at the centre of the blow
and how many tons of topsoil to the acre have been blown away to end up
away out here?*

While trying to digest this, the newsreader from the wireless in the
wheel house was talking about the snow-clad New Zealand high-
country turned red from Australian dust. He was glad his life was out
at sea — it might be rough and wet at times but at least it was clean
and the wind couldn't blow it away.

Heart-rending accounts of hardship faced by the dust-bowl cotton farmers in America sprung to mind, as blinded by dust, they watched their country blow away while foreclosures forced an army of bankrupted farmers to pull out and begin walking the roads. Wasn't there a similarity here — it all had a familiar ring about it.

Parts of Australia's arid southern inland were literally on the move from soil erosion and sand drift, forcing many broke land-holders to walk off their runs with nothing but the dusty clothes they stood in. Emotive words like 'land degradation', 'desertification' and 'ecosystem collapse' had not yet been invented, though sensational newspaper reporting had devised plenty of others, equally imaginative to stir the minds of bustling city dwellers. On the land where it was all happening, the story was very different. No longer was it the farmers' and graziers' exclusive problem; scientists too were grappling with the fragmentary evidence coming in from innumerable sources and wondering where to start.

Theories came and went, as fact was sifted from fiction and the misinformed eventually gave way to the informed. It was a slow process as always and, in the meantime, to those of us who were working the country, they were years that wouldn't be forgotten in a hurry. For much of the time, graziers were little more than caretakers for the city-based wool brokers who controlled everything we did, even down to what we ate. There was a wagonette load of jam, treacle and bullocky's joy (golden syrup) in one corner of our store because it was the cheapest stuff you could buy and cases of rancid tinned butter, blown up like footballs from the heat, that you weren't game to drive a tin-opener into. The 180-pound hessian bags of flour were often a mixture of mouse dung and weevils; and the 60-pound bags of sugar, a solid block from being wet along the road somewhere by the time the six-monthly stores arrived on the wagons (later lorries) from the rail head. The bags of sugar had to be broken up with the axe and the mouse dung, weevils and grubs sifted out of the bags of flour through sheets of wire gauze.

All the light soil mulga and poplar box country was, in general, severely over-stocked and for many years was stretched way beyond its capacity to cope with this level of use. Surface soils were pulverised into fine red dust around watering points, woolsheds and yards, holding paddocks and all along stockroutes by the sharp hooves of millions of sheep. In hot dry weather, the slightest wind lifted clouds of this fine red dust that reduced visibility to a few hundred yards. Dust storms were so frequent in the worst years that people got used to sweeping out half a kerosene tin of dust and dead leaves from homesteads every morning.

Dad's father ('Grandfather') loved the bush and always came out from Brisbane on holidays to stay with us at Thrushton. He took we three boys out on long daily walks through the spinifex country where the wild heath flowers were out and through the belah and mulga country too. He made a cypress pine seat under a big bulloak tree (*Casuarina luehmannii*) on the edge of the spinifex, where we'd sit while he smoked a cigar and listened to the music the wind made as it whistled through the drooping needle-like pendulous leaves. Our eyes brightened as he took a little packet of jellybeans and peanuts from his waistcoat pocket for us to eat while he smoked a cigar and had a spell.

He'd insist we sit perfectly still while he whistled up tiny birds that came right up and sat on branches just above our heads and twittered away to one another. When he finished his cigar, he broke off a twig and screwed the cigar butt on the end of it. By the end of his holidays, every small branch round where he sat was decorated with a cigar butt like a Christmas tree. We were fortunate in that our parents and grandparents on both sides were great nature-lovers and spent a lot of time admiring the flowering bush plants and calling up birds that frequented the bush. Grandfather had no sooner arrived on one occasion when a dust storm began. A howling westerly wind whipped up blinding clouds of red dust that thickened as high dust blown from further west moved in and blotted out the sun. When we took in his early morning cup of tea, his white hair and moustache were as red as beetroot and the white sheets on his bed were lined thick with the same red gritty dust. He found it hard to understand the sudden change of weather which is a common feature of droughts.

Grandfather was a very right-thinking, strict old gentleman with deep religious convictions and had everyone singing hymns round the piano most nights. He sent out a new hymnbook some months before he arrived so we could learn the hymns we were supposed to sing with him. Dad and Doolie were too busy to consider such things so we couldn't help him much. When he asked to see the new hymnbook, it couldn't be opened. Hornets had built a whopping big mud nest right across all the front pages turning them into a solid block, probably a few days after it arrived. Sort of gave the game away a bit, but I think old Grandfather had given up on us all by this time anyway, though he kept on trying and hoping for a win.

As youngsters, the hurricane lamp was kept burning all day in our little schoolroom under the Thrushton house, sometimes for several days at a time until the dust storm had subsided. At no time could the sun be seen through the thick dust. Even in the middle of the day it was only possible to see the bare dim outline of the sun when it was directly overhead. During this critical fifteen-year period, enormous changes became obvious to even the most inexperienced observer. Whole districts became a tangle of dead branches and fallen trees from ringbarking for more grass, and scrub-cutting from daylight till dark to feed starving stock. Most youngsters in that period were brought up with an axe in one hand and a rifle in the other, and every spare moment was devoted to scrub-cutting, ringbarking and suckering, interspersed by shooting roos and emus to keep the tucker up to a mob of hungry station dogs.

By the early 1930s, hundreds of square miles of tree skeletons littered the landscape on all sides as the ringbarking gangs worked their way through the eastern sector of the scrubby mulga country, now aided by arsenic pentoxide for a better percentage kill and to reduce the level of suckering. But the new-country flush was short-lived owing to the nitrogen- and phosphorous-deficient nature of the soils, the below-average rainfall period and heavy stocking with sheep immediately following ringbarking. Drought followed drought and, in the absence of competition from ground layer species and a lack of fire because there was no grass to burn, inedible shrubs like acacia, eremophila, cassia, myoporum, cypress pine and eucalypt seedlings began to colonise the bare open spaces. By the mid-1930s, shrub regrowth had reached such proportions in some areas that three-year-old ringbarked country was so unusable and so uneconomical to treat that the normal follow-up suckering had to be abandoned. This is what we now refer to as the 'woody weed' invasion. It has been with us ever since we first started developing the eastern sector of the 'soft' shrubby mulga country, but gradually thickened up as seasons improved and soil moisture ratios increased. Also, heavy stocking meant greater pressure on the more palatable species which were hard pressed ever to complete a proper seeding cycle. This allowed the less palatable, prolific seeding wire grasses to take over most open space which wasn't already occupied by shrub regrowth as soon as relief rain had fallen. Full wool fleeces from sheep removed from heavily infested wiregrass holding paddocks were so densely matted with the barbed seeds that they bounced like sheets of bark when thrown out on the wool-rolling table. The density of this very poor grass was much worse in the eastern scrubby soft mulga country than it was in the lower rainfall hard mulga country further west. But it eventually became a problem there too, along with woody weed regrowth like Charleville turkeybush (*Eremophila gilesii*), silver turkey-bush (*Eremophila bowmanii*), butterbush (*Cassia nemophila*), sandalwood (*Eremophila mitchellii*) and turpentine (*E Sturtii*).

These are some of the many aspects contributing to declining productivity, soil erosion and general land degradation throughout most of Queensland's light-carrying red soil mulga wool-growing regions. Pastoral research on wool and frame development of merino sheep, blowfly strike, internal parasites and related problems had been the focus of attention for many years by CSIRO scientists working from their research base at Gilruth Plains near Cunnamulla. When the Charleville Pastoral Laboratory was later established in Charleville and its scientific team began land use and pastoral studies in western Queensland, the earlier CSIRO work was gradually phased out and Gilruth Plains eventually was closed down.

The research programs into woody weed regrowth, plant nutrition and soils in the western division by this team of dedicated scientists has been an outstanding achievement. A great deal of work on the woody weed invasion and its distribution in the mulga lands and the use of fire as a management tool has brought a much better understanding of the resource and its management problems. It has built a framework for wiser land use since the 1970s by identifying core problem areas where changes in management and property size are crucial. Only by serious consideration of all data and options is there any possibility of sustaining the long-term use of these important, though low-carrying, pastoral lands.

We shifted over from horses to wheels. Just before Frank joined the RAAF in about 1942, we were in Bollon at Bligh Khan's garage getting a wheel bearing replaced in the utility when we noticed an old motorbike leaning up against the netting fence alongside, covered with creepers. It was an old Coventry Eagle, a British bike of World War I vintage (probably a 1914 or 1916 model). It wasn't much bigger than an ordinary pushbike, with two brake pads round the rim of the back wheel and a tiny single cylinder engine with a square tin as a petrol tank on top. Both the tyres were flat and the seat had rotted off, but we dragged it out and Frank pushed it around for a bit.

'Do you think you can get it going?' Frank asked Bligh.

Everybody folded up laughing at the very idea of it. But they put in a couple of hours on the old wreck and, at last, in a cloud of smoke and backfires, she sprang to life with a whine like a nest of wasps. They pumped up the tyres and put on an old bicycle seat and away Frank went up the road leaving a trail of blue smoke behind. You'd have thought he had a Rolls Royce he was so pleased with it. He gave Bligh five pounds and headed for home, too flash to come back with me in the utility now! So I gave him half an hour's start and then followed, keeping an eye on his tracks to make sure he was still there.

Sure enough, about ten miles further on, here she was, leaning up against a sandalwood tree with Frank a lather of sweat and a hole dug in the ground where he'd been kicking away at the thing trying to start it again. We couldn't get it going so put it in the back of the utility and took it home.

We got to know everything about this contrary contraption over the next few months, as we had to keep pulling it to bits every time it broke down — which was every few miles. Frank would start out for a tennis party somewhere, all togged up in his whites like a pastry-cook, tennis racquet tied over his shoulder, a bottle of water and all, and the bike purring away like a cat. Then, a few hours later, ting-a-ling-a-ling would go the phone and the voice on the other end would say: 'This ★!?(★`~?+★= thing has broken down again — can you come and get me — bring some water with you too. I don't know whether I've still got a tongue or not. I can't feel the blessed thing!'

We got the bug with bikes. We had a hair-raising ride down dog netting fences from Clonard to Rutherglen with Frank riding his old bike and me hanging on behind on a couple of rolled-up corn bags — could hardly walk for a couple of days after. I'd bought a 1927 model nine horsepower Harley Davidson and sidecar (a pine box like a coffin hanging out one side over an extra wheel) from the manager of Rutherglen and we were on our way to pick it up. What a trip. It was thirty odd miles, but when we got there nobody was home and we had no idea how long they'd be away. So I left the fifteen pounds purchase money at the door with a stone on it, knowing that if we waited around we'd have to stay there the night and we had no tucker or swags.

We knew nothing about this old bike with fowls camped in the sidecar and dogs chained to the wheels, but after a lot of kicking and swearing, she suddenly backfired and began bellowing like a scrub bull. Talk about a din! There was no muffler, just the open exhaust. So we took off, backfiring all the way like a cannon because we had the magneto advance and retard lever in the wrong place. The sprocket was so badly worn there were hardly any points left and the chain clattered over the blunt points with a noise like a jack hammer. We finally hit home, the last few miles down fences over logs and things in the dark. The old Harley used to get so hot in the summer it boiled the petrol out of the carburettor. The inside of all my trouser legs were burnt into strips from rubbing against the hot cylinder fins. I was telling Spinifex George about it one time, and he said: 'That's good, mate. Yer won't never need a headlight when she gits dark.'

The manager of Rutherglen also had another Harley of the same model in bits and pieces in a piano case, so for three pounds I bought it for spare parts. Every week saw worn bits pulled off one and replaced by not-so-worn bits from the other. There were two long thin upright metal tubes at each side of the front wheel. As the front wheel was rubbing on the fork I thought adjusting the nuts on top of the tube might reposition the wheel, so began screwing — the wrong way, of course. Suddenly the cap I was *unscrewing* at the top of the tube let go with a noise like a shotgun blast and everything inside that was under enormous pressure from the compressed spring went high in the air like shrapnel. Didn't ever find some of the bits — just as well I didn't have my head in the way, though a bloke would have to be thumped on the other end to have affected his brains. As old Teddy (Friggin') Trivett always said when anyone did something stupid: 'Dopey bastard, if 'is brains wez bloody dynamite they wouldn't blow th' friggin' wax out of 'is ears.'

The bikes were very handy on the place once we got used to their cranky habits, most of which we were able to rectify quickly as time went on. For small jobs around the run they saved a lot of time running in horses out of big paddocks and then riding miles to fix a fence, ride boundaries, bore drains and telephone lines. The sidecar held most of the gear I needed for most jobs. The old Aboriginal station hand working with me perched himself up on top of the gear with the dogs. He thought it was just Christmas as we tore through the scrub and followed pads along fences, the wind blowing his hair all over the place. But he changed his mind when the bike suddenly broke down and he remembered we'd left the waterbag behind! The old Harley was used for years going back and forth to where I was working cutting scrub, ringbarking and fencing on both places.

Eddie Beardmore from Rose Hill came over to get Harry and me to help him draft up a mob of sheep he had on agistment on Breena Plains, which had got boxed up with a travelling mob someone had let loose in the stockroute. As usual, it was hot and dry and the yards were so dusty you could hardly breathe and could only see a couple of yards in front of you. The sheep milled around the forcing pen in a thick cloud of red dust with Harry and the dogs in behind and me hunting them down the race to Eddie on the drafting gates.

After a while, Eddie roared out through the dust: 'Pull 'em up, pull 'em up. Dust, bloody dust — bloody scandalous. Man's wool won't be worth two bob a bale.' A short silence followed, with Eddie leaning on the rail panting and spluttering like the dogs.

Then Harry's voice came through the dust from the back of the yard, heard but not seen: 'I finkt, boss, we get lot er little dust coat and put on 'im 'tat bloody sheeps, yer know boss'. And Eddie —

'Yes, yes, wonderful idea — hunt 'em up, hunt 'em up.'

And, of course, I got the giggles at the very thought of old Eddie and Harry struggling to put three thousand 'little dust coat on 'im tat bloody sheeps, yer know boss'.

It's sad to realise that such a short time ago it was the lonely first settlers who followed the tracks of equally lonely explorers as they spread across a land occupied for thousands of years by the Aborigines. It is now the isolated lonely Aborigine who treads his former land. The roles have been reversed. I think it's time we acknowledged the harsh and sometimes brutal treatment of Aborigines during European Settlement. We also should understand that, so long isolated from other lands, far more Aborigines died from introduced diseases like smallpox, measles and influenza than were ever deliberately killed in battle.

When we were fencing in some of the watercourse box country (old alluvial duplex soils) the ground was so hard you'd only get down a few inches at a time with a crowbar. And it was so hot in the summer you couldn't touch the thing if you forgot to cover it each time with a bag. We carted petrol tins of bore water along the line in the sidecar to pour in the holes, then came back each morning and dug out a few more inches of the damp soil until the holes were the right depth. Being a 1927 model, the Harley Davidson, although cheap to run, had a number of irritating drawbacks. Vaporising in fuel lines and carburettor from overheating and loss of spark in magneto and plugs caused most of the stoppages. Also the old model bikes had beaded rim tyres which couldn't be replaced when the beading stripped of. We had to lace the beading back with wire, which didn't last long.

Spinifex George was a little jockey-type drover. He spoke very quietly in a slow drawl. Boss drovers, of course, always liked little ringers in their camp because they didn't eat much tucker and took up little room. Their swag was generally small and light too, a big advantage on the wagonette always short of space. By the time five or six men's swags, bags of ropes, tuckerboxes, cooking gear, buckets, wash basins and billies were packed in, there was precious little room left. The cook had to fit up there too, because he drove the horses and put up the ropes to hold the sheep at night when he got to camp in the afternoon before cooking tea. On the big open treeless plains, firewood also had to be carried, tied under the axles of the wagonette and, where water was scarce, it had to be carried too. The cook had to be careful not to waste water or burn too much wood, or he was in trouble. With so much loading and unloading every day, the plant had to be well-organised and everyone had to pull their weight and stick to their allotted jobs or the camp was in chaos. Good horse-tailers and cooks were always up and washed in the dark. The horse-tailer then set off to find the hobbled horses and brought them in to camp ready for saddling up and the cook had the fire going, billy boiled and tucker out ready by the time he got back. In the meantime, the rest of the gang had a wash and rolled their swags ready for loading. They all squatted down around the fire with one foot

underneath for a seat and had breakfast. The horses were then saddled, the break pulled down, ropes rolled up and the mob slowly
moved off camp and spread out to feed. The sun was just coming up
as the camp broke up and the youngest of the team (on this occasion,
me) stayed behind to help the cook clean up, load the wagonette,
harness the horses. The cook headed off on the loaded wagonette for
the dinner camp and I rode off to catch up with the mob and take
my place on the tail. The mob was allowed to spread out feeding for
most of the early part of the day and by the time the cook's plant was
caught up with at the dinner camp, the mob was content to settle
down.

I soon learnt there were two important things that had to be
rigidly adhered to if you weren't to fall foul of the camp. The first was
that every morning when you got out of your swag, you immediately
washed hands and face and combed your hair. The second was that
you *never* came back to the fire empty-handed. The fire was the
central feature of the camp to which you brought back wood and laid
it beside the fire for the cook, who was boss of the outfit once the
camp was set up. And you had to be careful not to mess with the fire
either because the cook was boss of that too. To break this invisible
code was the unforgivable sin. Not understanding the importance
drovers placed on that early morning wash, I missed out on my first
morning because it was so cold. During the day I realised I was deliberately being shunned — I wasn't being spoken to. I had no idea what
I'd done wrong until late afternoon when one of the drovers rode up
beside me and said: 'You didn't have a wash this morning. Make sure
you don't do that again. You have a wash first thing tomorrow morning, right. It doesn't matter if the water turns to ice as it hits the dish,
you have a wash and comb your hair the same as the others, right.' —
and he rode away. I'd just had my first lesson on the road!

I always made sure not to be caught in my swag after daylight. I
woke with a start noticing a glow just above the horizon through the
mulga scrub surrounding the camp and thought the sun was coming
up. I flew out of my swag and began filling the nosebags with chaff

and cracked corn and was on my way over to the yard to start feeding the horses when the cook yelled out —

'What yer doin', yer mad young bugger?'

'I'm feeding the horses because the sun's coming up,' I said.

'That's the bloody moon, not th' sun. It's only 10 o'clock, yer galah. Git back in yer swag an' let a man git to sleep,' the old cook yawned.

Spinifex George got on well with everyone because he was such a wit about the camp and looked so small and comical in his outsized balloon jodhpurs with stovepipe legs into which his own little thin bandy ones were rammed. The balloons stuck out from each hip like miniature sails and made him look deformed. Drovers are often solitary types who don't talk much. And their life and everything about them is at a slow pace because their work is slow, being governed by the pace of the slowest sheep or cattle in the mob being driven. Sometimes they walk, leading the horse, sometimes they ride and, if the weather is dry and hot as it so often is and the wind is from the wrong direction, they can be in dust most of the day. The swarms of pestering little bush flies crawl all over you — in your ears, eyes, nostrils, over lips — and don't let up till after dark. The horses are nearly driven mad too. A thick knot of little black flies constantly suck away at watering patches they've eaten out of the corners of the horse's eyes. In good seasons, plagues of mosquitoes nearly eat them alive too. If the plant stops for any length of time, such as the dinner camp or in the evening, dung fires are lit so men and horses can stand in the smoke to get a bit of peace for a while.

Old Spinifex worked for us, off and on for years in between droving jobs. But he had one pet aversion. He was terrified of snakes, which became a great joke with all the men in the camp. There was never any shortage of snakes and they and old Spinifex always seemed somehow to find one another.

The plant had shifted camp and Skid Cole, the cook, came over to where Spinifex was putting up the ropes to hold the sheep at night. 'You seen any snakes pokin' about yet George?' — and George —

'Snakes, don't talk to me about bloody snakes — I wasn't 'ere five minutes before the bloody dorgs nearly run one over th' top of me!'

One time the plant was on the road with a mob of dog-poor cattle in a bad drought, shifting them to some agistment country about 100 miles away. The weather was hot and dry and the horse tailer was Broody Rooster. Broody had a big thirst up and every time he felt like getting on the grog, which was about every month or so, he'd suddenly get a 'terrible bad attack of harthuritis' and limp around the camp, getting worse by the day. When the mail coach arrived, he'd be so crook they'd have to help him into the cabin to see the doctor in town. A week or so later after he'd finished his bender and run out of money, the mail coach dropped him off at the camp which had shifted to a half-dry swamp some miles further on in the meantime. Broody, completely cured now and noticing the men down at the swamp, walked down to see what was going on. They were struggling with a bogged cow and trying to lift her back on her feet. Spinifex had the tail over his shoulder, Tom had the head and Claude had a rail lever under her stomach trying to break the suction of mud. Just as Broody arrived, the old cow gave a snort and a bellow as she struggled to her feet, and, like all bogged stock, the first thing they want to do when they get up is charge you. But Broody didn't wait. As she struggled to her feet with a snort, he took off at high speed and went straight up a leaning box tree at the edge of the swamp about fifty yards away like a goanna with the dogs in behind. When he looked back, the cow was lying flat in the mud again and everybody doubled up laughing.

After tea that night they were all quietly sitting round the fire looking into the coals, when Spinifex started off: 'Yer know, they must 'ave a terrible good doctor in that town. I see a bloke a while back, all burred up so bad with "harthuritis" they 'ad ter nearly roll 'im up a set of skids ter git 'im inter th' truck ter take 'im ter th' doctor. A week later he's cured 'im so good 'e coulder won th' 'Limpic Games foot race, specially if it wez hup bloody trees!'

Back at camp, the horses were all tied up in the shade and the dogs were having a snore-off too while the men boiled up and had dinner. The talk was all about the war as usual and what Broody, very game from this distance, was going to do with Hitler if only he could get his hands on him for a while.

'I jist want arf an hour with th' bastard with a butcher's knife an' a bag of coarse salt, that's all I'm askin'. Jist wanter hear th' mongrel beller while I hack little bits of hide orf 'im an' rub in another 'andful of coarse salt. Pickle th' bloody mongrel, that's what I'm gunner do if ever I git me 'ands on 'im.'

And Pappy, a bit further along the log they were sitting on, very serious when discussing strategic positions on the battlefields in France in the First World War, is explaining the importance of the 'rearguard action' in defensive withdrawal.

And old Spinifex, from the butt of a tree alongside, struggling in the wind to roll a cigarette with dry powdery tobacco, is saying — 'Th' only rearguard action ever I seen was th' fastest bastard in front and th' slowest behind!' —

But by this time, old Tom, a bit laid back with a full gut now, begins to snore.

Towards the end, old Spinifex went a bit queer, spending most of his time camped away from people and just talking to his horse and dogs — you never quite knew whether he was talking to you or to them. It was probably very largely the effect of a life of isolation and, like so many other old bushmen, he was happy to poke away by himself as he got older. He took less and less work too and just wandered about the bush with his horse and sulky and his dogs. He died in a lonely camp on a waterhole out on the Nebine not long after we left Clonard and was not found for a long time because he'd purposely kept out of touch and, of course, nobody missed him when he died.

Most of the old bushmen died in poverty-stricken circumstances. Though many had a grown-up family in some other state, they found letter writing such a difficult task that they gradually lost touch altogether. Many could not read or write. Those I knew over the years had no religion at all and were quite content to simply lie down in their camp or under a bush somewhere and die when their time came in the same way every other animal does. They had no hang-ups simply because they hadn't bothered cluttering up their lives with material things they couldn't cart about with them and looked on death as a purely natural event — the end of a cycle, as it were — and this is exactly how I see it too. It seems to me more rational to face things as they really are rather than fantasising about what is or isn't up in the sky or down below. As old Freddy Grey once said: 'Yer know, matie, I don't believe all this stuff they go on with about blokes burnin' for ever in them big fires down in hell. A man'd never stand it, would 'e, aaaaa?'

Lenny Kibble was an old bearded Thrushton kangaroo shooter whose right thumb and half one finger had been blown off by a sniper's bullet at Gallipoli. He made short work of the Turkish sniper who was in a tree a bit to one side: 'I dropped the bugger before 'e 'ad time to reload an' he hit th' ground like a bag er spuds and never even bounced.'

Lenny had an old 1923 model Overland utility he'd extended a bit so he could camp up in the back on top of his kangaroo skins as a mattress. He covered the top with canvas like the covered wagons of the prairies and when the skins got too high for him to fit in on top, he sold them to the local skin buyer and started all over again — this was his life. He smoked cigarettes night and day and stuck the butts by the wet end to the frame inside until it looked like a dried arrangement in the finish. He and his black and tan kelpie dog he called Johnny were never more than a foot apart. He couldn't start the day without a pannikin of very strong black Turk's Head coffee — I often wondered if this brand reminded him how lucky he'd been that morning at Gallipoli!

Another old Thrushton stockman was Charlie Clark who worked with us for many years. He was middle-aged and completely illiter-ate. If there was something that required his signature, the place was marked by a large unsteady cross. A couple of times a year he'd ask me to write a letter for him, never more than a few paragraphs and always to some old flame from somewhere in his distant past. It always seemed to be some barmaid he'd met across the counter in some back-country pub years ago and was probably the closest he'd ever come to a relationship with a woman. All the letters eventually came back unopened. It was sad. I'd have to guess what I thought he wanted me to write because he was too bashful to say. Reading the letter back, he'd just sit there dumb with embarrassment and scratch away at his pipe while avoiding my eyes. Finishing off the letter was the hardest part. He'd be all of a twitter. I knew he wanted to say 'With love from' but the very thought of mentioning feelings of a personal nature was quite impossible. The thought of having to actually say it himself was enough to nearly have him buckling at the knees, but if I said it for him, that was different. So I wrote, 'With love from your old friend Charlie', which left this simple old bushman quite drained and almost wriggling off his chair with embarrassment. He'd filled his pipe and raked her out a dozen times during the ordeal. He thanked me and made his way to bed where he couldn't be seen until morning by which time he'd be back to normal again and the matter would never again be mentioned, not even when the letter was returned unopened weeks later with 'Whereabouts Unknown' scrawled across it.

He was one of the many bushmen from the past who were disadvantaged, especially in a social sense, from a lack of education. Even if they wanted to learn they couldn't because those around them and those they worked for were often also illiterate. There were no wireless sets or schools out on the runs and most wouldn't have known what a book was if they saw one. Many, like old Charlie were leftovers from large bush working families in the back blocks somewhere, with illiterate parents from a poverty-stricken background. Most of them went straight from their parents' camp, never having been to a school, to work as off-siders for bullockies, drovers or ringbarkers for next to nothing from an early age.

Another old hermit who shot kangaroos for years through all that western country was Victor Hurst. He also had been at Gallipoli and was minus one eye. Some said a Turk gouged it out with a bayonet, but others claimed it was clawed out in a fight with a big old grey buck he'd wounded. I didn't ever get round to asking him what had happened because I knew he'd have told me something else again. He and his old lop-eared spotted dog, Snakebite, poked about the bush in a beat-up 1926 model Chev. utility. You could find them camped along any bore-drain in the south-west mulga country. Years later when coming back from St George one afternoon with a load of horse feed, the sump sprung a leak and I was running short of oil in the old truck. I knew where he was camped some miles down a drain between Wandit and Boolba, so followed the drain down until I came to his camp. He was pegging out roo skins when I arrived. While we had a drink of tea I asked him if he could lend me some oil to get me home and I'd return it on the next mail coach.

'I never use oil but you can drain it out of the utility,' he told me. 'I won't be using her for another week or two.'

So I unscrewed the sump plug and, slowly, out came about a quart-pot of thick black oil like a rope — you could nearly cut it. I put it in the truck engine (I think it was too thick to get through the hole where the rest had gone!) and got home with the bearings still intact. I told Victor he should change the oil once in a while.

'Orrr, she runs as flash as a bloody sand goanna, matie,' he said. 'Terrible good car, ole man. I've 'ad 'er for years now an' never 'ad ter put a jam tin of oil in 'er. Runs on the sniff of a oily rag — on th' smell of an oily rag, ole man, that's wat I say and never lets me down, aaaaaaaaaa?'

On a brief visit to see Keith and Frank in Brisbane just before the war started, Frank took me to meet the staff at the solicitor's firm where he was a trainee articled clerk. I noticed they all sat around the table in the lunchroom and opened and sorted the mail while they had morning tea. It seemed too good an opportunity to miss. Frank was always playing pranks on everyone so I thought I'd play one on him.

We had a lot of wild scrub goats on Clonard and, while mustering,

I came on a mob of these and selected a big old stinker (billy) with long curly horns. I ran him down, flew off the horse and grabbed him, took my knife out of the pouch and knocked the agates out of him then hacked off his beard — the most putrid thing you ever smelt, set hard as rock and gone rancid from years of old nanny goat urine.

I carted this ripe old fuming beard home in the saddle pouch, rolled it up in a brown paper parcel, registered it, and mailed it off to Frank. When the mail arrived, all the girls at his office raced to open the parcel, saying they wished they had a kind brother to send them surprise presents like that. The weather was hot and the ripe old goat beard had been fuming away rolled up in the parcel for a week before it hit Brisbane. When they opened the present on the table, the fumes filled the room like gas and everyone ran for cover holding their nose. Frank had to brave the fumes, sneaking up on the offender where she lay in the middle of the table and lead her out to the garbage can like a cranky dog on the end of a chain.

CHAPTER 8

The War Years

JUST before the Second World War started in 1939, I was fortunate to have mated up with a couple of unusual scrub-cutters who'd recently arrived at Thrushton and a jackaroo from Rutherglen, all from Brisbane and not long out of College. With no work available anywhere around the city, they came out on the advice of the wool brokers to work on these two properties. All were older than I was and had a good education. They seemed very knowledgeable and perfectly comfortable talking and arguing on all kinds of subjects new to me. I did a lot of listening and learnt a lot about 'book stuff' that was foreign material up to this point.

They talked about religion, politics, industry and trade and the way these were manipulated from behind the scenes and brought on wars aimed at the domination of other people's countries and resources by all kinds of sinister means. It was the age-old conquest of the weak by the strong as links were forged between other powerful industrial nations as a means of keeping power out of the hands of the working people. They were probably what many would have termed socialists. They claimed the uneducated masses had no way of learning the real truth because news was always carefully sifted and the real truth kept well away from popular newspapers of the day. They maintained that popular newspapers likely to have a wide circulation were always filled up with sporting results, petty scandals and all sorts of inconsequential sensational nonsense to keep the mob happy by stopping them from thinking. These young people and later Moodgie's thoughts on these same topics had a profound influence on my life and thoughts. I started to think a bit too — on more serious and far-reaching things than animals and the daily routine of bush work that always dominated male conversation wherever you went.

Firmly fixed in the mind of most station bushmen at that time, especially the younger ones, was an underlying animosity towards wealth and position and the arrogance that often accompanied it. Those who aspired to false behaviour by smart or eloquent talk were instantly recognised for what they were, especially what they termed the 'snotty nosed half-axes' straight out of private schools who thought they were a cut above everyone else. They saw these kinds of people as spoilt upstarts who strutted around with their noses in the air like they had a broken shovel handle jammed in their arse. I couldn't count the times I've heard the old hands say, 'They don't 'arf think their shit don't stink.'

Many working people saw the product of private schools as examples of unearned privilege and position. The silver spoon or the old school tie often foreshadowed the elevation of vastly inferior people to positions of power and authority over those from state schools with a working class background, yet often with superior integrity and ability. Others with intelligence, but who lacked social position and education, often spent a lifetime trying unsuccessfully to get off the bottom rung of the ladder in order to gain some semblance of public recognition and acceptability.

At station homesteads, owners, managers, overseers and jackaroos dressed for tea at night in collar and tie, the ladies often in evening frocks, while the men ate out in the kitchen with the cook. This class distinction in such a small isolated community, where men had to perform similar work together on the same place every day, had the potential to breed discontent and foster feelings of inferiority and resentment, which it sometimes did. It was an awkward situation that I felt was largely insoluble under those conditions at that time.

Owners and managers understandably needed a life of their own with their family. Many station hands would possibly have felt uncomfortable had this been any other way, the fence dividing the two groups, the privileged from the non-privileged, the educated from the uneducated, had been firmly in place for so long that each had little in common with the other. It was probably as much an education gap as anything else. Changing attitudes, a Depression, a war and technology began to iron out the gaps and form a more equitable society. Boarding schools, to which owners and managers had to send their children, tended to be seen by many working people as institutions of privilege, continuing traditions from the infamous Colonial era no longer acceptable or applicable to the changing times.

We had four camps of men scattered about on Thrushton cutting scrub when the war started, mine being one of them. I'd been in to the homestead to get another load of stores for the camps and, as usual, camped the night with Dad and Doolie at the homestead. After tea the wireless told us the sad story. Hitler's forces with a thousand tanks were on the move and as a consequence of broken promises to British Prime Minister Neville Chamberlain, and 'peace in our time' (whatever that was supposed to mean), we were now at war with Nazi Germany.

As I rode round the camps to spread the news, hats and waterbags were thrown in the air along with axes and billycans in jubilation. The general retort was: 'I'm gunner be with th' boys, by Christ I am. Bugger th' bloody sheep, the bastards cin bloody well starve.'

They looked on it all as a wonderful and exciting opportunity to break the hopeless monotony of their lives. Many of these young bushmen raced off to enlist because it gave them the first permanent job they had ever had and at the same time they suddenly became war heroes anxious to fight for their country. It was in fact the first time anyone had ever made a fuss of them, which helped the ego no end. They suddenly were hosted by the RSL and by station owners who wouldn't have said 'good-day' to them the week before. As they left on the train from Dirranbandi or Thallon, a guard of honour awaited them, with the odd bugle blowing and the CWA ladies waving flags. Such are the joys of war. Patriotism or what the war was all about didn't concern them. 'We're going to be with the boys on an overseas trip in a big boat, all at the government's expense, and be actually paid to do it too, be Christ.'

Most of them just took off, collecting their cheques on their way past the homestead and kept going. Don't know what happened to most of them, but I did get a letter some years later from a stockman who was working cattle runs outside Alpha somewhere. It was almost impossible to read the letter, which claimed that he and Ken Maynard (one of the scrub-cutters) were mates and had camped together while in mustering camps before Ken started with us. The letter said that before Ken joined up, he had promised to leave his horse, saddle and dog to him and, as I had them, would I now send them up. I tried to work out what this order was all about. Ken had come to us on the back of the mail lorry with nothing but his swag that he took with him when he went. The only thing he left behind was a leaking old battered quart pot, one of the things he threw in the air when I told him the war had started. I sent a letter of explanation and heard nothing more. Ken had joined the Navy and was one of many who lost their lives in the battle involving the cruiser *Sydney* off the West Australian coast.

So, with nearly everyone gone, Dad and I were left with one old hermit who said he was 'too old an' didn't go for fightin' an' killin' anyhow', trying to feed four thousand head of hungry sheep with their ribs sticking out. After the war started it was impossible to get scrub-cutters anywhere. In desperation, like many others, I went to the police station in St George after a weekend to look over the inmates of the lock-up as they were turned loose from the pen on the Monday morning, hoping to find someone who could swing an axe. Whether their black eyes and split lips were from beltings up by the police or by someone else, I didn't know. I brought some of these poor blighters home occasionally, but the grog had a terrible hold on them. They weren't much good and certainly didn't like axes and if you didn't camp with them to drag them out of their swags each morning to start work, they'd stay there all day and do nothing. It was hard work just trying to keep them moving and nothing much ever got done. Most of them left after they got their first cheque and didn't come back. So we had to cut out roughly the number of sheep we thought we could handle, try our best to feed these, and let the rest take their chances and hope for some rain before they got too weak to walk. The younger stock that could travel, we took back to Clonard again, but lost a lot of the older breeding ewes.

Keith joined the RAAF in 1940 as a wireless operator/air gunner, later serving on operations in France, Germany and Italy. According to the pilot Bluey Hershall, they were rescued after ditching in the North Sea and were lucky to survive and later, their badly damaged plane crash-landed in the Libyan desert. Keith was repatriated at the end of the war just before his promotion to Squadron Leader came through.

After the Japanese had entered the war in the Pacific, Tom Duffy rode down to see me one day. He'd just had a letter on the mail coach from Chalker, a young cove who'd been horse-tailing for him on the road several months earlier and had left the plant one night to ride into Cunnamulla to join up. Tom was in a real flap — said he hadn't realised the war was so bad and that the Japs were so close.

No doubt hoping to impress old Tom with his game attempts to halt the Japanese invasion and probably taking a chance on Tom's weakness for geography, Chalker's letter announced:

I jist come outer th' fox holes on the front line at a little place called Bribie Island . . . Terrible 'eavy fightin' — dead Japs layin' about everywhere — 'ave ter git back to the front line again now an' knock over a few more Japs. Hopin' this letter finds you in the pink like it leaves me.
Chalker
(Your friend at arms fightin' for 'is country)

When I told Tom that Bribie Island was only a few miles north of Brisbane and the bloke was pulling his leg, Tom got wild and snorted around for a while.

'I didn't think it sounded like Chalker — you could never prise the lazy bugger out of his swag in the morning to get the horses. You'd stand him on his feet and shake him awake and next time you looked round he'd be back in his swag again snoring. The cook hooked the cart mare to the end of his swag one morning and dragged it a couple of hundred yards over tussocks and logs before the dopey bugger woke up. He wouldn't have been able to knock a bloody condensed milk tin off a stump twenty yards away if you gave him a shotgun and a box of bullets, the dopey bugger. The army's the best place for him and I hope a Jap jabs a bayonet in 'is bloody arse too.'

Frank also joined the RAAF, mostly stationed at Renmark while in training as a fighter pilot. The war was well advanced by the time he was old enough to join up and finished before he could be sent overseas. It was always great to have him home on leave to break the loneliness and boredom of continuous hard work. He always seemed to be getting into strife by playing the most outrageous pranks on somebody, nearly always on poor old Doolie and Pappy who were easy meat for his particular kind of skills. Back home on leave towards the end of the war, Frank turned up with a big heavy .45 Colt revolver he'd pinched from a hole under a cliff on the beach where someone had planted it, no doubt intending to retrieve it. Frank decided to save him the bother. He bought some bullets and looked around home for something to try it out on. It had a kick like a mule and every time you pulled the trigger she'd blow your hand in the air nearly up to your shoulder. The first things he saw were the fowls with Pappy's prize Black Orpington rooster strutting very stiff and correctly and shining like a piece of new porcelain at the centre of his wing of ladies — just the perfect picture, but far too peaceful for Frank. For the first couple of explosions, nothing much happened except dust kicked up in a few places. Rapid action which would denote any kind of unplanned chaos in the mob was well under control until the rooster, necessarily very erect with dignity under such crisis conditions, suddenly parted company with his pope's nose amidst a shower of feathers. Pandemonium broke out amongst the chooks as they tried to charge off in every direction at once. Dogs barked, the horses bolted, heads came out of windows and Pappy roared. The normal bush order and tranquillity was suddenly disrupted, as it generally was when Frank was around.

By the start of the war, with everyone now turned over from cattle to sheep, wool carting and shearing contracting became a pretty tough occupation with all kind of competition and fights between rival contractors for sheds. We had finished mustering and had all the small holding paddocks full of sheep ready to start shearing on the Monday morning after the contractor, George Ashwin, arrived with his gang on the Sunday. On the Saturday night, the whole shed and most of the yards suddenly went up in flames and all the machinery and wool packs with it. We knew something had gone wrong but it was only later we heard that our contractor had a fight with a rival over who should have had our shed and this was the way the other bloke had got even with George. It put us in a real fix and we ended up having to shift everything over to a neighbour's shed miles away and shear there. This was a hard decision for a neighbour to make in a drought. To have his country eaten out by thousands of other people's sheep was hard to take, but in times of trouble, there was nothing else he could do — it was an unwritten law that you couldn't let your neighbour down in an emergency.

Eddie Twidale was one of the biggest wool carters around Bollon at that time. He wasn't very popular with the smaller carriers with old lorries battling to compete while Eddie bought new heavy rigs and trailers on behind. Eddie was a powerfully built man with arms covered in tufts of hair like stunted spinifex, singed off in places from poking around in campfires. He worked like a bullock and had drivers on other trucks doing the same. Everyone thought he was making a fortune. His lorries were going all day and half the night while shearing was in progress. But he told me one time that all you ended up with in that game was a fleet of broken-down, worn-out lorries and a big overdraft. You had to cut the price so low to get the work, there was nothing in it.

He had a house in the Bollon and pulled up there late one night with a big load of wool and rolled into bed. Just on daylight next morning he was up on top of the load twitching up the bales that had loosened on the rough road the night before, a pannikin of tea alongside him on one of the bales. The twitching was almost finished when there was a bit of shuffle in the dust down below as the Broody Rooster arrived on the scene. Broody was a little sawn-off shrivelled-up drover with more hide than a thousand head of bullocks — couldn't stop talking, like a rooster can't stop crowing.

Looking up three tiers of bales to where Eddie was twitching the wire rope on top, Broody starts off: 'You run over my bloody dorg when you come inter town last night — bloody good dorg too. You wez goin' like the hammers er buggery — man got no right goin' that quick with a big load on comin' inter a town.'

Eddie looked over the side, 'What th' bloody hell yer talkin' about, I never seen no bloody dorg'.

And Broody — 'Well, yer run over 'im any'ow and kilt 'im dead. Man can't afford to lose a champion dorg like that — worth a fiver — good dorgs is 'ard ter git, you aughter know that — man no bloody good without a good dorg.'

Eddie getting a bit stirred up now: 'You'd be no bloody good if yer had thirty head of th' bastards. Anyway, th' useless bloody thing, all it ever done in its bloody life was piss on car wheels and chase Clarry's bloody fowls.'

And Broody — 'Done matter, 'e wez th' best dorg ever I seen with a few head er sheep, an' you gunner pay fer 'im too — can't jist run over a man's champion dorg an' git orf like that.'

But Eddie, with bits of hide knocked off his knuckles from the wire rope, had had enough. He tied the twitch stick handle and began climbing down. 'I'm comin' down, yer yappin' little mashed-up turd an' when I git me feet on the ground, there's two things I'm gunner do with you. The first thing I'm gunner do is screw yer melon head orf yer shoulders, and the second thing I'm gunner do is ram it up yer bloody arse along with your dead dorg with that crowbar over there.'

But Broody, with such undignified threats of mutilation to his person, didn't wait to look 'over there', he was gone, and I don't think any more was ever said about that 'champion dorg' — not within Eddie's hearing anyhow.

Billy Lock and his team took over the bore drain delving contract in our district and other work with his bullocks after Alf Smith died. Like most of those old coves, all he ever talked about were bullicks, 'orses and dorgs and was always on the lookout for another scrubber to run down and break in for the team. I made the mistake of telling him I came across a small mob of cleanskins while mustering a big scrubby 12,000-acre paddock and there was a young down-horned bull amongst them. Right or wrong, Bill wanted that bull to break in for his team — didn't matter how wild it was. So early next morning we started out at daylight to ride the nine miles to where I last saw them and start tracking down the mob. As soon as we caught up with them they took off full gallop through the thick mulga scrub in a cloud of dust. The scrub was too thick to head them off and there was no open country where they could be rounded up and held in a mob. So we just followed their dust, trying not to gallop into a tree or be dragged out of the saddle by overhanging limbs — you could only see a few yards in front of the horse. It wasn't long before they started to knock up, as one after another, they peeled off the mob and began charging the nearest horse. The bull, being the strongest, kept going in the direction of a thousand-yard tank about a mile away. He hit the water with a mighty splash and began swimming out into the centre where he bailed up. Bill went in after him on the horse armed with a long dead branch. After a wild fight, the bull came out the other side and started charging my horse every time I tried to head

him off. He bailed up again, facing me with blazing eyes and tail
thrashing from side to side. Bill, pretty wild and a bit toey at any time,
was getting stirred up now. He tied his horse up and armed himself
with a great limb of dead mulga and started heading in the direction
of the tail-thrashing bull that he'd already named Charger.

'Get back on your horse you mad bugger — the bloody thing'll eat
you,' I called out.

But Bill kept on walking. 'I'm gunner knock 'im down and then
we'll tie 'im up,' he said. 'We'll bring the bullicks down here tomorrow an' chain 'im ter one of the big old workers — that'll straighten
some the kinks outer the cranky bugger. After 'e's been dragged
around for a week in coupling, I'll knock th' stones out of 'im an' cut
'is horns off, an' after a red hot brand singes the hairs off 'is arse, he'll
be talkin' Christmas turkey!'

But Charger had other ideas. He waited until Bill was about
twenty yards away, then gave a roaring liquid snort and charged
straight at him. Bill was still struggling to get this great log down fast
enough to belt him between the eyes when there was a loud thump
and Bill went flying in the air and hit the ground with the log on top
of him and the bull kept going. I was sure he'd be dead — but no, this
bloke was tough. He got up plastered with dust and dead leaves, got
back on the horse and ran the bull until he bailed up again. Another
log and the same thing happened again and again until it got too
dark to see and we had to declare Charger the winner of the first
round. I'd never seen anyone take such a hammering and keep on
going.

Bill was a bit beat-up and not quite so flash next morning, though,
with great mulberry coloured blotches across his chest and ribs and
hide off his nose, ears and cheeks. But he still insisted we take the
bullocks back as coachers next day and run him down again. We
finally succeeded in getting Charger, half-dead by this time, into a
small holding paddock with some old working bullocks for coupling
next day in a set of abandoned yards they'd done up a bit. A few
years earlier, the bore-drain had broken over and flooded the area and

a dense scrub of box saplings had grown in the waterlogged soil. The saplings were only about two inches thick, straight as a gun barrel and about twenty feet tall. Bill tied the horse up at the fence and was walking over to open the gate into the yards while his mate rode round the other side to hunt the bullocks up.

Charger must have been sulking under a wilga tree close by and couldn't be seen. When Bill was halfway over to the gate, there was a switching snort from behind. Bill took a quick look and here was the bull with tail over his shoulder coming straight at him. No time to do anything but look for a tree, and the only trees were these thin saplings. He flew at the nearest one like a wild cat and started to climb, but when he was up five or six feet, it started to bend over with his weight. Anticipating what was about to happen, Bill started to bellow to attract the attention of his mate, who fortunately hadn't gone far. As the sucker bent down, the mickey hit him from underneath and shot him into the air, straight over the other side, where 'bang' again and over old Bill went again. This happened four or five times before his mate galloped back and Charger took to him, while Bill had just enough time to hobble back to his horse. He can thank his lucky stars the mickey had down-horns and that he ended up with only bruises instead of holes in his butt end.

There were very few horse teams in the South West when I was young. It was the slow but steady bullock teams that did most of the heavy work. They pulled heavily laden wagons, delved the bore drains, snigged logs to the steam-driven sawmills, posts for yard building, and dragged ploughs and scoops, tank sinking and opening up new bore drains. Their main drawback was the amount of feed they ate to keep their strength up for the hard work they had to perform each day. In dry times, the bullockies rode all over the place for miles cutting out all the widely scattered currajong trees they could find, then drove the bullocks around, a couple to each tree. A big working bullock needs a lot of feed just to keep it going and as most teams, with a few spares, generally had between twenty and thirty bullocks, the men cut out all the currajongs in no time, then had to fall back on the less palatable mulga. Nobody liked losing all their currajongs in this way because they were big shady trees that were needed for their own stock-feed during dry times, so there was always a degree of ill-feeling over this.

The only horse team in the Bollon district at that time belonged to Fred King who seemed to have plenty of work all the year round until one day at the Sixty-fiveMile yards he was castrating a big half-draught colt. They had the rope on him trying to drag him up to a post when the horse pulled back and broke the greenhide rope. He reared right over backwards and Fred couldn't get out of the way in time. A big horse's head is a virtual battering ram coming down at that speed. As it slammed into the ground with Fred's leg underneath, his leg was smashed in several places. Too impatient to wait for it to knit properly in the hot sweaty plaster in the summer time, he hacked the plaster off in bits and pieces with the axe and a pair of fencing pliers. The leg knitted so crooked that the toe of his boot stuck out sideways and was always getting hooked up on logs and tree branches as he waddled about the bush behind the horses. The few remaining teams fought to survive as motor lorries took more and more of the work because they were faster and cheaper, so he decided to sell the horses for dog meat and get out.

Some of the more stubborn old bullockies struggled on for a few more years because this was the only life they knew. But their days were numbered when the first hard-tyred motor lorries began to appear and started undercutting cartage prices. And, of course, they couldn't compete with crawler tractors that began taking over tank sinking, bore drain delving and snigging logs to local sawmills. Time had suddenly become a major factor and everyone wanted the work done quickly. Also stations got sick of having to feed a mob of hungry working bullocks when they rarely had enough feed for their own stock, so every grazier was pleased to see them finally go.

Even so, loyalty to the old timers was strong and the phasing-out period stretched on into the 1940s, eventually terminating for good by the end of the war. These days the only reminders of the old teams are brightly painted wagons on roadsides approaching western towns where they act as relics of a bygone era for the tourist industry.

Dad's brother Hugh left the land and returned to live in Brisbane about 1943. Dad and I, with a couple of station hands continued working both places in conjunction and, as the homesteads were about twenty-five miles apart, we moved back and forth between the two places wherever the work happened to be. Looking back on those years now, I realise that about half my life out there was spent on the end of an axe, ringbarking and cutting mulga to feed starving stock. The only break for months on end each year was knocking off on Sundays to cart rations round the camps and giving Dad a hand to muster sheep into where we were cutting mulga in those big paddocks. If there was a shower of rain, sheep left the cut mulga to race around after the green pick that could barely be seen, yet was eagerly chased for variety from the monotonous mulga diet. Unless mustered and brought back and held on the scrub, they wouldn't come back until they were just about dying, so it was a pretty constant job. As there was hardly any mulga on Clonard, we had to keep shifting stock over to Thrushton which was predominantly mulga scrub whenever there was a shortage of feed, which was for months at a time in those drought years. When we weren't cutting scrub on Thrushton, I camped most of the time at Clonard with a married couple we had there, as this is where most of the improvements were taking place and where most of the work was.

Travelling backwards and forwards became such a bind that we put another married couple on Thrushton and shifted down to live permanently at Clonard until I was married a few years later. As things had been pretty tough-going for a long time, and Dad and Doolie were just about knocked up, they at last agreed to take a well-deserved month or six weeks' holiday.

★ ★ ★

I was batching while they were away and was returning to Clonard from Thrushton where I'd been camped down the back paddocks mustering for shearing. As I came to the night paddock gate, a saddled horse was tied up to a tree near the men's hut and another one carrying a pack saddle was feeding alongside. As I pulled up in the utility, a big old stooped man with a beard the same colour as the red dust came slowly to meet me, dragging his feet along in a pair of filthy worn-out flapping rubber-soled boots minus their laces with tongue dragged forward over the toes. I had no idea who he was or what he was doing camped in the hut without permission. But he approached with outstretched hand and, peering intently, stopped a few feet away.

'You'd be young Gasteen wouldn't yer be? Me name's Phil O'Shea an' I thought I'd pull up an' 'ave a blow with yer fer a bit, if it's all right. I used to be doggin' for your father on th' other place up there years ago.'

He pointing his thumb over his shoulder somewhere to the north. I couldn't believe it. Old Phil O'Shea — where the blazes had he come from in such a dilapidated, tattered state, carrying next to nothing? Not having seen him since I was a young kid, I certainly didn't recognise him now. He *really* was an old man now, not as I'd pictured him all these years. Anyway, he moved in and camped with me until Dad and Doolie returned from holidays. I cleaned up a couple of rooms in the hut and gave him a bit of tucker to go on with and a few bits and pieces of cooking gear out of the shearers' mess until something could be sorted out. Although nothing was ever said, he settled himself in and camped there for the rest of his life.

We didn't really mind, even though he was a bit of a nuisance at times, because he was a good old cove from a long way back and did odd things around the place to help. One of the jobs he gave himself was clearing the new night paddock that hitherto had been so scrubby it was a great haven for the roguish night horse to hide in just when you wanted to catch it in a hurry. It was watercourse country heavily timbered with poplar box (*Eucalyptus populnea*) trees and sandalwood (*Eremophila mitchellii*) shrub understorey. He'd been using fires for different purposes all his life and was a past master at cross-burning. It didn't matter whether trees were green or dead, it was all the same to Phil. He'd butt two limbs together on top of a big green log and bring a shovel-full of coals from another fire. In no time, he'd have them smouldering away. He'd keep twenty or thirty of these going night and day, getting up a few times during the night to poke the ends together so they wouldn't go out. I cut down all the live trees and Phil did the rest, cross-burning all the long limbs into shorter lengths to pack around the stumps until they were all burnt out. After about twelve months he had the whole paddock like a tennis court and the night horse had nowhere to hide. In fact, you could drive all over it in the middle of the night without hitting a stump or getting a puncture on sharp roots and sticks.

When his hair got too long, he'd get me to cut it and trim up his long bushy singed eyebrows and hack the forest of curly grey hairs that protruded in great tufts from his ears and nostrils. I'd have him perched up on a petrol tin under the shade of a tree while I attacked him with a pair of old blunt clippers. Everyone else generally kicked up a hell of a din during this operation, with me on the end of those old antiquated clippers. But it was like shearing a stinking old billy goat. He had a huge wound at the back of his neck, a deep furrow nearly from ear to ear that was lined with blackheads and half full of gunger and scales of dead skin. A dense growth of long curly grey hairs were growing out of this rich nutrient bed so I'd have to give her a bit of a scrape out before driving the clippers into it. I think Phil's nerves had been all burred up for years because he showed no signs of ever feeling anything — just as well too. On the first of many such sessions, I asked him how this great wound came about. Because it was very obvious to me, as it would have been to any other roo shooter using sawn-off .303 bullets for years, that somebody had shot him with just such a bullet — probably in some drunken brawl out in a back-country pub somewhere.

Like a flash and without hesitation, he said, 'It was a terrible big carbuncle, boy, with twenty-nine cores!'

I didn't like to ask him if it had smoke coming out of it too! One thing was clear though. During many a fight, he'd made enemies and was sure one of them was about to sneak up and do him over at any time. He wouldn't go ten yards, night or day, without his rifle — even kept it loaded with him in his swag at night. I often wondered whether he'd spent some time in jail.

When Frank was out on holidays from school, we used to have fun with this now docile old scrubber. There were a lot of rabbits with burrows on a sandhill about a mile from the house. Phil was going to show us how to poison them with chopped-up carrots and strychnine. We pulled up carrots from Pappy's vegetable garden about sundown and chopped them up and mixed in Phil's measurement of strychnine, then scattered the baits around the burrows. We were camped with Phil in the men's hut at the time.

'We'll turn in real early, boy,' he said. 'Because we've gotta be up before th' "cocks is crewed" to run th' baits before the crows an' hawks cart all the rabbits away.'

We didn't know Phil and his rabbits. At about half past two or three o'clock in the morning we were wakened by a hell of a din coming from somewhere out in the night paddock and sat up, half-asleep, to listen. It was old Phil trying to catch Roany, the roguish night horse we had there. Hell, it was funny — I still laugh about it. Don't know how long he'd been at it before we woke up, but as we listened, we'd hear old Phil scraping past dragging his spurs along the ground from his flapping rubber-soled boots and the jingle, jingle of the bridle as it was swinging about on one arm. Then a bit later there'd be two or three loud snorts and a long drawn-out explosion of farts and a clatter of hooves as the night horse charged off full gallop to the other end of the paddock. Phil was left roaring a string of oaths in the dust behind and, a bit later, another string of oaths as he fell arse over head in the bore-drain he'd forgotten was there in the dark. He'd drag himself out of this and rattle on past the hut, mumbling as he continued in the direction the clatter of hooves was last heard. Then silence for a good while. We'd be just about to get up and give the poor old blighter a hand. Then there'd be another almighty thunderous explosion of farts and another string of loud snorts and the clatter of hooves as Roany galloped full pelt to the other end of the paddock and stood there in the corner looking back with a few more snorts.

Old Phil, voice a bit cracked in the vocal machinery now, was roaring a frightening array of threats and oaths a long way behind in the dust haze. Just as well Roany couldn't understand bush English and what was going to happen to her butt end 'd'reckly', or she might have gone clean over the fence and kept going. Don't know how many times this happened, but we couldn't do anything for laughing. The sideshow kept on but eventually we got up and gave him a hand to catch Roany. We boiled up and had a drink of tea, got the other horses in and were out to pick up all the rabbits just on daylight — but not a single rabbit, not one. Phil blamed the weather: 'We'll hit 'em again d'reckly, boy, after a shower er rain when they git a bit 'ungry.'

The Bush Brotherhood used to send out one of their travelling parsons a couple of times a year to instruct us on the Lord and his doings. At first they came in a horse and sulky, then, as times improved, graduated to motor cars. If at all possible, we kids always made it our business to get them bogged somewhere before they'd gone too far. One of the more recent parsons of the Bush Brotherhood in our region was Mr Winslow, who had taken me on my first holiday to Sydney when I was fifteen. He turned up at Thrushton about six months later and spent the night with Dad and Mum before moving on next day. He got directions from Dad on how to find my camp some eight miles down the run and drove all that way on a bush track over stumps and sticks through half a dozen wire gates to say hello.

Georgy and Billy Lock, father and son, were the bullockies delving the bore drain and, seeing my camp under trees near the water, decided to camp the night and have a yarn. They were unyoking the bullocks along a nearby fence and, of course, Georgy's mud-larking bore-drain clothes were stiff with mud and bullock hair and Billy's were the same. Just as my mate and I walked back to camp with axes over our shoulders, Mr Winslow arrived. After greeting him, I noticed Georgy peering at the stranger over the neck of the bullock he was unyoking, so thought I'd better introduce them.

Georgy was a short wiry little bloke with very bandy legs from years in the saddle and burnt nearly black by the sun. His huge bushy, singed eyebrows overhung a pair of tiny sunken little beady eyes that seemed to peer out at you like a fox looking out of a hollow log. Walking over to the bullocks, I said —

'George, this is Mr Winslow from the Bush Brotherhood come out to see us.'

And Georgy — 'Jesus bloody Crise, Jimmy, never shook 'ands with one er them little parsons before — 'Ow yer goin' boss — terrible dry ain't it — might git a drop er rain d'reckly, aaaaaaa?'

And with that he fastened on to Mr Winslow's soft chubby little pink hand with his gnarled, claw-like fist and began swinging it from side to side with the little crushed paw inside. With noses an inch apart as Georgy, short-sighted, got in close to get a better look, the swinging stopped, the claw opened and the little hand fell down at the Reverend's side like a pink-iced bun just stood on by a horse. Mr Winslow's hands were probably more at home holding fancy teacups at the CWA ladies' tea parties back in town. He said he couldn't stay long so we boiled up and gave him a drink of tea and a couple of chunks of Bill's emu egg brownie and away he went.

'Th' little parson didn't stop long, aaaaaa Jimmy,' Georgy noted. 'Muster took fright at gittin' lost openin' all them wire gates in th' dark and gettin' bogged in the bore drain, aaaaaaa?'

As soon as we'd finished shearing at both places late in 1942, Dad and Doolie went away to Brisbane to have a few weeks' holiday with their respective families. Phil and I had been drafting up the young stock and shifting them into different paddocks. When we finished I took the utility and joined Moodgie, my fiance, for three weeks or so at her home in Lismore where she was on holiday from Sydney University, intending to pick up Dad and Doolie on my way home. Phil and I had been batching at Clonard, so before leaving, I killed a sheep and cut it up and salted it so he'd have plenty of meat while I was away. If he got lonely or crook, he could always ride the several miles over to drover Tom Duffy and his gang at the Sixty-fiveMile and camp there. Poor old Alf had recently died and Tom was cleaning up the bark hut and sorting out the few things he'd left behind. Anyway everything seemed to be in order on the place, so I loaded up and headed for Lismore, camping the first night just over the border at Boggabilla. From here I sent Phil a couple of tins of tobacco and some khaki handkerchiefs for round his neck as a present for the poor old bloke back at the place by himself. The day before I was due to leave for home, the parcel arrived back in the mail with the word DECEASED scrawled across it in red letters. I didn't even know what the word meant until Moodgie told me it meant he was dead. I went cold — couldn't believe it. No good ringing because nobody was at Clonard and Thrushton wasn't on the phone.

I collected Dad and Doolie and headed for home, calling in at the police station in St George on the way past. Here, they told me what had happened. I've often wondered if Phil perhaps got crook and rode up to the Sixty-fiveMile only to find nobody there. I later found that Tom and the rest of the plant had gone west of Thargomindah to start back on the road with several thousand head of sheep. Phil evidently got a bit light-headed, caught his horse and rode away — where to, I couldn't guess. It must have been straight after I left for Lismore. He took no tucker either, for everything was just as I'd left it and all the stuff in his meat safe on the hut verandah was mouldy and full of ants. He was later found in a state of exhaustion wandering along the Culgoa River below Dirranbandi without a hat or anything else, by one of the station stockmen riding the boundary.

Phil's horse was tied up to the boundary fence that had blocked him. He climbed over and continued on by foot. The man thought this strange, so followed his tracks and came on Phil about a mile further on where he'd hit the river and started going round in circles. As he didn't know who he was or where he'd come from, the man took him home and phoned the Dirranbandi police sergeant who came out with a young constable from St George who was there on a stock thieving investigation. Unable to establish identity because Phil was making no sense and was obviously pretty crook, they put him on the train and took him to the old people's home in Toowoomba. He rallied enough to say his name was Phil O'Shea but the poor old chap died in his sleep the next day. It closed another fascinating chapter in the history of a tough old bushman who had roamed the back country, like so many of his kind for more than seventy years. Just as well I put my name and Moodgie's Lismore address on the parcel I sent him from Boggabilla or his death would have remained a mystery for ages.

CHAPTER 9

Wedding Bells

MARJ (I nicknamed her Moodgie) was the eldest in her family. She had two sisters, Joan and Ted, and a brother Bert. The family was brought up in an intellectual household where integrity and the importance of high moral and social values were always paramount. Moodgie was a born student and very bright and strived always to give of her best. At sixteen, with the New South Wales Leaving Certificate from the Northern Rivers High School in Lismore under her belt, she started studying medicine at Sydney University. As medicine took six years and we wanted to get married before then, after the first year in Sydney, she switched to the three-year science degree course and moved to Armidale for a year. Here, she became a resident in the classic old Booloomimbah homestead that was to become the nucleus of the new university complex of New England University. After the Japanese submarines finished shelling Sydney during the war, Moodgie moved back to Sydney University again to complete her studies.

Doolie had invited Moodgie to Thrushton for a holiday before starting university. She didn't want to come. She was a shy and very private person and Thrushton was away out in the bush where she knew nobody and there were no other girls nearby. As my brother Frank was home on school holidays from Brisbane at the same time, wondering how to entertain her was at least partly overcome. I soon found she took up very little space and was quite capable of entertaining herself for hours with reading and writing and with work that had to be done round the place. We'd seen one another a few times before this as kids, which didn't mean much. Now we were older, she sixteen and I seventeen, we must have looked at each other with different eyes and seemed to find excuses to be together whenever possible and soon became good mates. On that first visit, we must secretly have decided to team-up at some future stage, though neither of us, being so young and shy, had given any indication of this at the time. We only saw each other once a year but wrote numerous letters, a pretty difficult task for me but second nature to Moodgie. Every time another of these great bulging letters arrived on the weekly mail coach with that neat flowing hand, I reluctantly compared it with my own scratching and blotted attempts full of spelling mistakes. The comparison between my mess and her neatness shamed me into a determined effort to improve and I'm sure this is what taught me to write. In the summer time, I'd sit at a table with perspiration trickling down every part and the ink drying on the pen nib a dozen times before I'd decided what to write next or how to spell the next word. As I dipped the pen in and out of thick half-dry ink in the bottle with the sediment building up on the nib and forming a crust across the point as it dried, each page began to look like something the fowls had walked over with muddy feet. I was a hog for punishment and gradually improved with time.

You had to be careful not to let some of the old illiterate bushmen see you reading or writing anything — that was sissy stuff not to be associated with *real* men. I remember a young chap who was off-siding for bullocky Billy Lock while delving bore drains. Bill had caught this young cove reading a book he'd brought along with him, rolled up in his swag. It was in the fire in five minutes.

'Don't let me ketch yer doin' that again, boy — plenty of work around the bloody camp without wastin' time lookin' at that bloody stuff — it won't learn yer nothin'.'

After a long association with these rough and ready types of old illiterate bushmen and working with them for years, it became obvious their feelings of inferiority and resentment ran deep when in the presence of educated people. Their lack of education where 'book learning' was concerned made them feel vulnerable and uneasy. To a minor extent this rubbed off on me, as did some of their outlook and attitudes to life. I can still see the look of total disbelief on Moodgie's face, not long after we were married. I had embarked on a correspondence course, Principles of Diesel Engine Design and Maintenance, through the Diesel Engineering College in Sydney. One day when I was surrounded by books and assignment papers, the dogs barked and I saw two strange horsemen and a couple of dogs approaching the night paddock gate. Instinctively I flew in the air and began stuffing books and papers under mattresses and things to cover up any evidence that I'd been reading before they reached the house. Never having been made to feel guilty about wasting time on such things as reading and study, Moodgie couldn't understand my reactions. On occasions when I was on the road droving stock somewhere and the mail lorry was going past, I collected the mail and rations. If any of these old types were around, I'd have to wait until they'd gone to bed a bit after dark, then sneak out into the scrub with the hurricane lamp, get it going and spend half the night reading Moodgie's letters. Some were too big to fit into one envelope so came in two instalments and, though they took me ages to read, were all that kept me going from one week to the next. I once rode fifty miles in a day to pick up one of her letters that had gone to the wrong property by mistake.

Being so isolated, with nobody of my own age to talk to most of the time, I was pretty much a loner, or maybe I'd have been that way anyhow. Both of us were fortunate in that respect, I suppose, because Moodgie's natural reserve placed her in a similar category and we got on well. The loneliness of working in the bush didn't bother me much until someone came and I realised how good it was to have company for a while. Probably being too serious-minded, I've always felt distinctly uncomfortable at parties where people generally seemed to devote so much time to small talk, witty puns and off-colour yarns.

Sometimes I'd be lucky and find some old bloke camped nearby and spend the time during the party yarning to him at the fire in front of his camp — I found that much more interesting.

Moodgie's father, Dr Russel Pearce, was Medical Officer (Pathologist) in charge of the Commonwealth Health Laboratory in Lismore. He was a very gifted person and a dedicated student of advanced science, particularly in the field of preventative medical research, comparative religions and social and political change. He was totally dedicated to his medical work and spent much more time in his laboratory than he did at home. He took a diploma in mining engineering and degrees in both science and medicine. After graduating in medicine from Sydney University, he was involved with the hookworm campaign while stationed at Thursday Island and Townsville and in medical work in Melbourne, Sydney and Brisbane before settling in Lismore.

Her mother Edna Pearce (Peberdy) was quite an extraordinary person too. She was one of the early women Master of Science graduates from Queensland University. Her first assignment after graduation was researching the cattle tick while stationed at Toowoomba. She later turned to high school teaching as a full-time profession. She had a wide circle of friends with similar interests in music, gardens and literature, but she would not become involved with politics or religion and strenuously avoided being caught up in controversial issues. She had a great sense of humour, often at her own expense. She recalled snoring through a lecture by the famous physicist Sir Marcus Oliphant:

To be sure of not missing a single word, I arrived early and sat in the front row directly below the lectern. But while waiting for the lecture to start, I must have dozed off. What an awful embarrassment. Just imagine, that poor man having to gaze at my open mouth and compete with my snores all the time he was speaking. When an attendant woke me, the hall was empty and everyone had gone home!

She and her homely old Lismore friend, Mrs Creighton, passed many a jolly afternoon at a table under shady camphor laurels in the rambling back garden. While they drank tea and ate scones straight out of the oven with strawberry jam and cream, they chuckled away at all the pranks the children got up to while growing up. Mrs Creighton had seven wild boys and a girl in her large family and was saying —

'You know, Mrs Pearce, (no first names in those days) we kept 12 fowls and a rooster in pens out the back of the house. The fowls did an awful lot of cackling but laid no eggs — we had none at all and Dad was out of work again too. But what luck. I read in the Women's Weekly one morning that castor oil was just the thing to make fowls lay. So I bought a bottle from the corner store and had the boys catch all the fowls. What an ordeal it was because fowls, like children, hate the taste of castor oil. Anyway we got the lot drenched, a dessertspoon each, thinking how lovely it would be to have our own fresh eggs again. But unknown to me, the boys sneaked out and bought 13 eggs with their pocket money and put them in the nest boxes. Oh, what excitement there was next morning. The 12 fowls had laid *13 eggs* so one had actually laid *two*. I told all my friends about this wonderful recipe which they all tried out immediately. But it didn't seem to work for them and ours stopped laying again next day too. Those little villains — it was months before I found out what really happened but in the meantime, the grocery man said he'd sold right out of castor oil!'

Moodgie's mother played the viola in the Lismore Municipal Orchestra, often practising after tea at night in the lounge room. But her sheet anchor was her large and lovingly tended green leafy garden, full of fragrance and humming with bees. This is where you'd generally find her — old battered hat, boots and all, garden fork in one hand and the hose in the other, the cat and the rake lying on the lawn alongside. I've often thought since she died that she was one of the loveliest people I have ever known. I don't ever remember her uttering a harsh or unkind word about anyone, which must be the greatest compliment anyone can be paid.

My intellectual inadequacy in such a household made me shudder. After we were engaged, I spent part of my annual two or three weeks' holiday in Lismore to be with Moodgie. I used to be terrified that her father would ask me a question on something scientific or political. I had never before been in the presence of such a brilliant mind and the experience really terrified me. Ours was not that kind of household. Dad and Doolie were educated people, of course. Dad read a lot of astronomy and archaeology and, coming from a very conservative and religious background, had made a study of the Christian religion and its application, of which he was most scathing to say the least.

Doolie read a lot too. They belonged to the Queensland Bush Book Club. This organisation was founded to supply books and other reading material to people in remote areas who had no access to libraries or other forms of intellectual pursuits for relaxation and who were handicapped by the length of time between mail days and distances from towns. Members could state the kind of literature they were most interested in and back would come an exciting big box of books on mail day several weeks later. It was like looking forward to Christmas, waiting for the arrival of parcels and things you'd ordered by catalogue weeks before. This was a wonderful service, of great benefit to many lonely bush folk, especially some women who felt trapped by distance and loneliness.

Both Dad and Doolie were very musical and had a wide selection of popular and classical records that we constantly played on the old wind-up gramophone. Their reading tended to be newspapers that were a week old before we got them, popular magazines and novels. The *Bulletin*, a Queensland journal regarded as the 'Country Party Bible', that Dad devoured from cover to cover as soon as it arrived, certainly wasn't designed to foster a deep analytical appraisal of social and political events. Many saw the *Bulletin* as a conservative propaganda sheet that mixed in a bit of news and some funny stories to make it look less blatant. Consequently their leanings were towards conservatism and their reading concentrated on the 'right wing' opinions and literature emanating from such sources. To have done otherwise would have put you outside the clan, as it were.

Our life was isolated away from the mainstream, especially from those with an education. Like most other landholders, we were trying to cope with the massive overdrafts after the Depression years and rock-bottom wool prices. Each day was the same monotonous pattern of hard work and there was so much of it that there was precious little time left over for reading or studying anything. I had always found reading a pretty slow and difficult task and generally managed to find a horse to handle, a saddle that needed restitching or a gapped axe that needed filing or a broken handle that needed replacing — anything, in fact, but lie down under the house reading like the others during the hottest part of the day. Also, the weather was so hot in the long dry summers that sweat just trickled down every part of your body, even at night, and the flies gave you no peace at all until after dark. It was anything but conducive to study or thinking too deeply about anything. There were no refrigerators, only charcoal coolers and drip safes. A pad was worn back and forth between the shade and the waterbag while your main thoughts revolved around how to keep cool enough to sleep at night.

On holiday at Moodgie's place after we were engaged, the anticipation of being questioned at any moment on almost any subject at all by someone of her father's brilliance was daunting. How could you make a favourable impression when anything you said was bound to sound stupid, ignorant or both? The whole place was lined with books. They overflowed the bookcases and grew up the walls, precariously balanced one on top of the other; they covered tables and chairs — I couldn't even read the titles of most of them, let alone understand what was inside. I used to be absolutely petrified at breakfast time and tried to become invisible as he tore open the latest big brown paper package of medical and political books that had arrived in the previous mail. He'd be finishing dressing in the dining room during breakfast before leaving for the laboratory, using the sideboard mirror at one end of the room and walking back and forth between it and his office table, the dining room table midway between the two.

Balanced on top of a foot-high pile of books that covered his office table was a little brown portmanteau holding all sorts of bits and pieces necessary for the completion of this scientific operation. It contained studs, cufflinks, ties, tiepins, gold-linked things that went round his arms to hold his sleeves in place and clips to stop his trouser legs getting caught in the bike chain while riding into town to collect mail from the post office box. He didn't own a car and had never learnt to drive. I watched the progress of the operation in total fascination. I hadn't previously imagined any human mind could be so sharp or as retentive as this. He had one of his enormous textbooks open alongside his steaming hot porridge on the corner of the table almost under my nose. He'd take a spoonful of porridge while glancing at the open pages full of graphs and tables and continue reading out loud as he walked to the sideboard mirror to fiddle with a stud for a while. On his way back for something else, still talking, he'd glance at the next two pages and turn them over on his way past and keep walking. He'd continue reading aloud those pages he'd simply glanced at without a break or a pause. Jaw-breaking words flowed out of him like tea from a teapot.

On his way past the next time, he'd stop for another spoonful or two of porridge. He'd scan the next two pages for a second or two, turn them over and go on reading them for another five minutes until another visit to the old portmanteau was necessary for the next step of the operation. This went on at the rate of ten to twelve pages in fifteen minutes until he was properly dressed and all the porridge was gone, after which he left for the laboratory, much to my relief.

Before leaving the bush for Lismore where Moodgie was waiting for me, I'd spend hours cleaning myself up, filing and cutting off corns and trimming cracks, scrubbing my hands and arms, scraping gunger from under cracked and chipped fingernails and filing them into something like a normal shape with the axe file. But how could you make yourself *look* intellectual in a household where intellect and improvement of the mind so outweighed anything looks and dress could possibly produce — and in any case, a bloke only had to open his mouth to highlight the fraud! My working days were filled with not much more than horse breaking, roo shooting and sharpening axes to cut down half-dead mulga, dried caterpillar shit showering down on my half-naked sweaty body all day and feet squelching in boots saturated with sweat.

Moodgie graduated with a degree in science in 1944 and worked with her father at the Commonwealth Health Laboratory in Lismore for some time. We were married by Mr Winslow in his little church at Tabulam, only a short run from Lismore. Moodgie was twenty, and I was twenty-one. When much younger, I had jokingly told Jack Winslow that if I ever got married, I'd get him to do the job — to put the hobbles and halter on a bloke, so to speak, and I kept that promise. Friends of ours had just spent their honeymoon on Heron Island and recommended it as a delightful quiet spot, so we decided to go there too. As the boat left early next morning, we stayed the night in a cheap guesthouse in Gladstone. Moodgie wanted a bath so I got the old rusty chip heater that warmed the water going, then nearly died of fright. Just as the flame began to roar up the long chimney pipe a huge water rat like a blazing torch came hurtling down the chimney with sparks flying off it. It flew out of the chip hole and began galloping round the small bathroom in a pall of smoke. It was my first encounter with a rat and certainly the first with one that was on fire.

We found Heron Island a beautiful little unspoilt coral atoll off the Queensland mid-central coast several hours' trip by motorboat from Gladstone harbour. You could leisurely walk round it in less than half an hour and on the eastern side was a picturesque lagoon shallow enough to wade about in at low tide. The clear blue-green, thigh-deep water in the lagoon covered a magnificent garden of different coloured corals set amidst patches of snow-white sand. Huge clams with delicately coloured mottled green and blue jaws squirted water high in the air when their jaws slammed shut as we approached. Baby turtles scurried in and out of knobs of sponge and coral set among waving sea plants. A seemingly endless array of tiny rainbow fish and many different kinds of beautifully coloured spotted fish darted amongst crabs and starfish of all colours, shapes and sizes. There were cowry and a host of other interesting shellfish everywhere while beneath every rock and piece of loose coral was the home of an octopus in company with a multitude of other curiously shaped and colourful aquatic things I couldn't believe existed.

Moodgie had studied marine biology and knew most of the things we were looking at; but for me, who'd spent most of my life in the drought-stricken western country and had rarely been to the coast, it was all a completely new and fascinating world. There was practically no development on the island and the accommodation and food were pretty rough and service non-existent. The only buildings were the remains of the old turtle factory which acted as a storeroom, kitchen and dining area, with several small one-roomed huts strung out along the beach above high water under weeping sheoaks and big spreading, large-leaved tropical trees full of bird nests. The island was formed of coral sands honeycombed by muttonbird burrows below a dense growth of scrambling type shrubs and vines. Turtles crawled up the beach at night, dug holes and laid their batch of eggs and were gone again before daylight. We were often on our feet during the night to investigate the strange scratching noise under our beds, only to find tiny young turtles that had got lost on their way from their nest to the lagoon and had yarded themselves in our hut. They were remnants of an earlier laying period.

The twenty or so of us on the island were made up of American air force and army officers, who, like us, had just been married, and a few from the Australian forces on leave. I think there were only one or two other civilian couples apart from us, either on holiday or honeymooning. The fishing boat went out every day when weather permitted. It was a wonderful fishing spot for those interested in the sport and everyone caught so many fish most of them were thrown back into the sea. In the absence of trained cooks on the island, big coral trout, red emperor and other prime fish caught from the boat were just boiled in a twelve-gallon copper until someone scooped out the stringy mess with a wire-netting scoop attached to a mop handle and slopped them on enamel plates. We tried cooking our own down on the beach with another couple, but the wood wouldn't burn and the wind blew sand into everything, so it was back to the turtle factory again. But we were young and in love, it was all exciting and new, so the quality of the food didn't bother us — there was plenty of it: that was the main thing.

One night we had wild weather from a tropical cyclone off the coast. Walking out of our hut right on daylight the next morning I propped in my tracks as the towering rust-stained iron plates of a large boat dominated the view in every direction. I woke Moodgie and we began exploring this wreck, high and dry in the shallow water on the beach, hardly believing what we saw because it hadn't been there when we went to bed. A rope was dangling down the side so I climbed high up and over the railing onto the deck. Nobody was left on board but I'll never forget the eerie feeling as I tiptoed about what remained of the decks and along narrow alleyways with goose pimples up my spine you could have knocked off with a stick. I thought of pirates and half-expected to have one charge at me with a knife from round a corner at any moment — I lost no time getting down that rope again! Before long a few other people began turning up, including the owners of the burnt-out boat. There had been difficulty landing people on Heron Island because of choppy seas breaking over shallow water covering the coral reef at low tide, some of the women having to be carried ashore so they arrived in a dry condition. There was talk of blasting a narrow channel through the reef. So the owners had bought this burnt-out hulk with the intention of sinking it seaward from the opening to the channel as a breakwater to avoid large waves coming through the opening and eroding the beach in front of the huts. We were told that the ship had been strafed and set alight by Japanese fighter planes during the battle of the Coral Sea. There were dozens of very large live pom-pom bullets lying about the decks. The boat was taken in tow and anchored at Townsville to be sold as scrap and eventually bought by the owners of the Heron Island Resort. During the tow from Townsville, they ran into the cyclone as they approached the island. The towline snapped in the big seas and the hulk was washed up on the island during the night. A big sea the following night washed it further round the beach where it remained for many years. For me it was like Robinson Crusoe all over again. I'd not been on an island before and only rarely to the seaside. A few yards behind the turtle factory was the wreck of one of the early fighter training planes. We were told the trainee pilot was getting practice shooting up the turtle factory but forgot to pull out of the dive in time and bored into the sand at the back of the kitchen. They carted his bits away and left the wreck behind. The larger pieces too heavy for tourists to take away as souvenirs are probably still there. Our wonderful three weeks' honeymoon on Heron Island came to an end and we headed back in the direction of Thrushton in the big straight-eight Auburn car we'd just bought from my uncle in Brisbane, who had imported it from America. During the war when petrol was rationed and very hard to get, he had jacked it up under the house and left it there. We bought it for one hundred pounds and started for home, calling in to have a few days with Moodgie's family in Lismore on the way, full of plans for the future.

We had brought a box of all kinds of coloured shells back from the Barrier Reef with us when we returned, not realising that as they dried out, most of their bright colours faded away also. Nobody in those days had even begun to think about conservation — most people I knew wouldn't have known the meaning of the word. But as everyone else was doing this and there seemed to be a never-ending supply of shells, we did the same. Towards the end of our long slow trip home, the box began to get pretty nuggetty and we were glad to get it out of the car. I emptied the contents over some ants' nests for the ants to clean out the edible flesh inside the shells. Two

Aboriginal stockmen on the place sat for hours just staring at all these shells as the ants went about their business. I'm sure they hadn't seen shells before and kept asking us what they were — probably to make sure we said the same thing each time they asked.

CHAPTER 10

Friends and Neighbours

AFTER a day or two in Lismore with Moodgie's family, our next main stop, apart from camping the night in Tenterfield (where we nearly froze), was with Dad and Doolie at Thrushton before continuing on to Clonard. Now that we were married, it was decided we would run Clonard as a separate unit, only returning to Thrushton to help during the busy times during shearing and crutching and other stock work and when we had to camp out there cutting scrub. It was only a station track down dog netting fences between both places with numerous gates on boundaries and between paddocks.

The only homestead on the twenty-five mile trip was the home of our neighbours, the large Lee family. They comprised four big strong axemen sons who'd cut their teeth on ringbarking, scrub-cutting and fencing and four daughters who spent most of their time in the kitchen cooking to keep the tucker up to the mob, and old Herb and Mrs Lee. Herb was a rough uneducated old bushman who'd drawn the 40,000-acre Leawah block in a ballot. The track between our two places ran through Leawah and cut across their night paddock alongside the house, with a gate at each side of the paddock. This meant stopping and starting four times within a few yards of the house so there was no way of getting past without always calling in. But, of course, if you were travelling through country that didn't belong to you and using their station tracks to get to where you were going, you always called in at the homestead.

Always busy and in a hurry, we found having to call in all the time
a nuisance; and probably it was just as big a nuisance for the Lees as
well, but it was the done thing so there was no getting away from it.
We often hesitated because they had a big blue spotted cattle dog that
was always hiding somewhere waiting for a chance to fly out and
fasten on to your heels or the back of your leg when you least
expected it. It was generally running loose in the house paddock, and
they'd have to tie it up before we were game to open the gate.
Sometimes it was outside racing around among the horses. As the car
stopped, it would dive underneath and just lie there without a sound,
then nail you when your feet touched the ground as you got out.

Every morning in the hot weather the boys threw buckets of water
over the dirt floor under the house to cool it down a bit during the
heat of the day, which was siesta time when all work came to a halt
until the cool of late afternoon. When the water dried, which didn't
take long, this became the lounge room where the family weathered
the hottest part of the day sitting in the shade on old spring cart seats
around a couple of bullock hides and kangaroo skins and talked and
played with the dogs and cats.

Moodgie had met some of the family on previous brief holidays
and knowing we were just married, old Herb greeted her by fasten-
ing on to her hand and swinging it from side to side — "Ow yer
goin' girl, 'ope yer brought a drop of rain with you. Been scrub-
cutting for months now — terrible dry out 'ere yer know. Bare as a
birds harse, as th' sayin' is — flog a flea from 'ere to Burke an' back
an' never lose sight of the bugger. Been a crook week on top of all
that too, yer know. Th' car's buggered, th' wireless is buggered an' th'
harse is fell outer th' motor bike. But I sez to Mother, we've never
give th' young people a wedding present, so I sez ter Mother, we'll
give 'em a bloody rooster as the sayin' goes. Yes, that's what we'll do,
Mother, we'll give 'em a bloody rooster (with Mother and the family nodding heads in agreement!) 'E's a bit light on gist now from
flyin' round th' swamp an' not much feed out in the paddicks either,
yer know. But if yez put 'im in a pen an' throw in a bit of feed, 'e'll

be good eatin' d'reckly — always reckon th' best present's somethin' yer cin put in yer belly, yer know yer've 'ad it then.'

So down we all went in the blazing sun with a mob of dogs in tow. A big mob of fowls and ducks were feeding round the edge of the swamp, some camped up in trees and others flying like hawks. Herb got the dogs on to them, some running flat out half-flying and others up in the sky.

'Buggers' knock up d'reckly — won't go far before they start to knock up with th' dogs in behind them, then we'll grab one of th' roosters,' yelled Herb.

So everyone raced round in a lather of sweat and at last one of the boys came back leading a bedraggled red Orpington rooster for Herb's approval. He had about as much meat on him as some of the plovers and sandpipers that hit the sky with some of the fowls when the dogs charged in.

Away we went soaked with sweat, the rooster on the front seat between us. His beak was open and tongue was hanging out panting from a head with comb attached that stuck out of a hole we'd cut in a corn bag. We hoped he wouldn't die before we got home and emptied him out of the bag.

At branding time, Herb sometimes asked us to give them a hand to muster the cattle. They were pretty wild from running out in big scrubby paddocks where they were seldom handled. We young coves were always looking for a bit of fun when yarding a mob of wild cattle. We'd crowd the mob in hard at the yard gate so some of the mickies cut off the mob and charged off in the direction they'd come from. We'd be waiting, of course, and gallop our horses up alongside them and start shouldering them about the country surrounding the yards.

'Git away from the bloody tail an' give th' buggers a bit of room or there'll be cattle everywhere,' old Herb yelled.

But, of course, this was the whole idea, and in any case it was too late. Within seconds cattle were going in all directions, each one of us up alongside a beast full gallop shouldering them about in clouds of

dust with old Herb bellowing at us from back in the yard. Most of
the cattle were gone and Herb was there by himself now trying to
hold what was left of the mob. They finally beat him and all came
charging out with tails over their shoulders to join the ones we were
hammering round the paddock outside.

When yarding cattle, Herb always left the blue cattle dog chained
up back at the house a couple of hundred yards away because it had
no brains at all and was completely uncontrollable. It didn't care what
it grabbed hold of — any set of heels would do as long as it was heel-
ing something. This time, with cattle galloping about everywhere,
Herb was in a wild panic and wanted the dog in a hell of a hurry. He
bellowed to the girls over at the house to let it off the chain. But
the girls were all in the kitchen cooking as usual to keep the tucker
up to their big axemen brothers who could eat like draughthorses.
With all the talking and scurrying about and clattering of dishes,
they didn't hear Herby yelling, which stirred him up no end. He was
perched up on his horse with hands cupped round his mouth and the
bridle reins dangling from one arm as he bellowed like a scrub bull
— Let the bloody dog off. Nothing happened.

'What's wrong with the buggers, they all bloody deaf or somethin''
over there?' he bellowed.

There were cattle spread out all over the place going like the hammers of blazes with all us young scrub-dashers leaning out over our
horses' necks flat out in amongst them. Then the roars of old Herb
rattled our eardrums again.

'Let th' bloody dog orf.'

'Friggin' place'd burn down on top er th' buggers an' they wouldn't
know th' bloody difference.' But still nothing happened. At last a head
came out of the kitchen window, and a bit later the cattle dog, like a
blue streak, came heading flat out in the direction of the cattle yards
where all the dust was. With the cattle gone now, Herb was the only
thing left in the yard, still standing up in the stirrups roaring. With
all the dust he hadn't seen the dog coming. As the only set of heels
left close handy were attached to Herb's horse, boof-headed bluey

charged in and fastened on to them. The horse went up in the air with a startled snort and started kicking up and farting. Old Herb, still bellowing, was trying to hang on as it climbed into the sky with the blue cattle dog swinging out like a flag from a leg or a hock or anything else it could grab hold of every time a leg hit the ground. Herb's hat was gone — he'd lost a stirrup and had put a fang through his tongue. He looked about to explode.

But we'd had our fun and a good gallop around on the horses so we rounded up the mob and yarded them properly this time, then all went over to the house and had a drink of tea and a feed. There wasn't much talking but plenty of wild-bullock stares in our direction from Herb and the girls! We were about as popular as the boof-headed blue cattle dog until things cooled down a bit.

The Lees were good neighbours, though they lived a hard rough life. It was unavoidable because, like most of the country in that area, a lot of it was unimproved. Also it was low-carrying, poor wire grass and vinegar grass mulga country with the standard large over-draft to be serviced and ten big strong hard-working people to get a living off the place. It all took its toll. But they were all great workers and the girls were wonderful cooks. The boys were all good axemen and Ernie and Bill had won prizes in local wood-chopping events and Bill was a champion foot runner. They also were good tennis players and cricketers and played in the Bollon teams.

When I was only about seventeen or eighteen they sometimes invited me into town with them for a tennis or cricket match. I had fifteen miles to ride and nearly as many gates to open and close. This meant getting up before three in the morning to catch and feed the horse so I could get to their place by daylight. The horse had to be unsaddled and left in the yard with a nosebag of feed and hopefully I'd get a bit of breakfast before we left for town in the utility. The first time, I stood around at the bottom of the stairs with an empty gut, listening to the banging of spoons in plates as they wired into their porridge and stuff, waiting to be asked up for breakfast.

When they had just about finished, old Herb yelled out through a mouthful of stuff: 'Don't yer want no breakfast before yer go, boy? Yer don't jist stand around 'ere if yer want a bloody feed — if yer don't shoulder yer way in, yer won't git nothin' — it'll all be gone with this 'ungry mob tearin' inter it.'

When we were first married, it was a pretty hard and lonely life for a young girl straight out of university and not accustomed to roughing it in any way. We rarely saw anyone and there was no intellectual conversation whatsoever. Moodgie was used to classical music and keeping up with news items on the wireless, but you couldn't listen to the wireless out there in hot weather because of the constant roar of static. The telephone, when it was working, was the only link with the outside world, but this was a party line to which several other properties were connected. You couldn't phone anyone without all the others picking up the receiver and listening in to your conversation, then broadcasting it all round the district — it seemed to be their main source of entertainment.

Always busy, we rarely left the place, but did go to the pictures in Bollon one Saturday night. Pictures started showing once a week in a shed in the main street. It had four walls but only part of a roof and some adjustable canvas verandah chairs inside — you had a great view of the stars and moon while the show was churning away. I had only been to the pictures in Bollon a couple of times before, and each time the outfit broke down halfway through — which no-one took much notice of. When Moodgie and I went, a raging dust storm blew up and the flapping screen could hardly be seen through sheets of flying red dust. Before long the screen blew clean away altogether, so that was the end of that. We left and started to belt our way back home through blinding dust and swirling dead leaves from a strong gusty wind — it wasn't a real success.

If we went anywhere at all, it was generally back to Thrushton to have a weekend with Dad and Doolie. Even when I went out to the Sixty-fiveMile to pick up the mail and other stuff that was dropped off by the mail lorry once a week, I often left Moodgie behind if there were a lot of men camped there. I was trying to shelter her from all the swearing and rough talk amongst the men generally camped in and around the old Sixty-fiveMile slab and bark hut.

This was the home of drover Tom Duffy, who leased the 3,000-acre stock watering reserve that surrounded the hut and the Sixty-fiveMile bore. Most of the time, the place was surrounded by drovers, horse-breakers and any bagman who happened to be walking the roads at the time and wanted a feed and a bit of a blow. The old hut and yards used to be a Cobb & Co coach change on the Cunnamulla road midway between the FortyMile and Bollon. When Tom was away on the road with stock, Alf Claverton, an old burred-up whiskery drovers' cook, with constantly watering eyes almost turned inside out from glare, dust and fly bites, made his headquarters there to look after the place during Tom's absence. He had an enormous gut, laced underneath with a green-hide strap from which dangled an array of pouches. He stumped around on his heels because all his toes were burred-up from a wagon running over them when he was young. He'd wipe his watering eyes with a filthy khaki handkerchief tied round his neck and blow his nose with one finger every now and then while you were talking to him.

That was why I didn't take Moodgie if there were a lot of strangers camped there. Probably trying to be a bit too over-protective, I suppose, but when we were young we were always taught to have respect for women and not be rude or use bad language in their presence. Moodgie also stayed at home on shorter occasions when I was away mustering. We had no money at all so, to build up a few bob, I spent a good part of every winter camped away on distant properties I'd tied up for roo shooting.

I'd bought an old 1928 Model A Ford ton truck from under a wilga tree outside Bollon for fifty pounds. I got it going after putting in another clutch and used it to cart the gear and skins from place to place. The old cars were very different from those of today, and only dodged along at about twenty-five miles an hour. If something broke, you could always get yourself out of trouble as long as you had a good kit of tools with you. I was roo shooting out on the Nebine, west of Bollon, one time and the engine in the old truck overheated and threw the metal out of a big end bearing. I took the head and sump off and got the piston and connecting rod out and melted out the bit of remaining big end bearing babbitt over a fire.

The only possible substitute for a bearing was the thick sweat-hardened leather of the neck waterbag that was tied on the side of the truck. A neckbag is a canvas waterbag hung round a horse's neck and adjusted with a wide leather strap. Its thick leather backing keeps the canvas away from the horse's sweaty chest as it hangs in front while riding. After constant use in hot weather, the leather is constantly saturated with sweat and, no matter how well it's greased, it eventually sets hard as a rock when the sweat dries out. I cut out two identical sections of this hard thick leather to roughly the size of the crankshaft journal and soaked them in the bore drain overnight. Next morning the leather was soft enough to gently hammer out the moisture on the flat side of the axe head. By trial and error tightening of the bearing cap a few times and trimming off the excess leather after refitting the bearing cap each time, the job was finished. It lasted for years and didn't knock when the engine was running either. Removing the bearing cap for inspection six months later, thinking the leather must be just about worn out, I was amazed to find it hadn't worn at all, seemed as hard as the original white metal, and was shining like a mirror. I put it back and tightened the nuts and it was still in the engine when the old truck was sold a couple of years later.

My roo shooting camps were pretty rough because we were on the move all the time and never in the one place for long. We'd be gone by daylight every morning and shot until nine or ten o'clock, then back to the camp to peg out the skins during the hottest time of the day when the roos were camping out in the scrub. We'd start shooting again in the late afternoon, walking miles like emus and get back in the dark, boil up and peg out the skins till all hours of the night with the hurricane lamp. Into the swag for a few hours sleep and then we'd be up again in the dark, have breakfast and start all over again. When the roos got a scatter-up from shooting, we'd shift camp to wherever we found water — it was pretty rough going and you were always knocked up by the end of the winter. During these longer excursions Moodgie stayed with Dad and Doolie at Thrushton.

Even when back home, I was often pegging out skins into the small hours of the morning, Moodgie coming down every now and then half-asleep with a drink of tea. I knew no better then, but have often thought since what a wonderful mate she was the way she always stuck to me and never complained. In fact, life for me went on just the same as it had before marriage. I might have known a bit about handling stock, horse-breaking, roo shooting and swinging an axe (I'd had enough practice), but what I didn't know about women and marriage would have filled a library of books.

Soon after my introduction to a double bed, when I'd kicked the blankets and sheets off while spread-eagled all over the bed, Moodgie woke me one night and said —

'Can you move over and give me some room — I'm nearly falling out of bed'.

Half-asleep I said 'OK mate, hang on a bit till I git me hat!' (I've never been able to go ten yards without it.) Old habits took time to die but we finally buried most of them as we went along.

I had to ride the boundary one time after a wind storm and as the bike and sidecar were used for all the light work, Moodgie came with me for the ride. She perched herself up in the pine box sidecar on top of a petrol case and some bags and away we went. We'd gone eight or ten miles along dog netting boundary fences in great style dodging logs and stumps when a big red roo began hopping along the fence about a hundred yards in front. We'd been used to chasing anything that moved with the horses and the bike didn't seem much different — it's how we trained horses in scrub country for stock work. So I opened the throttle full bore and got into him. We were getting up close, with bits of dirt he was kicking up hitting us in the face when 'bang' went the sidecar tyre. The whole thing, tube and all, flew off the rim into the scrub. We broadsided round and nearly capsized as we jumped a log on the bare rim before pulling up, the old roo a long way in the lead now. With the buckled wheel past repair, we unhooked the sidecar where it was and left it there, continuing with Moodgie on the mudguard on some bags hanging on behind. It certainly wasn't an outfit designed for comfort.

I took Moodgie with me on a shorter trip of a few days to give her a break from the house for a while. There were a lot of roos on some big open brigalow and belah plains at the back of Clonard and I thought we'd camp on the edge of the plains while I got stuck into these mobs of big reds I'd been saving up for a good while. We loaded our gear, some salt mutton in a tin of brine, a drum of water and some bread and jam — and, of course, the .303 rifle and ammunition. To provide a level of comfort befitting a young lady, I threw in an old fibre mattress from the men's hut as we went past — that the stuffing was falling out of it didn't seem of any great importance. So away we went. There was a station track for the first few miles to the Mona boundary, but after that we just hammered and clattered in and out of melon holes and gilgais and over logs until the plains came into sight several miles further on. At the place where I intended camping, two big old scruffy-looking bulls were fighting, one on each side of the dog netting boundary fence. You could hear their roars a mile away. They were furiously rooting up the ground with their horns and throwing dust all over themselves as they pawed up the loose dirt. By the look of it, they'd been at it for days. It was mainly bluff, of course, but they really had the breeze up Moodgie, who wasn't too happy about camping there. So we poked on about another half mile until we came to a good wilga tree under which I threw the mattress. As it was nearly dark, we unloaded and while I took the salt meat out of the brine and threaded the chunks on a length of wire tied between two trees at the head of the mattress to air during the night, Moodgie rattled up a feed.

As the roars of the bulls still echoed round in the cold winter night, Moodgie was uneasy about sleeping there. So I showed her the bullets while I filled the magazine and put one in the breach, cocked the rifle and pulled back the safety catch. 'Now, if they come any closer,' I told her, 'all I have to do is knock off the safety catch and they're dead.' Settling down with the rifle and torch between us, I promptly went to sleep. But Moodgie couldn't close an eye — just lay there listening to the roars of the bulls.

Every now and then, she'd wake me up to say there was a moth fluttering round her face and I'd say, 'Go to sleep, mate, a little moth won't hurt you, they've got no teeth.' But this kept up and in the finish I sat up and turned the torch on to do battle with this blessed moth. For a while, couldn't work out what I was looking at. Suddenly I realised it was a big red fox, standing upright with a back leg on each side of Moodgie's cheeks while eating the meat I'd strung between the two trees, its tail brushing backwards and forwards across her face — hence the moth!

It must have been very hungry because when I sat up with the torch on, it galloped over to the dog netting fence about thirty or forty yards away, propped for a second, then came back full gallop to within a few inches from Moodgie's nose. I grabbed the rifle and passed Moodgie the torch, telling her to hold the beam straight on the fox. He galloped away again exactly the same as before, propped at the fence, turned and was on his way back full pelt. I lined him up in the sights and pulled the trigger when he was ten or twelve feet away, hitting him fair square in the gullet between both front legs with a sawn-off .303 bullet. He dropped stone dead in full flight and went bump, bump, bump as he skidded up on to Moodgie's pillow, his mouth opening and closing a couple of times with the last gasps. The rumble of the explosion echoed round in the frost on those plains for what seemed like five minutes. Even the bulls went silent for the rest of the night.

Moodgie reckons I pelted the dead fox off our swag saying, 'I'll knock the hide off him in the morning, mate, now go to sleep.'

Moodgie was a quick learner and, amongst all her other trades, she soon became a great protector of tucker. We couldn't work out why the fowls didn't lay any eggs, even though they always seemed to be cackling. Moodgie promptly set about unravelling the mystery. As I rode back from mustering one evening with the dogs, she was waiting at the night paddock gate.

'Come and see what I've got to show you,' she called.

She dragged out this enormous black and yellow spotted goanna by the tail — like a young crocodile and fat as a seal from living high on all our eggs for weeks. Getting a bit more suspicious with every bout of cackling, she had sneaked down to the chook pens with the axe to have a look and, lo and behold, there was the culprit with an egg halfway down his gullet. She very gingerly closed the door behind her and, bailing him up in the corner, got into him with the axe. You never saw anything with so many holes cut in it as this bloke had. Must have been a pretty frantic tussle and Moodgie was as cocky as a bandicoot for a fortnight after!

After every bad windstorm, I had to ride for miles along telephone lines and fences to clear off trees and fallen limbs. Also bulls and old buck roos were always sparring up with one another through the boundary netting and tearing great holes in it and roos kept lifting up the netting and crawling through underneath. I took the rifle and some tucker — you didn't go anywhere without rifle and ammunition in the winter when prices for skins were good. It was to take more than a fortnight's work. Someone had started a fire on the Mona (neighbouring) side, which had got away and burnt out a couple of thousand acres of cleared, heavily grassed, belah melon-hole country and much of the fence with it. The fence was in a real mess. Forty or fifty sandalwood posts had been burnt off level with the ground and many others had been badly damaged. Some of the netting was beyond repair too.

There were mobs of roos in the fresh green feed after the burn and we shot a lot while working on the fence. Continuing round the rest of the boundary when the job was finished, on the section joining Charlie Nixon's run, an enormous red buck stood up from the butt of a tree where he'd been camped. He was about one hundred yards away on Charlie's side of the fence and I knew he'd go if I didn't shoot immediately. So, without getting off the horse, I shot while sitting in the saddle and the bullet hit him in the chest. He dropped on the spot, but before I could tie the horse up and climb over the six-foot dog-netting, he had jumped up and unsteadily lumbered away. I knew he wouldn't go far so followed along his tracks and watched him about to lie down under a wilga tree about half a mile from where the horse was tied up on the Clonard side. I was sneaking up to finish him off when I noticed Charlie riding up from the other direction a couple of hundred yards away with his dogs. He'd heard the shot and as if drawn by some unseen force, suddenly turned his horse and rode straight towards the wilga tree. I knew the old red roo was close to dead but thought Charlie might frighten him away and I'd end up losing him. But, as it turned out, when Charlie was almost past, the roo gave a few dying kicks in the leaves and the horse shied sideways and the dogs started barking.

Charlie had been scrub cutting for months and looked a bit dehydrated. He hadn't had a shave or haircut for months. His toes stuck out of the end of old elastic side riding boots and his white shirt was red with dust and stiff with sweat, with darker blotches where the dust had stuck to patches of oil and fat. One sleeve was gone altogether and the other, still rolled up, was dangling down one side, held by a long strip of seam. His old felt hat was stitched round the top with baling twine and a greenhide strap stopped his dungarees from falling down and hobbling him. We had a yarn while I gouged the hide off this big old tough red. Charlie confirmed there were a lot of roos on the place and said that I could shoot there any time I liked, so I shot a couple of hundred there by the end of winter.

Charlie had a name all over the district for being a pretty wild old hermit who nobody seemed to know much about because he just camped in the bush with his stock and rarely left the place. Comical stories had circulated round the district about his exploits for years. Spinifex George often worked for us and had also worked for Charlie periodically since about 1928. He used to have me in fits telling me the things that happened when he was working there or had heard from other people.

The story went that Charlie became engaged to a refined English lady while over in the 1914–18 War. On returning to Australia, he eventually drew a block and wrote over asking the lady to come out and marry him. Her parents evidently were well set up in England. So Charlie thought he'd better build a bit of a house to replace the fly and few sheets of bark and iron he had leaning up against a half-fallen tree on his undeveloped scrubby run. The big day arrived and Charlie met his English lady on the mail coach at his turn-off near the FortyMile with his horse and cart and a mob of dogs. Whatever he'd told the lady about his land holdings in Australia, she hadn't expected to be trundling through dry dusty mulga country in the middle of a drought with heat and flies. By the time she hit the FortyMile, she had to be coaxed into the cart to finish the last stretch to the new house Charlie had nearly finished building. They camped with the flies and ants in the scrub at the side of the track to have a feed of cold salt mutton and damper. Bits of timber and corrugated iron lay scattered about in the scrub that came nearly to the walls of the house. To Charlie, the function of a house was to keep the dew off your swag at night and shade the waterbag and tuckerboxes during the day. The house was built with unpainted locally cut cypress pine and galvanised iron with bare walls full of knots and nothing much inside. As the cart approached the house, they were met by another mob of barking licorice-all-sorts dogs. Some jerked from the end of long chains tied round the house stumps amidst old rams' heads and a cemetery of kangaroo and emu bones right up to the front steps.

Spinifex claimed there was a bit of a tug-of-war between Charlie and the lady on the ram's head and dog turd meadow outside the door as he encouraged her to view the interior of the empty house.

But she'd had enough — wouldn't stay and went straight back on the next coach. Charlie took it very hard and wouldn't live in the house for years, but eventually got over it, finished off the verandah, and shifted in. I got to like old Charlie but, of course, he was a rough as bags old bushman.

He asked some of us to give him a hand to muster and brand his cattle one time. 'Camp over here with me — I got plenty of horses so don't bother bringing any — just bring your saddles and swags,' he told us.

The first horse he ran into the yard snorted and galloped around hitting halfway up the rails and fell down in the dust in the middle of the yard.

'What's this wurrung thing supposed to be?' I asked, but Charlie wasn't going to be put off.

'Orr,' he said, "'e's a good 'orse — 'e'll settle down after a bit. I handled 'im one night about twelve months ago with the hurricane lamp — good 'orse when 'e settles down!'

I didn't take much of a fancy to the first of Charlie's 'good 'orses', so decided to go back and bring our own. Charlie did have some beautiful horses, though, but many were just running wild out in big scrubby paddocks like brumbies. When the one he was riding knocked up or got staked, he'd run some of the others in and cut one out of the mob. He'd leave it in the yard with an old saddle on for a day or two till the sting was knocked out of it, then he'd give it a bit of a work-over in the yard before heading out into the run. His cattle were as wild as hawks too. They were rarely handled and would all but eat you in the yard.

Charlie got us over to brand-up before taking the fats to the trucking yards at Dirranbandi. A lot of wild cleanskin scrubber mickies eighteen months or two years old were in the mobs with fire nearly flying out of their eyes. We'd almost finished branding and were pulling the ropes off the last one, when someone dragged the head rope off before the leg rope was properly untied. The mickie got to its feet and went mad and put everyone out of the yard as it jerked at the rope still tied to its hind leg. Acting tough, Charlie flew in and grabbed a horn in both hands to throw the mickey and get the rope off before it broke it's leg or the rope. But the mickey was a big raw-boned bloke and strong too. The rope broke and with a couple of snorts and tail in the air, he threw old Charlie about three feet in the air and as he hit the ground, started rooting into him and rolling him all round the yard. With froth flying out of the mickey's mouth as it tore into Charlie and dust flying everywhere, it was impossible for anyone to get in the yard to do anything.

If it had gone on much longer, he'd have killed Charlie. All that saved him was the blue cattle dog that dived in and fastened onto the mickey's heels and while it charged the dog, we got hold of Charlie's boots and dragged him under the bottom rail just as the horns crashed into the rail alongside. With hardly any clothes left on and red stripes all over him, Charlie, still cracking hardy, staggered round in circles gasping for breath and wouldn't let anyone help him. Groans came out of his swag all night — you could hear them from a hundred yards away, but next morning he said he was 'feeling OK', so we got the cattle together and headed off for Dirranbandi ('*The Dooran*' to all the old coves on the road). But when we'd all gone with the cattle, I don't think old Charlie would have been too long out of his swag — he'd have been too sore to move for the next few days.

CHAPTER 11

A Farmer's Best Friends

THERE is much enjoyment and satisfaction in breaking-in horses and dogs — they teach you a lot while you're teaching them. Horse-breakers, in particular, are a pretty mixed bunch. Some are good but many aren't. The good horse-breaker is not necessarily a good buckjump rider. He doesn't have to be because if a horse is properly handled, it rarely bucks while being broken in. It's when a horse has been brought back from spelling for a few weeks to get over soreness during handling that you have to be careful and by then the horse-breaker has generally gone. There was always a lot of bravado with young coves when talking amongst themselves about horse-breaking and rough-riding and there was always much more talk than action. I haven't seen anyone too keen to get on a really bad horse if it could be avoided, unless there was a good audience round the rails to supply plenty of cooeeing or perhaps a few rare girls to impress. In my experience, most of the rough-riding was done round the camp-fire at night or over the pub counter when blokes got a bit turpsed up and wanted to tell everyone what they'd done or how good they were. I remember a classic example of this at a rodeo in Bollon one afternoon. Joe, a young half-turpsed up station hand was at the rowdy stage telling everyone in the old pub how he'd back himself to ride anything they could find with hair or hide on it and drag a wild cat up both flanks by the tail at the same time.

Somebody took up Joe's bet and suggested we try him out. Scotty had just yarded a big wild snorty-looking chestnut colt at a place a few miles out of town. He was going to put in the rodeo — reckoned it could buck a town down and we were keen to see how Joe shaped up with this big toey bloke. So we bundled him into a utility and started out with half a dozen other cars in tow to see the fun, but the closer we got to the yards, the crooker Joe got.

'Done know what's gone wrong but I got a terrible guts ache — Jesus, I'm bloody crook, yer know,' said Joe. 'Muster been all that hot rum I wez gittin' stuck inter.'

The car started to slow down, but a voice from among the dogs and saddles in the back yelled, 'Keep goin' — you'll be right, mate, when yer fly onter Scotty's buckjumper an' rake 'im up the bloody ribs with them big set of tacks.'

Advice came from all quarters, another voice adding, 'And if we can't find a couple of wild cats for you to drag up 'is flanks, we'll hook the dogs on to him if 'e looks like slowin' down.'

But Joe's sting and cockiness suffered a mighty blow when we pulled up at the yards and he got an eyeful of this big raw-boned, wild-eyed chestnut colt. It snorted every now and then as it hurtled stiff-legged round the yard in the dust with his tail in the air.

Joe suddenly announced he was too crook and would have to lie down fer a bit! 'Man can't ride when e's as crook as this — Jesus Christ, I'm bloody crook, yer know, mate — better go back to town and 'ave a yarn to the doctor, aaaaaa?' he groaned.

So that was the end of Joe's buckjump riding for the day and we all had to turn round and cart him back to the pub where he made a rapid recovery after downing a few more snorts of rum. But there was no more wild talk about all the outlaws he'd 'rode to a standstill after they'd pelted everyone else — an' coulder done it without a bloody saddle, too!'

I learned a lot from two outstanding horsemen when I was sixteen or seventeen. They were Ted Trivett and Les Joliffe. Ted did a lot of horse-breaking in western Queensland before and after the war. He was a top horseman and had won many buckjumping and bullock-riding championships, but he was also a good horse-breaker too. An article in the St George local paper, the *Balonne Beacon*, stated that noted Australian champion buckjump rider, Ted Trivett, had been captured during the Middle East Campaign and was now in a prisoner-of-war camp in Italy. Word reached Mussolini, who'd heard a lot about this Australian sport before the war and was keen to see this Australian champion in action. He arranged for the camp to put on a rough riding demonstration and turned up with his top brass to see the action. So Ted rode for Mussolini and was very proud of the fact too when he returned to Australia after the war.

While waiting between mobs of young horses for breaking-in or when the weather was too hot for handling horses, Ted made his living as a travelling saddler. His hands were at home with a side of tanned leather for saddling or greenhide for rope and whip plaiting. He often had several tanned kangaroo skins, dyed in different colours, going at the same time too, cutting them into continuous thin strands for plaiting whips and belts of different colours.

Les was also a good horseman but not up to Ted's standard. He moved around a lot and had been a ringer for years on some of the big Territory and Queensland back-country stations. When it got too hot for horse-breaking he checked out the bores, repaired mills and troughing, and rode boundaries to keep them up to scratch. The main trouble with watering points was that big goannas about five feet long spent the hottest part of the day swimming in the water troughs and sunbaking on the float arm with tail dangling in the water. This held the float valve open with water running to waste everywhere as the troughs overflowed and drained the tanks. Les's job was to ride round the mills hunting off all the goannas and to shoot as many as possible in the process. But there was no shortage of goannas and fresh ones kept coming back. Les was very wary of goannas, because for him they always spelt trouble. When riding over those open treeless plains, the dogs often start up a big goanna from the grass somewhere and chase it flat out all over the place. With no trees to climb for protection, goannas always make straight for the horse, which is the only upright thing above ground level on the plain. To escape the dogs, they often hurtle straight up the horse's hind legs with those long sharp claws and occasionally end up sharing the saddle with the rider. Riding young horses straight out of the breaking-in yards, goannas were dynamite to Les. The horse nearly turned itself inside out trying to shift the goanna, while Les reckoned the prospect of a twenty mile walk back to camp if it threw you was always incentive enough to make you stay with him.

As most of the big runs had huts and out-stations at some of the bores, Les had a lot of time on his hands when his work was done. Big stations with a lot of men killed a bullock every week for meat, which meant plenty of hides. Les used his spare time curing them with coarse salt and cutting them into strands for plaiting greenhide ropes and whips. He camped at the various huts as he rode round the waters which could be more than 100 miles if he was on big runs like Alexandria, Wave Hill or Victoria River Downs, each with areas around 8,000 or 10,000 square miles of country. It left him with time to perfect his leatherwork and when you saw its quality, you realised he hadn't wasted it. In particular, the whips he plaited out of kangaroo skins were art forms in themselves. Beautifully plaited and finished off with your initials plaited in a different coloured strand in the handle if you wanted it. The finished articles went to local western and city agents and overseas as well. I don't know how he heard I was in Brisbane, but he turned up at our factory at Stones Corner one day and asked to see me, but didn't give his name. When I went out he said, 'Yeh, I thought I'd still know you, even though I've never seen you with a tie on before.'

I immediately recognised him too — we hadn't seen one another for thirty years. He was carrying a sugarbag containing several plaited kangaroo hide whips and handles he'd just finished plaiting as part of an on-going order and wanted me to comment on their quality. They were sheer perfection, even better than the ones I'd seen him plait all those years before. Now retired, he was buying up old houses, renovating and reselling them in between turning out these masterpieces. He was a habitual wanderer and, like so many of the old back-country bushmen from that era, could have gone anywhere. He was never in the same place for too long but had evidently found living in the city more comfortable than out-station huts when he was getting on in years.

The good horse-breaker is a student of temperament and technique and is primarily concerned with applying each stage of proper handling on the ground before the horse is ridden and this is how it should be. Buckjump riders are more likely to be on top of the horse punching it about outside the yards before it's been properly handled, to conquer rather than train, but careful handling on the ground is the key to good horse-breaking. Teaching a horse how to be caught is the first important step. The horse must always be taught to face you and stand up properly when being caught. You can always tell the quality of the horse-breaker and those to whom the horse is passed by the behaviour of the horse. If it keeps moving away from you in the yard when you're trying to catch it and keeps putting its butt end between you and its head, you know some novice has been at it. I wouldn't put up with those antics from any horse, because making a horse stand up properly when being caught is the very first step in good horse-breaking.

I always broke in with a whip, using it not to flog the horse but to make it stand up properly by gently flicking it behind the front legs until each leg moved one at a time towards you, and the horse was facing you and remained facing you. If it turned away, the process was repeated, talking gently to it all the time until it stands still and then you can begin rubbing it down, still talking to it quietly the whole time. A similar procedure was adopted when teaching to lead, though some use a rope over the horse's rump above the back legs, pulling the rope and halter towards them at the same time. Most horses learn to lead quickly. The most important thing is teaching them to follow alongside you at all times and never allowing them to hang back — leading means leading, not dragging, and a horse should be left in no doubt as to which of these it has to do. This is where the whip has the advantage over other forms of handling. Some horses, like some people, are habitually lazy and, if given half a chance, will bludge on you for the rest of time. A flick with the whip at the right moment works wonders and keeps the horse up beside you and always alert. Constantly talking to horses and letting them smell you is important when breaking them in. Pat them a lot and rub them down often too, pick up their hooves and stroke their legs — it's very much a hands-on operation, but, above all, be firm in what you want done and make sure they do it, not next week but right now.

I made all my own breaking-in tackle and ropes, as well as halters for teaching to lead and tie-up and only rarely used hemp halters and then only after they'd been made a fixture as opposed to the slip-knot variety. Free-running ropes through loops as part of hemp halters can badly bruise a horse's jaw when it pulls back when tied up. If it's the running loop type and the halter is wet with sweat or rain, when the horse pulls back and the rope pulls tight, it locks in that position and won't let go, leaving the animal dangling, half-choked down at the end of the rope. Jaws can be badly bruised and the memory of this maltreatment can stay with the animal for life and make them throw their head about in the air (giggle-headed) at the least pressure in that region of the head. So don't use them. A mate of mine used nothing but a rolled-up chaff bag over the back of the horse's head with both ends of the bag tied together underneath the jaws by a double half hitch in the rope. I think it's as efficient as any other method and safer than most. After seeing it in action, I used it too. Teaching to tie up can be dangerous if proper care is not taken. I sunk a big heavy post in the centre of the holding yard (the small round-yard is only for handling) and cut a deep groove round the top of the post with the axe about five feet above the ground. The groove was then greased with mutton fat and I fitted a heavy ring to a length of twisted wire round the groove so it could turn freely. This avoided the possibility of a horse getting tangled up in the rope or choking down by winding itself round the post or tree until there was no rope left.

Using this method, whichever way the horse went round the post, the rope and ring had to follow.

Of all horse-breaking procedures, mouthing is by far the most important. Hard or insensitively mouthed horses are annoying and can be dangerous, especially if you're hard-riding to gouge wild cattle out of thick scrub country or mustering galloping horses. We've all struck them, of course, plenty of them. But with care and attention to detail during mouthing, this can be avoided in most cases. It's important that the mouth is damaged as little as possible to avoid rawness and bruising from the chafing and pinching of the bit. There are some good rules to follow. Never use ring bits. Use the heaviest bar bits procurable and bend the tips of the bars outwards to avoid damage to mouth and jaws during mouthing. Tear a thin strip of soft material about half an inch wide and wind it round and round right across the bit until its about three-quarters of an inch thick, then tie the ends firmly to the bars at opposite sides of the mouth. The bit is now made firm and soft with much less likelihood of damage when the horse's head is dragged back in tackle, or when being reefed about when being driven in reins, in and outside the main yard. Don't overwork or overheat the horse. If you have the time, do your work-outs in the early morning and evening and go through all the lighter training until the horse is going properly. Drive in a line of pegs and put the horse through them regularly in bending-race style until it's used to being pulled about before starting out into heavier work after it settles down. Always remember not to overdo things because a horse gets very sore and hasn't hardened up yet. Make sure the horse is adequately spelled (for at least a fortnight, or longer if possible) to get over initial soreness before starting out into heavier paddock work. Teach the horse to walk out freely at all times and never let it jog. After initial mouthing in tackle and while driving in reins, *never* turn a horse until you've first stopped it dead in its tracks by reefing back hard on the reins. Then and only then do you pull it round to turn. After perfecting this most important part of mouthing, a horse props and turns in the same motion. Although I've sometimes had a horse's legs go clean from under them when turning sharply when galloping around pushing cattle about or chasing horses, they soon learn to allow for the extra weight of man and saddle. You find it's a pleasure to ride and work a horse with a mouth like this. These are a few essential points necessary to good horse-breaking. But horse-breaking will always remain very much an individual craft — as most things are.

Like all men who have worked land and stock before motorbikes and four-wheel drive vehicles, I've had a lot of horses and dogs. Some have been good, some average, and others not worth feeding. But occasionally, very occasionally, you strike one that's so far above the general run that you never forget them. They become an extension of yourself and are a pleasure to work with. You trained them, worked with them and camped with them and became intimately acquainted with all their weaknesses and strengths, their ups and downs. It becomes a working partnership in which the animal knows you as well, sometimes better, than you know it, or yourself.

Your livelihood depended on them. When mustering sheep in scrubby country and, to a lesser extent, in yard work, a man was only as good as his dogs and was absolutely useless without them. Similarly, in cattle work, the horse maketh the man. A good horse-breaker has to be a good psychologist. Every animal is different. Their temperament, personality, ability and physical capability differs, one from the other, just as it does with people. The teacher, breaker or trainer needs to be observant and flexible enough to accommodate the subtle variations and to utilise each attribute in a way that is both acceptable to the pupil and promotes a bond of trust between the two. It is only by adhering to these principles that the best can be extracted from the pupil. What the outstanding horse-breaker and teacher have in common is that they are born, not made, but certainly can be made better with proper training.

There are few hard and fast rules and certainly no scope for oversimplification when it comes to personality and temperament. I made the mistake one time of drawing too close a comparison between animals and humans — though there *are* so many behavioural similarities. I claimed that if it were possible to manage people like we manage stock and safe carrying capacities, most of the world's problems would be solved. My mate and I were talking about horse breaking while we waited for the billy to boil. I was saying that if driving a mob of horses miles to a distant set of yards, I'd have them all taped by the time I got them there. All the flighty hypersensitive ones out in front of the mob, shying and darting about every time something moved or made the slightest noise. The sour cranky ones with ears laid back, charging backwards and forwards up and down the wing, snapping and kicking at everything that comes within striking distance. And all the dopey lazy ones scraping along in the dust behind the mob with heads nearly on the ground as they stumbled along over every log and stick in their path. I contended that if a line was drawn round the mob and all the outside ones were sent to the meat works, a bloke's troubles would be over — the rest of the mob would be easily handled. This splash of wisdom sounded pretty good to me. But my mate chewed things over for a while before saying —

'Ah, but if you used this rule with people, you wouldn't have your Mozarts, your Einsteins or your Shakespeares would you? You'd have the world filled up with muscle-men.'

Yeh, good point, I hadn't thought of that.

I broke in all the horses for both of our places for years, a few brumbies and some for other people. I've had a lot of good horses and a hell of a lot of duds, but only once have I had a horse that I'd class as quite outstanding. Sadly, he died, possibly from eating some poisonous plant (Birdsville disease, I was later told), just as he was reaching his prime as a rising six-year-old. I took a lot of care when breaking him in, especially when mouthing — you could turn him on a sixpence. He had a good kind eye, was quick to learn and always keen to please. He was an excellent walker and very fast and sure on his feet. He had to be — he'd learnt all his scrub-dashing skills from chasing kangaroos, emus and scrub cattle.

I lent him to drover Tom Duffy, himself a horse-breaker earlier on, when Tom was helping me muster one time. At the dinner camp, Tom came back with the horse a lather of sweat and foam, dancing about and chewing at the bit as he announced: 'Christ, this is the best horse ever I rode. Never before seen a horse so keen to work. Every time a kangaroo or emu or any other bloody thing jumps up, he's up alongside it inside a hundred yards — nearly been out from under me a dozen times already and the day's only half over!'

There was a rodeo and bullock riding competition on in the Bollon where all we young coves who reckoned we could ride a bit were going to meet up. They'd all be riding their best and flashest horse so I was going to do the same. Horses and our gear were very important. Everything came by mail order and all the big firms put out an annual bushman's catalogue. We studied the riding gear, especially saddles, for hours on end and tended to judge a man on whether or not he was a good horseman and rider and what make of saddle he had. It was his trademark of acceptability. My best horse, not long broken-in (the one I've just been describing) had been out spelling for a few weeks and was all shined up and full of feed and looking his best. I ran him in early in the afternoon and saddled up, aiming to ride the twenty miles into Bollon before dark. I had a big seven-inch kneepad buckjump saddle and had made a big heavy breastplate with huge nickel ring in front to go with it. The dress was important too. White beaver moles and check shirt with double pockets. Wide-brimmed ringer's hat rolled up at the sides, three-inch wide leather belt with nickel rings on each hip with three-inch nickel buckle in front, high-heeled elastic side riding boots, leather leggings and an enormous pair of spurs I'd made myself out of inch windmill hoop-iron. Even if you weren't as good as you thought you were, it was important to at least look the part!

This horse hadn't humped his back since I broke him in. In a hurry to get going, I reefed up a couple of extra notches in the girth and surcingle and swung into the saddle, expecting him to move off in his usual free style. But, as I hit the saddle, without even having time to get my foot in the other stirrup, his head went between his legs, his mouth flew open and he started to roar as he hit the sky. I couldn't even get hold of a tuft of mane — it was all down between his legs. I thought he was going to turn inside out as he spun round and round and from side to side as he bucked and kicked up. You'd wonder how a bloke could get pelted out of a seven-inch kneepad buckjump saddle, but I found it was no trouble at all. I hung on to him for a good while, but with only one stirrup, and the other one flogging me up the ribs every time he flew in the air, I got higher and higher out of the saddle and couldn't get back. He went clean from under me in the finish and as I hit the ground, kept bucking and roaring round and round so I had no chance of moving. He went stone mad and, with flying hooves, bucked from side to side and kicked up at the same time.

He finished upside down in the bore drain, with legs high in the air thrashing at the sky and my beautiful saddle buried in the mud underneath. As I struggled to get him back on his feet, his head slammed back and forth on the hard bank as if to bash his brains out, splashing mud and water all over me. When at last he clambered to his feet, shaking all over, he was a rare old sight and so was I, both of us plastered with mud and duckweed. The flash breastplate I'd spent so much time perfecting was torn in half, one stirrup was gone and the quartpot, still in its pouch, was squashed as flat as a flounder. Dad, hearing the roars and clatter, came out with the rifle and wanted to shoot the horse — reckoned it would end up killing someone. But it was my own fault. If I hadn't been in such a hurry to hit Bollon before dark, I'd have done what I usually do with a young horse straight in from spelling — saddle up in the yard and hunt it round for a while with the saddle on. There'd have been no trouble then. So I threw buckets of bore water all over horse and saddle and got things cleaned up a bit and went up and had a bath and washed all my precious gear. What a fiasco! I let the horse go and went in next morning in style in the utility. Although I worked this horse for another couple of years, he made no attempt to buck again. I wasn't disappointed either. They didn't come much rougher than this bloke!

Moodgie and I were returning from Thrushton where I'd been

camped for some weeks fencing with Dad. We only came back to
Clonard to check things over and intended returning early next day.
This same horse was running in a 300-acre paddock with some of the
other saddle horses. It normally wouldn't come anywhere near the
house unless forced to. But as we pulled up in the truck at the front
gate, he trotted straight up and started pushing me about with his
nose while I tried to open the gate. He tried to climb over me as he
raced round and round getting closer all the time as I tried to push
him away to keep him off my feet. I thought this seemed strange
behaviour but the horse didn't seem physically sick in any way so
I hunted it away while running the truck into the shade under the
house. Before we could get out, it had followed us in and began hammering on the running board with its hooves as it tried to get in the
front with us. I knew something was very wrong then. We hunted it
away again and were carrying boxes of groceries up the long flight of
back steps to the kitchen when it came galloping up the steps behind
us nearly on to the high verandah. I struggled to get it down again,
expecting at any moment to hear a bang as it slipped and broke a leg
between the steps. It was quite mad and had no idea what it was
doing. I'd heard of horses getting 'pea-struck' as they called this condition, from eating Darling Pea in the West Darling country hundreds
of miles away but had not seen it here before.

I was beside myself wondering what to do with this poor animal
to which I'd become so attached — he was a marvellous horse and
about the only thing he couldn't do was talk. There were no such
things as vets out in that country in those days, so I mixed up some
mustard in hot soapy water and tried to force it down his neck in the
hope it might make him vomit — but, of course, it's virtually impossible to make a horse vomit anyhow, so I was stumped. It got dark and
I finally had to hunt him outside in the paddock again but couldn't
sleep a wink and heard the poor frantic thing pawing at the fence and
gate for hours as it tried to get back to us. I knew he felt we'd abandoned him, but had no idea what to do. Went down with a light
several times during the night but he was so frantic it wasn't safe to

be near him in the dark. At last the noise stopped. Maybe he was over the crisis, I hoped. But as soon as it started to get light, I followed his tracks and found him dead on a sandhill in a hole he'd rooted in the sand about a mile from the house. He must have been in dreadful agony towards the end because he had holes dug up all over the place and there were signs he'd been rolling about in the sand. Sadly, I'd lost the best horse I'd ever had — or had ever seen, for that matter.

It was almost as hard to get a really good all-round dog as it was to get a first class horse. Though many of the general rules for handling horses also apply to dogs, dogs are easier to train than horses, mainly because of their size and the fact that they are small enough to be with you most of the time. For this reason, more time can be devoted to short intervals of snap training around the house paddock in the mornings and evenings or at any time during the day. A long rope should be used in the initial stages until the animal is properly under control and understands the various signals allocated to the different functions you want it to perform. If a dog doesn't come up to scratch by showing sufficient intelligence during training and working within a few weeks, get rid of it and replace it with something better. You can waste so much time and energy with a dud that's never going to be what you want. If you don't act, you'll be lumbered with the useless thing. Someone will feel sorry for it or fall in love with it and you'll be lumbered with it forever. You have to become hard enough to act quickly on this point if you don't want to be surrounded by a mob of useless barking dogs that aren't worth feeding. And don't forget they eat just as much as the good dog and you're the one who has to keep the tucker up to them — which is always an extra chore a busy person can well do without. You see it everywhere.

The outstanding dog is the rare exception and you go through a lot of duds trying to find it. Everyone has a favourite breed, but, personally, I wouldn't look further than a good kelpie as an all-round working dog in paddock and yard work. I've had a lot of border collies — there are some excellent dogs amongst them, of course, and they're pretty workers in open country. That's why you see so many of them in sheepdog trials, but most of the ones I've had would drive you mad in rough and tumble scrubby paddock work or when forcing is needed in yard work, especially when working with cranky old ewes and lambs. When a sheep bails up, the border collie is likely to be sneaking about peeping out from behind tussocks and trees and dancing away a bit further every time the old ewe stamps its foot. The kelpie would have already been in there and knocked her arse-over-head and be putting her somewhere. That would be the end of that and there'd be no more messing about from then on.

The good all-round dog is what everyone hopes to get hold of but they're few and far between. Some are pretty workers but won't force. Some work too close for paddock work and split up the mob and leave half behind. Some bite and others are just halfwits that bark and tear about, more often in the road than not. Others are always in the wrong place at the wrong time and don't seem able to anticipate a sheep's next move until it's too late. When handling touchy stock, there's a critical 'no-man's zone' between man and animal into which you must not enter. The animals will stand still, facing you, while you observe that critical space. If the animals look like turning away to rush off, you must retreat a few steps — turn your back on them even, until they feel comfortable in that safety zone again. If, on the other hand, you try to hurry things along by encroaching into that critical space, just one foot over that invisible boundary line is sufficient to have the mob turn tail and take off. You're then faced with going through the whole procedure of heading them off and settling them down again. The good stock-handler, man, horse or dog, understands the importance of observing this 'open-space' zone — it's the key to handling stock. The dog that understands it is outstanding. Just observe a bright young pup working a batch of chickens. The pup that understands that critical zone at an early age is always going to be a good dog. It will keep the chickens in a neat little knot without any of them trying to escape, while it works them closer and closer to the tin or box it intends putting them in. When that dog is old enough for paddock work with sheep, it has already mastered the essentials of properly handling animals.

A group of musterers all together with their mobs of dogs can be a catastrophe and, if not so annoying, would be hilarious at times. Most of the dogs and some of their owners wouldn't know what *training* meant. There'd be dogs charging about like maniacs looking over their shoulders at the ones behind. Five or six trying to piss on the same tree at the same time and others racing around sniffing arses, some trying to mount one another and blokes roaring and yelling in an effort to get some sort of control.

It reminds me of the old drover's cook on the road with a mob of sheep one time. It was just on daylight and the billy and some chops were sitting beside the fire to keep them warm while the men were away getting the hobbled horses. The cook was sitting on a log filling his pipe when, out of the blue, this ginger dog turns up. He thought he'd try it out on the sheep still in the rope yard to see if it was any good. As soon as he put it through the ropes it flew in amongst the mob with a string of 'whoophs', sending sheep end-for-end in all directions. It came out the other side of the mob with wool hanging off every tooth, then bolted back through them again with a few more 'whoophs' and sheep upside down in a cloud of dust and some out through the ropes.

The cook was just looking for a good sort of a stick to knock it on the head. But, before he could, a jackaroo straight out of college and all togged up a treat, rode up from the head station to see the drover and his mob through the run. The jackaroo was perched up on the old nag like a bag of pumpkins. He had brand new shining leggings, spurs, elastic side boots and a hat that was three sizes too big.

The old cook looked up as he stoked up his pipe and got her going. 'Now a smart young up-and-coming station manager like you'd know a real good sort of a dorg when 'e sees one, an I'll bet you'll wanter buy this one too when yer see what 'e cin do,' he said.

The old cook got hold of the ginger dog and put him back over the ropes into the yard again then yelled out, 'Split 'em.'

The ginger dog flew in amongst the sheep again with a few more loud 'whoophs' with sheep arse-over-head in all directions in a cloud of dust.

When the dog came out the other side of the mob, the cook bellowed out, 'Split 'em again, an' bring back a bit er wool with yer.'

And the ginger dog wheeled and tore back through the mob again with another string of 'whoophs' and sheep head-over-turkey, dust flying everywhere and half the ropes knocked flat, and came back with wool hanging off every fang.

Very impressed by the action-packed display, the jackaroo, full of excitement, exclaimed: 'By Jove, but look, this is the most incredible dog, what. I say, by golly, what an amazing animal. He's almost human. Understands exactly what you say. How much do you want for him?'

As it was with horses, I've had many good dogs but only one you could class as quite outstanding and he was a black and tan kelpie called Boxer. I bought him, virtually untrained, from a jackaroo about to leave Rutherglen, our neighbouring property. After seeing Boxer working, I could see a potential champion in him if he was properly handled. He started off at two pounds ten shillings but I must have shown too much interest and the price kept on going up until it hit five pounds, an extortionate price in 1939 when the price of an average 'handy' dog was between one and two pounds. He was a different dog in six months and it wasn't long before I began to wonder who was training who. He could nearly talk and was as good as two men in a paddock when mustering. I could put him on a fence with three or four hundred head of sheep or with just a small mob of a dozen or so; it made no difference. He'd take them to the nearest yard, provided the yard was on the same fence, it didn't matter if it was ten miles away. I'd muster in to him all day. As he saw me coming with each little lot, he'd come over and, completely ignoring me, take possession and push them over to the main mob he was driving and keep going. I'd come over to the fence about lunch time and if there were no tracks, I'd light a fire and put the quartpot on to boil while I waited. After a while, along he'd come with the mob and we'd have lunch — I always had a mouthful or two for him as well. After lunch I'd get on the horse and ride away and off he'd go with the mob again, blocking the lead every time it got too far in front and some of the tail looked like knocking up. It didn't matter what size the mob was, he was always in position before the sheep had even decided its next move — it was uncanny to watch. He was tougher and had more energy than any other dog I've seen and was never sore-footed. You couldn't stop him from working and using twice the energy he needed to use. Riding out to distant paddocks to start mustering, he had a set routine, almost like a robot. He'd trot on ahead of the horse for about fifty yards, turn, and trot back again to almost under the horse's head, then turn and trot back again and continue repeating these antics until you reached your destination.

Moodgie and I came back from Thrushton where we'd been mustering and crutching for a couple of weeks to check things over at Clonard and to get a killer. There'd been storms across that country and the young wethers were in good condition on all the fresh young feed. If there was a piece of country in Queensland that always seemed to miss the rain, it was Thrushton. Some big fat wethers were running with a couple of thousand other mixed sheep in the Long Plain paddock on Clonard. Though it was nearly sundown and a 17,000-acre paddock, we drove along the station track in the old truck hoping to see some of them before dark and leave the rest to Boxer. I'd just wait there until he brought the mob back then grab one and load it on the truck and take it home.

Boxer always rode in the same position, jammed in between the mudguard and the bonnet on the driving side with his nose sticking out from under the headlight. The truck couldn't move without him — he even looked part of the outfit. We came out on some small broken plains surrounded by thick belah and wilga scrub with sheep scattered about all over the plains feeding; you could just make them out in the fading light. As soon as they heard us coming, they took off for the scrub full gallop as only fresh young wethers can. Don't know how far Boxer had to go before he got round the lead of the mob. Might have been half a mile or more, but we waited and waited for a couple of hours and still no sign of him and not a sound either. They could have split into two or three mobs before he could get round the leaders during the chase in the dark. I suddenly realised that if he kept seeing sheep, he'd keep working them together until he mustered the whole paddock and we'd be there all night and the next day too. Not much good waiting any longer as we only had one very dim headlight. We decided to pick our way slowly home, hoping Boxer would already be there, and that he hadn't staked himself on the head of a fallen tree during the chase. But he wasn't home and when he hadn't turned up by after ten o'clock, I really started to worry.

We whistled and called from high up on the verandah with no result. At last, just before midnight in the cold frosty night, Moodgie, who has a better set of ears than mine, said she could faintly hear a dog barking a long way away. So we got the old truck started and slowly sneaked back to the exact spot where the sheep had bolted for the scrub. There were eyes shining everywhere as several hundred sheep began milling round the truck as we tried to get out. A moment later Boxer was beside us wagging his tail, with eyes shining then straight back to the mob again to hold them together. All I had to do was bend down and grab a leg and throw a big fat wether on the back of the truck and tie him down. As the engine started and we headed for home, Boxer was there in his usual place on the mudguard as if he'd never left it. He'd been holding them there half the night, no doubt wondering why I hadn't waited.

When we were mustering the bottom paddocks on Thrushton, we camped out there as it was seven or eight miles from home. Our camp was in sandy spinifex country near an old set of yards. These were between two small paddocks for holding horses at night and previously mustered stock for shifting out next day. Our swags were rolled out in the open where we slept, covered with bags and bits of an old fly to keep the frost off at night. A small fly nearby was stretched across a ridgepole to cover saddles, clothes and towels and a small table made from cut rails for the tuckerbox and cooking gear and for washing up on, a bore drain alongside for water. Though winter nights are generally very cold in spinifex country, we were camped there one particularly cold winter when everything was snow white with frost every morning and ice lay thick on everything wet or damp and hung in long transparent fingers from the end of every leaf. The soft sandy spinifex country was frozen hard, making horses' hooves ring as if on a bitumen road when being brought in to have their nosebags put on. Clear cloudless skies and crisp cold frosty nights with warm sunny days typify the normal winter weather pattern. But things change rapidly as soon as the sun gets up and the temperature starts to rise. Horses begin bogging fetlock deep in sand that was frozen hard a few hours before. Everyone begins shedding layers of woollen clothing and hanging them on trees or fence posts as you ride along, to be picked up and put back on again on the way back to camp late in the evening. A hot sun bored into you all day to emphasise the two extremes. Every morning, without fail, just as the first faint glimmer of light began to appear in the eastern sky — you could set a clock by it — Boxer would wake me by dragging a cold wet paw surrounded by frozen sand, down my cheek. The only parts of him that weren't white with frost were the tip of his shiny wet black nose and his bright beady eyes. Sometimes I'd wake before the paw got to work and see his dim outline lying there about a foot away with front feet neatly placed out in front, just staring at me without the slightest movement, as if performing some thought trans-ference experiment. For all I knew he could have been doing it for hours — and probably had been.

He had given me so many years of faithful service I wondered how I'd ever get by without him. There's a saying, 'An old dog for a hard road', and this certainly applied to Boxer as he got cunning with old age. He gradually went deaf and almost blind with cataracts. He'd start off in the morning following me with the other dogs mustering and after a mile or so I'd notice he was no longer with us. Moodgie used to be amused to see him trotting back home a couple of hours later and plant behind a big box tree a hundred yards from the Clonard house, peeping out every now and then to make sure the coast was clear before settling down for the day. I went over to look and found he'd dug himself a comfortable little daytime camping spot, just far enough away to feel safe from any possible chastising by me for bailing out from the day's work. I had bought him in 1939 as a two-year old dog and he died in peaceful old age in 1948. When I asked Dad to send down my other two dogs when we went back on the land at Wuuluman near Wellington, I left Boxer behind because of his age. Dad wrote and told me he had died in his kennel one night. I'm glad it was from natural causes because so many very old working dogs end their lives under the wheels of a car or bitten by a snake or kicked by a horse. If there's some secret place where all good faithful working dogs end up when they die, I'm sure old Boxer will be there with the best of them. I've never had a dog like him and never likely to either — they're one in a million.

CHAPTER 12

Pigs, Roos and Cockatoos

WE had no money as usual and were trying to make each day a winner during the winter months when things were quiet on the place and kangaroo skins were a good price. I loaded the truck with a big tuckerbox, a drum of water, rifles and ammunition and, taking stockman Charlie Turner from Clonard with me, headed for Moonie Ponds to shoot roos. This was a sheep property between Nindigully and Thallon, about a hundred odd miles away, where it was said there were hundreds of kangaroos. Moonie Ponds was in an area of beautiful open coolibah and belah flooded black soil country. It was a bit too open for getting up on roos, there only being a big old man belah or coolibah tree every hundred yards or so and no shrub understorey to provide cover while sneaking up on the mobs as they fed about the plains. Still, with hundreds of roos everywhere, I wrongly imagined we'd be able to come back home with a good load of skins on the old truck in the month or so we intended being away. What you don't know about different country!

We loaded up with stores as we passed through St George and camped on a sandhill on the outskirts of the flooded country in Moonie Ponds several miles off the Nindigully road. As it was late afternoon and Charlie was feeling a bit crook with a touch of 'flu' or something, I left him back at the camp while I had a walk around to size up the country. Within half a mile of the camp I ran into mobs of big red roos and shot five of them. As it was nearly dark, I skinned them and, all excited at the prospect of at last getting enough skins to buy some of the many things we needed but couldn't afford, I headed back to camp. It was late and pitch dark but Charlie had a fire going so I could find the camp. There was no tucker out though and, being too sick to be bothered eating, he was stretched out in his swag like a goanna. So I left pegging out the skins until morning and, after a quick drink of tea, rolled into my swag too.

Don't know what time it was, but Charlie woke me to hear the noise from mobs of fighting pigs away in the distance eating the roos I'd shot earlier. The row kept on for a long time, then abruptly stopped when everything was probably eaten and the mob headed in the direction of our camp. Charlie, still feeling crook, really had the breeze up about these wild pigs and started telling me about the bloke camped on the Doondi Waterhole. The jackaroos from the head station on the opposite side had noticed a tent high up on the sandy bank of the Balonne River for more than a week, but hadn't seen anyone moving about or smoke from a fire. The boss sent them over in the boat to see who it was and if they were all right, but all they found were bones with no meat left on them strewn about in churned-up sand like a sheep yard. The pigs had cleaned him up while he slept at night or maybe he had died first — nobody ever found out. By the time Charlie had finished, I was as breezy as he was, especially as we began to hear the odd stick crack as it was stood on and occasional grunts out in the dark surrounding the camp.

Charlie was all for loading up and getting out straight away but I kept thinking of the roos we'd come all this way to get, so suggested we drag our swags under the truck where the pigs couldn't get at us. We did this and I went back to sleep, for how long I don't know. The next thing I remember was Charlie's .303 going off about a foot from my ear. I flew in the air with the end of a U bolt holding the springs underneath the truck hitting me between the eyes and nearly knocking me out. A .303 makes one hell of a din on a cold winter night and the pigs took fright and bolted in all directions like a mob of cattle — there must have been droves of them. I was feeling a bit cranky as I wiped the blood from where the U bolt had gone in. Charlie reckoned he shot at a big boar trying to get at him under the running board, but it was pitch dark so it could have been anything. Anyway, to be on the safe side, we pulled everything except the tuckerbox off the back of the truck and threw our swags up on top and camped there till morning. Charlie felt a bit better, so we started out early to attack the roos. As soon as it got light enough to see, we noticed humps of feeding roos sticking up all over the surrounding plains. Only a roo shooter knows how exciting a sight like this can be. Two men never shoot together, of course — that's like two blokes riding the same horse — so we started off in opposite directions as usual. We soon found the pigs were there in hundreds and white cockatoos in thousands.

We'd start away from the camp at daylight and have barely time to shoot six or seven roos in the first mile or two, when great mobs of cockatoos latched on to us. They began circling a few feet above our heads with a continuous piercing screech like an air raid siren. They followed us all day like this and only let up when we got back to camp about dark, not having seen a single roo that wasn't travelling flat out in the distance. The monotonous screech, which really got to us by the end of the day, was the warning signal for roos. I began to realise this was why the roos were so thick in this open flood country. Everyone else had a go at them too, with about the same success we were having. Pigs surrounded our camp every night in ever-increasing numbers, fighting and getting cheekier all the time. We couldn't even peg out the skins because they'd have been torn up and eaten before morning. We called it a day and got out while we were still in front, deciding to move further south to Narine.

Like Noondoo near Dirranbandi, Narine was a big Company-owned run on the New South Wales side of the railway line in Queensland, north of Mungandi and Hebel. I thought we'd try our luck in that big belt of fairly remote country. It came up like rain and not wanting to be bogged and trapped in this black soil country for days or even weeks if heavy rain set in, we headed for a dry camp at

Dunwinnie Siding. This was a tiny one-roomed hut affair with a rain-water tank at one end and a bit of lean-to at the other. It was built on a bed of gravel that raised it a few inches above the surrounding scrubby plain, with one open side facing the railway line a few feet in front. We found the siding was the permanent home of a mob of goats. It was dark when we arrived and, as the goats weren't fussy about sharing their camp with us, we ended up having to flog them out with bags before settling down for the night. It certainly wasn't a night for sleeping, for they came back and walked all over the top of us and dropped pills all over us as well for good measure. Dunwinnie Siding wasn't exactly a home away from home. Goats seemed to be all round us so I switched on the old truck headlight (it only had one very dim light) and their eyes shone in all directions. They were so tame we wondered if they'd been fed and kept in yards round the fettlers' camps for meat and when the camps moved further along the line had been left behind. We hunted them away again and ran the truck in front of the opening, hoping to keep them out long enough to get a bit of sleep. It was then that we noticed a single light away up the line towards Thallon. It turned out to be the old goods train on its way to Dirranbandi, dragging a string of empty trucks for loading at the railway trucking yards.

It was sneaking along so slowly it didn't seem to get any closer for ages, but eventually pulled up with steam blowing everywhere. The engine driver and his fireman mate jumped down to have a yarn. They said they'd seen our light from miles back along the line and thought it might have been some of the fettlers going into town on the pumper. The pumper was the three-wheeled trolley the fettlers used to propel their gear along the line from job to job by pushing a T-shaped handle backwards and forwards in front of them. If the train travelled faster than a walking pace they thought they might run over the thing in the dark. They said they could do with a drink of tea and a feed, so we stoked up the fire and had a yarn while they cleaned up most of our cooked tucker, surrounded by the mob of pop-eyed goats. How times have changed. It would be hard to imagine any train these days pulling up in the middle of the night miles away out in the sticks somewhere to have a feed with a couple of scruffy looking roo shooters they'd never seen before.

After they'd cleaned up all our cakes and biscuits — strike, they could eat — they threw a few more shovel-loads of coal into the engine firebox and waited for the steam gauge to go up. At last they slowly moved off amidst clouds of steam and smoke saying if there was any tucker or anything else we wanted from town, they'd drop it off for us on their way back with the load next day. But, as it turned out, what with the goats, cockatoos and pigs, we didn't wait there that long. We didn't get much more sleep either but were up early as usual and, with goats everywhere watching us light the fire and have breakfast in the dark, we loaded up and headed for Narine. The country was a mixture of heavy black soil plains interspersed by strips of sandplain and lightly timbered red country — just the right mixture for roos and we'd seen plenty of tracks everywhere as we drove along. Our hopes were high because, although we'd seen lots of pig tracks, we hadn't seen many during the day and the cockatoos didn't seem as thick as back at Moonie Ponds either. But you could never be sure until you started getting around the country on foot. Luck wasn't on our side this time. We only shot a few roos before the cockatoos found us there too, which made any further shooting a waste of time. Pigs were also just as thick as back on Moonie Ponds. We called it a day and headed back to the scrubby mulga country we were used to and felt at home in.

Though I'd shot kangaroos from a very early age when big enough to carry a rifle — thousands of them, in fact I didn't like doing it because they're such beautiful animals. Also, to be a good shooter you really had to study a roo's behaviour until you nearly became a kangaroo yourself, and when you added the rifle it gave you an unfair advantage over the kangaroo. Even so, in heavily timbered scrubby country, roos were never in danger of being reduced below about forty percent of their numbers because of their natural shyness and cunning. In scrubby country there was so much protective cover and so many bush-warning signals to announce your presence that, as often as not, roos had the upper hand. Even if their numbers have been reduced by drought and shooting, after a couple of good seasons they're back to their former population. This rapid re-productive ability is why kangaroos can be safely control-harvested like any other crop.

Learning to sneak up on a mob of roos to get a clear shot without being seen or heard while they're feeding in scrubby mulga country is bad enough, but in open plain country with only an odd tree here and there, it was much more difficult — almost a science. If there were only two or three, it wasn't so bad; with a mob, there were so many that had to be watched all the time and one mistake was all that was often needed to have them take off and scatter. If there were several roos in a mob, you knew there was nearly always a 'spotter', generally a bit to one side of the mob whose job it was to keep watch. If the mob hadn't seen you, the spotter had to be found and kept an eye on, or you were in trouble. There were the signal birds to contend with too — the lousy jacks (apostle birds), noisy little sooty-grey birds always packed together in a mob. They are often called 'happy families' because they never stop chattering away to one another. At the slightest sign of danger, they all fly up into trees making a loud and continuous harsh squawking din and every roo within hearing distance is either gone or standing up on tiptoes ready to take flight at the slightest movement. Other signal birds were mickies (soldier birds or noisy miners) and muttonbirds (white-winged choughs). These three were the worst in the south-west mulga country, just as the white cockatoos are the plague of the black soil plains close to water. It was rarely that roos and their signal birds were far apart — they both seemed to rely on one another. If the spotter roo or any of the others saw you first, you'd have to freeze in that exact position like a stature for a quarter of an hour at a time, often caught on one leg with the other one halfway over a log. Ants would be crawling all over you and biting the more sensitive parts while the ever-present flies crawled all over your eyeballs in droves, in your ears and up your nostrils. You often wondered if it was all worth the agony, but it was all part of the game and there was no other way of making a bit of extra money to supplement the low wages, so you put up with it.

Later, when I became a full-blown shooter, I often used horses to get around on and to lump skins about. I soon realised you didn't waste precious time sneaking around for half an hour to get a couple of roos, or, if you missed the first shot, probably none at all. You only had a few hours in the early morning and late afternoon for the best shooting and had to make the most efficient use of that time. I'd shoot as many as possible in the early morning and wouldn't waste time skinning them as they were shot but would return later as the temperature rose and the roos were looking for a place to camp up during the day. I'd follow my tracks back, find and skin the roos shot earlier, cart the skins back to camp and peg them out, ready to start shooting again in the late afternoon. You had to know a roo's every movement intimately; their favourite feeding places, where they camped, the bush warning signals that gave your whereabouts away, wind direction so your scent was opposite to the way you were shooting, and the types of grasses and herbs they preferred. Kangaroos are fussy eaters and, like all marsupials, they look for the type of country that grows short grasses and a wide variety of herbage. In the mulga country these areas are always the sandalwood (*Eremophila mitchellii*) gilgaied hollows and run-on areas (lower ground and broad shallow drainage depressions). They gather around the edge of spinifex country too, in the merging zone between the red earths and red sandy loams of the mulga country and the yellow earthy sands of the spinifex. It was like compiling a reference manual, the contents of which became second nature. Also you had to know the exact places to aim for so the animal dropped and wasn't wounded, even though in scrubby country or long grass it was often hard to do.

Like many beginners, I started off with single shot .22 calibre Winchester, Remington, Stevens and BSA rifles and, with age and strength, progressed through the full range of larger calibre repeaters

like the .32s, 32.40s and .32/20 Savage Hi-Power rifles, finally grad-
ing into magazine Army type .303s. When camped away in the bush
shooting, we buried an old axe head in the ground with blade facing
upwards for cutting the points off steel- or copper-cased .303 bullets.
The nose of the bullet was held over the blade and hit with another
axe or hammer. If the points were left on, the bullet went straight
through, leaving only a small hole the size of the bullet with little
internal damage. Too many animals were wounded in this way. When
the top half of the bullet is cut off, the bullet fragments as it hits and,
although this often makes a damaging hole in the skin of a small roo,
or if the roo is hit high up in a narrow place like the ribs, you rarely
wounded anything. Roos generally dropped as soon as the bullet hit.
Cutting the tops off in this way was rough and the bullet was always
squashed a bit out of round between the point and the shoulder. But
as long as it wasn't out-of-round on the main body of the shank that
came in contact with the rifling inside the barrel, it couldn't damage
the rifling. Time was always a factor and you were generally so short
of it you looked for the easiest and quickest way out. Also, as most of
our shooting in scrubby country was at fairly close range, the shape
of the bullet didn't seem to make any difference to the accuracy
over that distance. Getting a clear shot was often the biggest problem
because animals always seem to have the knack of being behind a
stump, a bush or down behind the brambly heads of fallen trees and
it doesn't take much to turn a bullet off line.

Although kangaroos were plentiful enough in the 1920s and '30s
and had to be kept under control because they ruined fences and
ate an enormous amount of feed that was always in short supply, it
was hard work shooting more than eight or ten a day. Only later, as
additional artificial watering points increased and widespread land
clearing and pasture improvement developed the land, did kangaroo
numbers build up to the plague proportions they've reached today.
Though their only value in those days was for their skins during the
winter, a freezing works to handle frozen carcasses for export was
established in St George in the early 1930s and some roo shooters

closer in patronised this new outlet. But prices were so low, there was very little profit margin. Carcasses had to be brought in to the freezing works regularly every day or so because nobody had a properly set up outfit to keep the carcass fresh and free of flies that were always present to blow the meat. Even in the winter, because the days were often pretty hot, shooters had to travel long distances to the freezer every few days over rough dusty roads in clapped-out old utilities. You'd never be off the road and have no time for shooting, to say nothing of the petrol bill at the end of the season. So, although the freezer was operating for years, it only struggled along because it was much easier to just shoot for skins.

I was talking to an old rabbiter and roo shooter who worked the sandhills along the Bulloo and Paroo Rivers and took the load to a local freezing plant once a week in a clapped-out old 1927 model Dodge utility. The rabbits were gutted and hung by threaded legs or on wire hooks attached to rails in a homemade frame on the back. I said — 'How the blazes do you keep the flies off them during the week and dust off them on the dusty tracks all that distance to the freezer every Monday — they'd be covered with maggots and dust, wouldn't they?'

'Orrr, bloody maggot's,' he said, 'yer don't take no notice er them buggers. I jist pull up at a bore outer town a bit an' throw a few buckets er hot water over th' ole rabbs, then give th' rails a bit of a rattle an' most er th' maggots drop orf. Th' blokes in there don't seem ter take much notice anyway — give ole "rabbo" a bit of a bath before they freeze 'im, yer know — them city people wouldn't know the bloody difference any'ow.'

As a boy, I often got all soft-hearted when sneaking in amongst a mob of feeding kangaroos — you got pretty expert at it with plenty of practice and it was always such a peaceful setting. Everything was sparkling on frosty winter mornings. Tiny pendulums of ice hung immobile like glistening diamonds from every still leaf and blade of spinifex while the sweet scents of moist sand, damp heath and spinifex wafted above a faint frosty mist that hugged the top of each clump. The old bucks would be sparring up with one another and barking every now and then. All the does had emptied out their joeys, which were hopping around flat out chasing one another through the clumps of spinifex while getting their early morning exercise as the old girls had a feed in peace. Joeys often came flying past nearly over the top of me, then returned for a better look. Sometimes they came right up if I didn't move, their little black noses twitching as they picked up the unfamiliar scent. The old girls looked up with a grunt and off the joey went again, flat out in the direction of mum's safety and comfort. As they approached, she'd straighten up and, sometimes in full flight, the joeys speared straight into the pouch entrance, head-first like a dart, ungainly legs and flapping tail following. How could you possibly shoot them and break up such a happy family enjoying the early morning sunshine in such lovely peaceful surroundings? I'd sneak back out again so they weren't disturbed and go home with nothing.

Unfortunately, you had to get hardened to death. You were surrounded by it all through the western country every day during droughts. Dead and dying stock lined the stockroutes, as, too weak to keep up with the travelling mob, they were left behind. In every station paddock where starving stock were being fed on cut mulga scrub, it was the same. Bore drains and water troughs became clogged with dead and dying sheep. Too weak to stand after a gutful of water, they collapsed where they were, and within five minutes the crows had picked their eyes out as they struggled to get up. The animal would just lie there waiting to die, with empty blood-stained holes where eyes had been only minutes before and smothered with ants that weren't even going to wait for it to die. Of course, you'd put the poor animal out of its misery with whatever you had with you at the time. It could be an axe, a knife, a rifle or just a lump of wood, but, whatever it was, the result was the same in the end. Killing became just another job that had to be done.

Australia is host to a large family of macropods. The two most common species of the larger macropods of the inland are the reds

(*Macropus rufus*) and greys (*Macropus giganteus*). Both these belong to the family of larger kangaroos and are distinctly different in growth, colour and temperament and in their preferred habitat. I've always loved the old red bucks and the blue does. Very occasionally you'll get a blue or reddish-blue buck and, more often, a red doe; but, as a general rule, the bucks are red and the does are blue. (At least, that's the colour we call them but in fact, the 'reds' are a mixture of red and ginger and the blues commonly range from a delicate slate or smoky blue to blue with a ginger 'rinse' through it.) The fur is short and soft and the fibres closely packed together almost like wool. When the blue doe's fur is parted, the colour close to the skin is always red and is quite dissimilar from most other breeds. They tend to stick to themselves and rarely mix with greys from choice and prefer the western plains or the more open semi-arid heavy soil country with short grasses.

Reds never frequent the south-western spinifex (*Triodia mitchellii*) country if there is an alternative. Yet they appear not to have this difficulty so much in some northern and central regions where the spinifex species is either *Triodia pungens* or *Triodia basedowii*. Where spinifex is the dominant plant community over large areas of country and there are only small areas of open black soil plains, reds have no alternative but to enter spinifex country to feed or starve. Reds are such beautiful, docile, non-aggressive and sensitive animals, very shy and timid and always alert and ready for flight. They often appear to be feeding when, in fact, they're only pretending while watching your every movement the whole time — even bobbing their head about to imitate feeding on a grass stubble all the time you're sneaking up. Then, without warning, as if a plug was pulled, the whole mob scatters on a front and takes off in the opposite direction from where they've seen you. Accompanying their rapid take-off is a drumming on the ground from two hard-soled feet at the end of those big powerful legs.

I've often heard people talking about kangaroos thudding their tails on the ground. It should be noted that kangaroos *never* hit their tails on the ground when hopping. The tail is used as a balance to enhance hopping, and is only on the ground when used as a lever for moving about feeding, where it takes most of the animal's weight every time it makes a forward movement. This is why it's such a powerful and indispensable part of a kangaroo. The tail also is used for balance when in a standing position and as a prop they lean back on when standing on tip-toes fighting.

The red's common warning signal is the thudding of feet on the ground, telling the rest of the mob to get out fast. I don't remember grey kangaroos using this method of warning. In very open country it is common to see a group of disturbed red kangaroos hopping slowly across the vast plains for mile after mile without stopping. This is why they're so hard to shoot in daytime in open plain country if they've previously been stirred up. They'd be feeding all over the plain, but you were lucky to get more that a couple of shots in before the whole plain emptied within minutes. No good following the mob because they'd be 'right on you' the second you were seen coming over the horizon. The only way was to retreat until out of sight, then circle the whole mob by keeping well outside their vision until you got right round and could come back at them from the other direction. But this entailed a lot of hard walking and, before you started, you knew it would be the same old thing all over again — one shot, two if you were lucky.

Space and distance protected red kangaroos until technology made inroads into their western domain. Night shooting became a lucrative occupation as four-wheel drive utilities with powerful spotlights and high-powered rifles fitted with telescopic sights were introduced, and motorbikes took over from horses. They made easy work out of a formerly tough slow job. The grassy open plains were soon to become a blood-stained battleground in which the shy and sensitive red kangaroo, that most beautiful of all native animals of the vast black soil plains, found he was no match for modern aggressive man and his technology. Red kangaroo numbers began to dwindle as a new industry blossomed and numerous freezing works were installed in key districts to process carcass meat to feed the hungry pet food market. It was to become a very one-sided affair. Kangaroos out feeding in the open were mesmerised and blinded by the powerful beam of spotlights on vehicles that roamed the plains all night. The roo sits upright for ten or fifteen seconds, transfixed by spotlight glare and engine noise. Its head, greatly enlarged in the high-powered scope, already fills the screen, the crosshairs in the scope are centred and the trigger is squeezed and it's all over. The vehicle stops just long enough for another beautiful red kangaroo to be thrown on the pile in the back and continues on for the next shot.

Mechanised night shooting wasn't for me — I couldn't be part of this kind of slaughter. I have often found that when technology moves in to make things so much easier and faster, it kills the simple pleasure of studying the movement of animals and observing and appreciating the natural world with all its complex subtleties and fascination. Speed and detailed observation just don't go together. Machines and the clock take over and life is never the same again.

Red kangaroos don't possess the same efficient fighting weapons as greys. Their front paws are broad and dumpy with short blunt claws while the big single ripping claw on each back foot is also short and blunt. Their hopping pads too are quite different. Their track is in two distinct 'stubby' sections because the pad sections are thicker, leaving two distinctive marks in soft soil or mud. Their dung is different also, being oval-shaped like a thin egg with 'snipped-off' points at both ends. Their tracks can be easily distinguished from greys' from several yards or more away.

Grey kangaroos favour the more heavily timbered eastern shrubby mulga country. These soils are predominantly red earths and sandy loams. But greys also inhabit the higher rainfall regions in grassy eucalypt forest country closer to the coast on a wide variety of soil types. Unlike reds, greys can be found living permanently in sandy spinifex country from choice. They are aggressive and mean when bailed up and would tear your eyes out in a flash if given half a chance. They are made for fighting, with longer and thinner paws than reds, and claws that are long and sharp and can cut like a knife in battle. The big single ripping claw at the end of each foot also is long and sharp with cutting edges. The big grey buck is a very dangerous animal to approach when bailed up, as many a dog can testify. When being chased by a dog (or dingo), all roos invariably head for water if close at hand, swim out into the middle if it's deep enough and wait. Any dog silly enough to swim out to continue the battle is in for a shock — the roo holds it down under the water in a bear hug until it drowns.

Unlike reds in open country, when disturbed the grey will generally hop away for a short distance before sitting up to look you over for a while before making off again. This is probably because the more heavily timbered country they prefer to inhabit gives a sense of security from the surrounding scrub, which gives the protection greys seem to need. Their tracks are long and slender and their dung is always an oblong block with square blunt ends. Their fur is much longer and not as dense as the red's — twice as long, in fact, and is open right to the skin with none of the red's dense fluffiness on the skin when the fur in parted. But, like all native animals, they have a precarious hold on life during bad droughts when feed and water is short. Many die, leaving those that have weathered the ordeal to bring their numbers back in better times. Even in good seasons they face hazards like plagues of mosquitoes and sandflies that nearly drive them mad. We had to light smoke fires so horses didn't go crazy, but the roos didn't have this luxury. I came on a big old grey buck lying at the butt of a box tree one time. He didn't move as the horse and dogs approached. I rode right up to him and got off the horse and the dogs came up and sniffed all round him. Although he was looking straight at us, he wasn't seeing anything. He was just lying there unconscious, drained of every ounce of blood by millions of sandflies that formed a solid grey paste-like blanket over his entire body. When I cut his throat, no more than an eggcup of blood came out of his jugular veins — he was literally dying of acute anaemia and starvation in one of the best seasons for years. Dogs can also suffer the same fate and sometimes died in their yards or on their chains from plagues of sandflies and mosquitoes.

With land development for agriculture came better feed and more water. Kangaroo numbers exploded and graziers and farmers soon found they were carrying as many, and sometimes more roos than domestic stock. The drive these days, which is long overdue, is to utilise this natural resource to offset the declining viability of many inland properties. Kangaroos can never be expected to replace sheep and cattle as the principal source of income. They can, however, provide additional income by being made better use of than is presently the case. Kangaroos and emus are built in much the same way, in that their two large legs are by far the most valuable parts of the carcass. When legs are cut off, and gut, liver and lungs emptied out, there's not much left. The upper half provides only limited amounts of meat and the small front paws are thin and light by comparison with the lower half. Certainly kangaroos have only two legs that do less damage than the sheep's four sharp hooves. We've been studying the damaging effect of these on surface soils for years and know all about it.

It's all to do with animal population and concentration. Sheep are by far the most productive and efficient animals we have. By concentrating on frame development and wool production over the years, we now have a well-balanced carcass animal that's almost as good in the front as it is behind. It breeds well, produces a valuable and durable fleece and is a remarkably adaptable and hardy animal. It also produces a good carcass of sweet tender meat for the overseas and domestic markets. What we have to do in the future is learn to run sheep in ways that are less destructive to soils and plants. This can be done more effectively if we start practising what we've been preaching for the last forty or fifty years and strenuously enforce recommended guidelines on safe carrying capacities so country is not constantly over-stocked and is spelled for adequate periods, particularly in dry times.

CHAPTER 13

Up Against the Mulga

SHEARING had just finished at Clonard and was about to start at Thrushton. It was so hectic and the weather so hot I felt Moodgie needed a break with her parents while I was camped out on stock work. At Dirranbandi she boarded the train for Brisbane where she could catch a bus to Lismore. After camping at Thrushton for three or four weeks of mustering, shearing and shifting sheep around, I packed a bit of gear into the Auburn and headed off for a brief holiday with Moodgie and her parents. I anxiously watched big clouds building up in the east, hoping I wouldn't run into heavy storms on the way to Lismore. By the time I got to St George it was looking very like rain and there was talk of heavy falls further along the road. But I was in high spirits at the thought of a holiday with Moodgie, the first since our honeymoon. I wasn't going to worry about a bit of rain and mud. If things got tough, I had a big powerful car and a heavy set of chains for the back wheels. She'd go through anything, or so I thought. I didn't take any tucker because I expected to make Goondiwindi the first night and stay at the pub.

Before I hit Nindigully it was pouring, and the road, with deep wheel tracks where lorries had been bogged, was under water for long stretches at a time. I put the chains on and battled through mud and bogs, arriving at Talwood just on dark. I dragged the garage man out of the pub to fill me up with petrol. He wanted me to hurry because the main road through Welltown was out for traffic, with miles of water over all the gilgaied lignum flood country. He suggested the back road to Boggabilla through Boomi.

So away I went, with a packet of biscuits to chew on the way. Hadn't been this way before — just a dirt road like the others, but with patches of low black soil hollows in places and some flooded country. With the chains flogging and having to be tightened every now and then, I crossed the Weir River in full flood from heavy rain across the catchment further up. Water was lapping the crown of the road in the few formed-up sections. I should have camped the night at Talwood — but this meant spending money we didn't have for needless luxuries like pubs. So I struggled on, in the dark now, with the road disappearing under sheets of water for a hundred yards at a time and very dim lights covered with mud. The Auburn had a very long wheelbase and I couldn't keep the rear end on the crown of the muddy road. Broadside on now, with the nose on top and chains on the back wheels in a foot of water down in the water table chewing at the mud like a thrashing machine, we came to a standstill with the diff. buried in the mud underneath. That was the finish. It was pitch dark and still raining heavily. I ate the biscuits, curled up on the front seat and called it a day, hoping for a blue sky in the morning. Some time during the night I woke, soaked through. The old canvas hood, bowed down with the weight of water, had gone into small holes and water was coming down on me like a shower bath. So thought I'd light my pipe and have a smoke while sorting things out a bit. Reaching down to where I'd put my pipe and tobacco on the floor before going to sleep, I froze with horror as my hand went into four inches of water that was halfway up the seat. Hell, I must be in flood country and the water was rising.

I didn't know what to do in the dark so just waited, hoping it didn't get any higher. With no clock or wireless, I hadn't any idea of the time. But the rain at last stopped and after a while stars could be seen. How wonderful — but how was a bloke to get out of this mess with no winch and probably no trees close enough to hook on to anyhow. Mess all right — daylight revealed a vast sheet of muddy water with the telephone posts sticking out of it. I didn't know the country but realised there was no time to waste. The Weir River I'd crossed near Talwood the night before was in full flood and was probably over the bridge by now. So I headed in the direction of Boomi, floundering along nearly waist-deep in low places in the water table as I followed the road clearing and telephone posts. A bit further on the country rose a little — and what a relief to leave the flood behind. A few miles further on, smoke could be seen in the distance and, as I got closer, a tent and fly too, with a yellow grader alongside. Two men were carrying a log to the fire — this was really something! I camped with this lively bunch of young coves, most of them from around Goondiwindi, for five days before we could get the grader in to drag out the bogged and waterlogged Auburn. We drained the sump, which was full of water, and refilled it with oil from the road camp. Away I went, happy to be on the road again, with Moodgie in Lismore wondering what had happened to me.

Though estimates of extent can only ever be approximate, mulga (*Acacia aneura*) associations, either as the dominant trees or as major landscape components, occupy around 500 million hectares of the arid and semi-arid zones of Australia. Of this, some 22 million hectares are in Queensland, invariably accompanied by emergent mixed eucalypts. These are poplar box (*E. populnea*), forest gum (*E. intertexta*), silver-leaved ironbark (*E. melanophloia*) and bloodwoods (*E. polycarpa* and *E. terminalis*). Less commonly they are accompanied by white cypress pine (*Callitris culumellaris*). Mulga often forms dense whipstick thickets in moist depressions and can remain in this form for twenty years or more until insufficient moisture in a bad drought eventually thins them out.

Acacia aneura is the most common mulga tree throughout the mulga zones, but several other mulga types do occur. These are turpentine mulga (*A. brachystachya*), bastard mulga (*A. stowardii*), horse mulga (*A. ramulosa*), Miles mulga (*Acacia aprepta*) and Bendee (*Acacia catenulata).* The common mulga (*Acacia aneura*) has an upright growth habit as a medium to low tree or tall shrub with thin, light-grey bark and thin yellow sapwood. The timber is extremely hard and tough with dark brown heartwood. The silver-grey foliage over sheets of yellow mid-height wiregrass forms a pleasant park-like setting in naturally open country or country opened up by scrub cutting or clearing. Elsewhere, in its natural state large areas of mulga country, particularly the western 'hard' mulga sector, form a monotonous drab grey landscape over red earth plains. The other mulga types commonly remain in low to tall shrub form and are generally found growing in massive red earths or shallow gravelly soils.

Mulga is Australia's most productive drought-relief fodder plant. It has been the lifeblood of the sheep and cattle industry in the mulga country since the country was first settled. Many inland pastoral districts in mulga regions would, in fact, cease to be viable if it were not for the mulga scrubs with low limbs and leaf-drop (leaf litter) on which stock graze. When scrub cutting during droughts, you soon learn the trees that stock eat and don't waste time and precious energy cutting anything they don't like. It was all axe work in my day, now replaced by chainsaws and bulldozers — the easy way. Scattered throughout the dominant mulga community is a constant sprinkling of other choice fodder species, generally present but never common. Sheep and cattle have a preference for many of these other species which were eagerly sought after as a variation from the constant mulga diet. The best of these are currajong (*Brachychiton populneum*), boonaree (*Heterodendrum oleifolium),* whitewood *(Atalaya hemiglauca),* plumb *(Santalum lanceolatum)*, myrtle (*Canthium oleifolium)* and bumble (*Capparis mitchellii*). Stock relished red quandong (*Santalum acuminatum*) too, but we didn't cut this useful tree. Common species like ironwood (*Acacia excelsa*) would be eaten if there was nothing else, but stock preferred the other species, especially currajong.

Nothing at all ate wilga (*Geijera parviflora*) in the 'soft' mulga country on Thrushton, yet in other districts, particularly if it was growing in heavier clay or duplex soils, every wilga tree (they normally droop right to the ground) would be eaten up as far as sheep could reach. They stand on their back legs and reach up four or five feet and trim every leaf like a clipped hedge. Thinking this may have had something to do with the acid to strongly acid soils on Thrushton, I made a point of checking this years later when classifying soils in these areas and found pH reaction to be around pH 5.50/5.75 in some Thrushton sites. Mulga thrived in these strongly acid soils but wilga was almost absent at this level of acidity. Its occurrence only increased as the country graded into alkaline soils down-slope towards run-on depressions and gilgaied hollows, many of which had pH readings of pH 7.50 to pH 8.50. Where wilga is heavily browsed by paddock stock, the soils appear to be only slightly acid — around pH 6.75 to pH 7.00 (neutral), but stock wouldn't touch wilga on Thrushton, even when the soils were alkaline, so it became difficult to reconcile these differences.

Every sheep in this country had black livers — I'd never seen a liver any other colour. When I saw a 'normal' pink liver displayed in a butcher's shop window in Goondiwindi, I thought it must have come from a diseased sheep. Black livers may have resulted from stock permanently drinking artesian water, though it also could have been the continuous diet of mulga and spinifex over a long period. After being fed on scrub for a good while, stock got to know every type of tree you were cutting by the ring of the axe in the different types of wood. Immediately an axe was driven into one of their favoured species, you'd have to get the tree down in a hurry because sheep came galloping up to start eating as soon as it hit the ground, even though uneaten previously cut mulga was lying about everywhere. We generally had a dog with us in currajong country because these often were pretty big trees and long before you got them on the ground you'd be surrounded by a mob of hungry sheep. We'd leave a bit of wood on one side so the tree remained erect while we dogged the mob out of the danger zone, then raced back to finish cutting it down, hoping to get it on the ground before they could get back — occasionally they beat you to it. We felled big currajong trees at

Part of Tom Duffy's droving plant waiting for the mail lorry at the Sixty-fiveMile Cobb & Co coach-change on the Cunnamulla Road in 1939. From left to right: drover Tom Duffy, me, cook Alf Claverton and horse-breaker Claude McDonald.

My old 1928 Model A Ford roo-shooting truck in front of the Thrushton homestead in 1940, with Boxer on the running board.

Moodgie, aged 18, at Rocky Creek near Lismore in 1942.

Me, aged 20, before I was married.

Moodgie, aged 19, before we were married.

The Pearce family. L to R: Joan, Bert, Teddy, Moodgie.

Moodgie photographs me with the old Auburn before we leave for a day in town.

Me during my horse-breaking days on Clonard. Phil's cleared night paddock is in the background.

Keith, marked by arrow in the back row, with the crew of their Wellington bomber in the Middle East in 1942.

We end up with our Buddy Stewart utility, tractor and jeep all bogged in Illgingerry Creek when taking Moodgie to hospital in Wellington to deliver baby Ian in 1947. Left to right: Clive Hough, a rabbiter and Greg Hough.

People from the land invariably end up at the agricultural and earth-moving machinery pavilion, including our family, while attending the Queensland Exhibition. L to R. Back row: Edna (Moodgie's mother), Moodgie, David, Jim. Front row: Ian, Keith and Lyn. 1956.

Wash day at the Woronora River boat shed. Moodgie is at the tubs surrounded by the copper, clothes trolley and clothes line. We used the boat to get groceries from the store on the other side.

Our homestead on Dalgonally, 1950.

Our house at 89 Longman Terrace, Chelmer, in Brisbane, 1958.

When I was a boy in the early 1920s, this was a whipstick mulga scrub about ten feet tall and so thick you couldn't ride through it. It has never been touched and is a good example of the way these scrubs sort themselves out.

The Wierbolla bore was sunk in 1920 with a flow of 1.196 million gallons of beautiful soft artesian water a day. Now the flow has dropped to about 270,000 gallons a day and the salt concentration is increasing rapidly, as illustrated by the white patches of salt in the foreground.

How times change: me (left) and Frank with the new sign in the spinifex at the boundary gate. Our old property Thrushton is now a valued national park, where in earlier times we nearly killed ourselves to develop it.

Frank holds up the last two posts of Dad and Doolie's old bark hut on Neabul Creek.

intervals along bore drains and cut out the soft pithy insides to make salt troughs — like native canoes. Most animals in that salt-deficient country have a craving for salt to make the mulga diet more palatable. Coarse salt was sold in two hundred weight bags or as rock salt lick. Drums of molasses or four-gallon tins of molasses and linseed, solidified as a lick, were also laid out along bore drains and around where we were cutting. This kept stock hanging around the cut scrub so they didn't have to be mustered back every time they got the wanderlust and scattered all over the place chasing after paddock feed that wasn't there. In long dry periods when there was nothing to eat except mulga and spinifex, sheep developed large fibrous balls like tightly compacted felt in the large gut (sheep have seven guts). In bad cases you could get half a hatful of these balls out of a single sheep. You could hear them rattling quite distinctly as the animals trotted along, especially if they'd just had a drink. Cattle, too, became pot-gutted, with the gut sagging down towards the ground. As they began to trot when driven, the extended stomach would flop up and down. Each time it dropped down, the exhaust end was sucked back inside, then blown out again with a loud noise as the stomach went up. Old Harry called them "im ole squawky-arse bullicks, yer know, boss.'

Scrub-cutting was hard work, especially in mature mulga trees full of knots which, like most arid zone timbers, are the among the hardest in the world. The axe had to be kept razor sharp all the time, yet not too thin on the shoulders or a hard knot could take a great gap as big as half a cent piece out of the face. Even if the axe wasn't gapped as badly as that, hours were involved in filing and finishing off with the carborundum sharpening stone. Though pretty skilled with file and stone from constant practice, scrub cutters avoided hard knotty trees like the plague. It was all a painful operation in winter with frost everywhere in the mornings. Hands became so sore with deep cracks between hard corns on every finger and on both palms that you had to grind your teeth for the first hour or so until you began the warm up and forget the pain as cracks opened up and often bled. The most painful was bruising underneath corns from axe handle jarring that always remained sore no matter what you did. Axe handles were heated over a fire and rubbed with mutton fat to keep both handle and hands pliable. A trellis of perpendicular dead branches protruded from knots round the base of many trees. They were as hard as the hobs of hell and very brittle. Before it was safe to swing the axe, these had to be cut off and cleared away to give a clear safe passage for the axe. On cold winter mornings the dead sticks were so hard and brittle they'd fly to bits as the axe hit them and tiny needle-sharp chips, each capable of taking a piece out of any part of the body they hit, flew in all directions. By the end of the day's work I always felt starving and looked forward to the usual huge meal Doolie would have prepared. In winter when it was cold enough to keep fresh meat for several days, there'd be roast beef or a leg or shoulder of mutton surrounded by crisp roast potatoes, pumpkin and thick brown gravy. In summer this changed to a huge piece of corned brisket or silverside, accompanied by cauliflower in white sauce with grated cheese on top, mashed potatoes, peas and beans out of Pappy's vegetable garden and beetroot. It's amazing how we got through it all, but you were constantly hungry from hard axe work and not a crumb was ever left on the plate. We were always healthy and strong. Hard work never hurt anyone.

I don't know which was worst, summer or winter. In the summer, we'd start cutting as soon as it was light enough to see and get as much scrub down as possible before the day heated up. You lost so much sweat, it was difficult to stop drinking. But bore water doesn't quench your thirst and having drunk a waterbag dry and several quartpots of tea as well during the day, you got the shakes by knock-off time from loss of salt. Some put salt in their waterbags and in their tea too, but I could never drink the stuff. You were just as thirsty after a big drink, even though your gut felt about to explode. Our only gear was the axe with sweat-slippery handle, hat, shorts and boots, sodden with sweat that you squelched about in all day. Slippery axe handles were the main cause of cuts to feet or legs. The slightest slip of your hands on the handle when tired and knocked up changed the axe face angle as it hit the tree, causing it to slide off at speed with the full weight of the swing. It was very dangerous and great care was needed all the time if you didn't want to lose half a foot. I only ever had one bad axe cut that put me in hospital and that was from a slippery sweaty handle. Dad also was in hospital with a bad cut that became infected.

In the 1930s and right through the war years, everyone was forever chasing around after good scrub cutters, always hard to get and harder still to keep on the job for any length of time. Dick Taylor from adjoining Rutherglen arrived at Thrushton early one morning in his old Model T Ford utility. He was on his way to ask some post cutters camped in Mourilian, the property that joined Thrushton in the south, if they'd come to cut scrub on Rutherglen. Doolie and I went with him for the ride — me to open and close all the gates. It was a long haul down dog netting fences, dodging logs and stumps. We skirted round a lake which had formed from the overflow of bore water from Thrushton's Wirrbolla bore drains which terminated in the Pup Holes, where it just ran to waste during the winter in those days of unregulated bores.

When the camp was eventually found, we were surprised to find two women there. They were the first women I'd seen in axemen's camps, miles from the nearest place. The first thing noticeable was their clean and tidy camp set-up, with much more comfort and care than the usual rough bushmen's camps. A large fly covered their eating space with bush-made sapling table and sapling shelves as a pantry and another sapling cupboard to hold cooking gear with rails on which to drain plates, pots, pans and billies — even a rail over which teatowels were draped to dry after use. Two large tents alongside acted as bedrooms with bullock hide double beds and more sapling tables for clothes and wash basin. While we waited for the men to come back from cutting, the women, with few words, sat down on bush sapling seats with a banjo each. For the rest of the afternoon they entertained us with a skilful rendering of old folk songs and the latest war tunes which they sang to the accompaniment of the banjos and a tin dish and spoon.

In the early 1930s, buckjump rodeos were the favourite sport in most of the western towns. All the young coves from droving plants or from surrounding stations who thought they could ride a bit tried out their skills, while professional buckjump riders followed the rodeo circuit about as an occupation. There were many outstanding riders and well run shows in those days. Lance Skewthorp, Thorpe McConvell and Tex Moreton were about the best. They were always on the lookout for new outlaws in the districts through which they travelled to replace those which had broken down or been knocked up. Big crowds always turned up to see the shows. Apart from buckjumping and riding tricks, whip cracking and rope throwing, some of the performers recited poetry, sang cowboy songs and yodelled. I remember being very excited one time when having lunch in the Bollon cafe when in walked Tex Moreton and sat at the next table, ordered some dinner and started yarning to me while they were getting it. To me, it was like royalty turning up. His outfit had just arrived and the men were putting up the tents for his show that night. He was very upset next day when he found the kids from camps along the creek had carved or scratched their names and drawn roos and emus along the sides of his sparkling new green 1937 Pontiac car.

Vince Kirby from Powrunner and his wife (he called her Pommy) worked for us on Thrushton for a number of years as a married couple. During mustering I camped there and had my meals with them. Their means of conveyance was a buggy made out of an old motor car. Everything on top had been pulled off and replaced by a cypress pine platform built over the chassis and wheels. A horse was harnessed to each side of the pole at the front end and with the addition of an old sulky seat, the outfit was complete. Vince had been on the road droving before starting with us and brought all his plant and mob of horses with him, so there were always plenty of spare stock-horses to replace those staked in fallen mulga while racing about mustering. Working horses had to be fed night and morning in a drought, while the rest, often low in condition, had to fend for themselves. There was a good style of a six- or seven-year-old black horse in Vince's mob. It was always fat because Vince wouldn't ride it. He wouldn't let me ride it either, even when the others were knocked up. He reckoned it was a dangerous horse, though it didn't look that wild to me. This seemed a bit strange so, when Vince and Pommy decided to go into town for a few days, I thought I'd try him out. As it took three days to get in and the same back, it meant they'd be away over a week. Bundling his wife and the dogs on top of the cart with his swag, Vince climbed up, yelled at the horses and away they went. I could hardly wait for them to get out of sight up the track before running this shiny flash-looking horse into the yard to throw a saddle on him.

We were all mad about saddles, the most common of which were Uhl's, Winecke's and Schneider's. We broke in horses and rode bullocks out of crushes and chased roos and emus about the scrub — we lived on horses and were all good riders. Vince had a beautiful rodeo-poly saddle, the first of this kind I'd seen, made by Werner Brothers in Rockhampton, which at that time had been voted best saddle in its class at both the Warwick and Rockhampton buckjump rodeos. I'd taken a great fancy to his buckjump rodeo-poly saddle, reckoned I'd ride anything in it, and was anxious to get it on this horse without Vince hovering around to make sure I didn't. Though the horse seemed quiet enough when running with all the others out in the paddock, when I got them in the yard and cut this bloke out by himself, he suddenly became a different animal and was so snorty I couldn't get near him, let alone catch him. So I got a rope on him and dragged him up to a post and blindfolded him while I got Vince's buckjump saddle pulled down as tight as I could with surcingle and girth. I flew on to him, pulling the blindfold off at the same time and everything seemed to blow apart. He went straight up in the air so high and fast each time I thought he'd never come down, while his head was jammed between his front legs, with roars coming out of him enough to put the breeze up anyone. The only thing I could see in front of me was the pummel of the saddle that I was rapidly growing out of and the rest of him underneath. I hung to him for a few flying bucks. Don't know how high in the air he went each time but he nearly scraped my boots in the dust every time he hit the ground side on, with his kicking hind legs over the top of my head somewhere. The next thing I remember was ploughing a furrow through the dung under the bottom rail of the yard! When I looked up he seemed to be as high as the six foot top rails of the yard with the stirrups flogging backwards and forwards across the seat of that beautiful Werner saddle nothing was ever going to shift me out of!

It turned out this was Thorp McConvell's top outlaw buckjumper that noted buckjump rider Teddy Trivett was frantically trying to stay with while giving a rough-riding exhibition one night. Crashing into the rope ring while nearly turning itself inside out as it bucked round and round the ring, the horse got tangled up in the ropes and began demolishing part of the tent as it went mad, kicking and struggling to get out. Women and kids shrieked as the lights went out and the horse headed off full gallop into the pitch-dark night. Ted bailed out, minus bits of hide as he went end-for-end on the hard ground and burrs. He came limping back just as they were getting the lights going again but the horse could not be found. Some months later Vince and his droving plant were camped with a mob of bullocks out on the Mungalala and the horse wandered in amongst his hobbled saddle horses and stayed with them from then on. Where he'd been in the meantime, nobody knew, but the saddle and halter were no longer part of him! Vince no doubt had tried him out too with the same result, and, as far as I know, the horse was never ridden again. Probably ended up in the meatworks somewhere.

CHAPTER 14

Shearing Days

IN dry times with weak stock scattered all over big scrubby paddocks, it was impossible to ever get a clean muster in the mulga
scrub on Thrushton. Clonard wasn't so bad because there was no
mulga, but the dense wilga and belah scrub with sandalwood shrub
understorey in most of the gilgaied box country made it nearly as
bad. Paddocks ranging in size from 12,000 acres on Thrushton to
17,000 acres on Clonard meant a lot of riding and tracking to get the
stragglers together after the main bulk of stock had been mustered.
During the drought years in the 1930s, no animals were fat. They
graded from low in condition to store quality at best. We'd have to
knock off scrub cutting at shearing time and muster those strong
enough to be driven miles to the woolshed and main yards. The rest
had to be gathered together for a straggler shearing later in the year
with the hope for a fall of rain that might strengthen them up a bit
in the meantime.

Straggler mustering was always slow and time-consuming because
there were rarely more than ten or twelve in a mob. They'd be
scattered all over the place, often miles apart. In heavy undergrowth
or thick scrub, with visibility down to less than a hundred yards in
places, they'd hear you coming before you saw them and take off full
gallop. You'd get the dogs straight on to them, but by the time they
got round the lead they'd be a quarter of a mile away. The weak ones
that couldn't keep up the pace, and the rogues that had been through

it all before, peeled off the mob and planted under any bush they could find and lay there until you'd gone past, then jumped up and raced off in the opposite direction. You just had to let them go, stick to the few the dogs were holding, and hope you could get most of them to the nearest set of yards. Those that remained could be scattered about all over the place in twos and threes. You'd work the water and criss-cross the sweetest pockets of country every day, knowing they'd eventually turn up there and leave tracks. You'd get on any fresh tracks and follow them until they were caught up with. Sheep that cut off the small lot the dogs were holding had to be run down and shorn on the spot. We always carried a pair of shears in a pouch on the saddle and a few chaff bags into which the wool was stuffed. The wool was carted on the horse to the nearest station track or fence line to be collected later.

From the time I left school in 1936, Dad and I worked together with scrub-cutters in camps around the run and did all the straggler and ram shearing. This was often three or four hundred head. We generally did a lot of the crutching on both places, amounting to thousands of sheep as well. Crutching is very hard work when you have thousands to get through and straggler shearing isn't much better. Some would have missed a couple of shearings and have two years' growth of wool, full of sand, sticks and burrs, which meant blunt combs and cutters that needed constant grinding. You're bent double all day while struggling with hundreds of hot sheep, often with fleeces matted with wiregrass seed and galvanised burr thorns. When the seed is bad, your arms and underarms and all down the left side get rubbed raw by millions of needle-sharp barbs. In the stifling hot conditions of a woolshed, you're perpetually dripping with salty sweat that's rubbed into all the raw places by wool-abrasion and burrs. It felt like being scrubbed down with sandpaper and coarse salt. At the end of each day you're so sore and your back is so stiff it takes a good while and a lot of determination to straighten up to a normal position. Most shearers end up with crook backs.

Crutching in a bad fly time must surely be the filthiest of all sheep work. In a good season, sheep get scoured with the fresh green feed and blowflies strike the constantly sloppy areas around the tail. Body strike can also be severe if grass is long. Heavy morning dews saturate fleeces while sheep are grazing. In these conditions, flies can strike any part of the wool that is wet, especially behind the shoulders (body strike). Saddlecloths and woollen garments hung up to dry after washing can be white with flies' eggs and maggots long before they're dry when flies are bad. When sheep are blown, the maggots generally start off in the tail and work upwards, spreading out as they go, keeping the blown area hot and moist all the time. The main bulk of maggots form a thick mass on the skin at the base of the wool around and above the tail, where they begin boring down into the flesh. Leaders break away from this main mass and begin working upwards along the surface of the skin in narrow veins through the wool, consolidating 'outposts' along the working vein as they go. These 'outposts' rapidly form into a succession of other thick masses of working maggots. If the sheep is badly wrinkled, a gluey yellow yoke forms between the wrinkles from heat and moisture which attracts fly strike and makes crutching a filthy, slow and back-breaking job.

For several years we bought our flock rams from a well-known stud in New South Wales. Our agents, Australian Estates, selected and purchased several truck loads of rams for their clients and off-loaded them at different destinations along the road at clients' properties. Being at the end of the road, we'd end up with all the culls from the original mob that everyone else had picked over along the way. These were always the wrinkly ones that nobody wanted. They should have been sent back, of course, but we were so far away and they'd been in the trucks for so long, Dad thought this would be cruel and didn't like offending anyone, especially the Estates, so we ended up keeping them and paying the price. They were absolute fly-traps and most of their lambs, apart from being smothered with body wrinkles, had a large wrinkle up the side of each cheek that nearly covered their eyes, making them wool-blind a couple of months after shearing. They were almost impossible to muster and after the first attempt ended in such chaos, I was determined it wasn't going to happen again. So every time one of these came through the yards during crutching or straggler shearing, I ran the machine straight through the wrinkle and cut it clean off. It looked a horrible sight with all the cheek muscles exposed. This could only be done when flies weren't bad because nothing was put on the wound to avoid irritation. Some of the worst cases we kept in a small holding paddock to see what happened and, within a few weeks, the skin had grown together. In another month or so, the scar was hardly noticeable and the cheek was left smooth and completely free of wrinkles. It was the best thing I ever did, though frightening at the first attempt. In the 1940s, the Mules operation, substantially the same and equally effective, was introduced to deal with breach wrinkles in the same way. Mulesing, after JHW Mules, the pastoralist who invented the operation, has since become standard procedure throughout the sheep industry, with enormous savings in time and waste of wool due to flystrike.

When machine shearing took over the sheds and replaced the old blade shears, the handpieces were similar to the ones I learned to shear with back in the early 1930s. Those old machines got so hot you could hardly hold them if the 'giggling pin' was worn or out of adjustment or if the machine wasn't in the wool all the time with plenty of oil. It was nothing to see hands bandaged with rag over huge burst heat blisters. A man had to be tough to keep working all day with red raw hands like that, fastened round a hot handpiece in the heat and sweat of a woolshed — but they did, plenty of them. Beginners often had a bucket of water alongside them on the board so they could keep dipping the handpiece in every time it began smoking. I used to feel sorry for poor old Dad, even though it was hilarious sometimes. He was short with a fair slab of gut out in front that he had to be bent over all the time. He always seemed awkward and never quite in control of a sheep.

The art of shearing is to fill the comb with wool and keep the machine in the wool and close to the skin at all times. Even the newer model machines can get hot from insufficient lubrication and start smoking if the fast-moving cutter that works backwards and forwards across the comb attached to the handpiece is allowed out of the wool for long, which is often the case with wrinkles full of maggots. From then on, every time you touch the sheep, it's like putting a branding iron on a beast; it kicks about all over the place at the slightest touch of the hot machine. Dad's handpiece often seemed to be in this smoking state with the sheep between his legs going clean berserk every time he touched it. And the longer its furiously kicking sharp hooves raked up and down his dungarees, the longer the machine was out of the wool and the hotter it got. In wrinkly sheep, if you weren't good with the machine and couldn't hold the sheep properly, it was a no-win situation.

Dad always seemed to have the crutch kicked clean out of his old dungaree shearing trousers. I was shearing in the stand alongside with his seat facing me. Every time I looked up at all the commotion, I'd stare straight into a monumental set of knackers swinging about like the pendulum of a grandfather's clock as they dangled out of the great hole kicked out of the crutch of his shearing strides. The sticky putrid mess where the maggots are working creates an unbearable itch that the sheep keeps biting at for relief. As the machine works through the nest of maggots, accentuating the itch, the minced-up bits fly up into your face, over your lips and in your nostrils. To relieve the itch, the sheep grabs hold of the first thing it can see, generally your trouser leg and starts chewing on it like a hungry dog. It's no wonder poor old Pappy got stirred up, because the first thing his sheep always saw was a thumping great pair of knackers swinging about in front of its snout. It immediately latched on to them and began chewing like a goanna stuck into a chop bone. Poor old Pap bellowed like a scrub bull and danced about holding the smoking machine in one hand while trying frantically to unlatch the sheep's jaws with the other. Those old knackers had a fair bit of chewing before I could reach over and pull his machine off. Human beings were never meant to work as hard as this, I'm sure. Nearly all the old coves were burred up and old before their time from constant hard work and financial worry, and often became embittered towards the end because they felt they'd wasted their life.

Ram shearing was a job nobody liked because rams are so heavy and strong and their horns are so hard as they swing them about against your ribs and arms. When flies are bad you have to be checking them all the time for cracked horns which are virtual flytraps. During endless fights over some old ewe that probably wished them all in blazes anyhow, they'd reverse back ten or fifteen yards, stare at one another for a bit while licking their lips, then charge straight in full bore. Then 'bang'; arses flew in the air along with dust and sometimes bits of wool too would hit the ground. With head on one side and a bit more lip-licking, they'd reverse back to the same position; 'bang' again. This often kept up for a quarter of an hour or more until one got knocked over. Fights often resulted in split or cracked horns into which blowflies laid their eggs, the newly hatched maggots working down the cracks into the core of the horn and round the ears and horn where the wool is always moist and sticky with a potent smell. We cut the horns off with a hacksaw, trying to hold the head still all the time to avoid breaking blades — not a very nice operation. You'd have to get the horn off as quickly as possible because several arteries around the inside core of the horn start pumping out blood as soon as they were cut. We made small wooden pegs and sharpened the ends and drove these into each artery hole in the hard core to quell the bleeding, then pressed a handful of powdered bluestone over the end of each horn and held it there until the bleeding stopped. By the time the operation was finished there wasn't much fight left in the old ram — not for a while anyway.

Mustering sheep out of gilgaied belah (*Casuarina cristata*) country, after heavy rain when flies are bad, was a terrible job. These are generally heavy cracking clay soils that turn into boggy glue-pots when the gilgais are full of water. Sheep have to work their way, often in single file, along the narrow soggy strips between each gilgai, turning them into a quagmire. After the first few have gone through, the rest end up on top of one another, half-buried in the sticky grey clay while you battle to drag them out, bogged to the knees yourself.

A few weeks before shearing was scheduled to start in the summer of 1944, heavy rain filled the gilgais and brought up a rapid growth of blow-away summer grasses (*Digitaria* and *Enteropogon* species). We had a couple of thousand full wool weaners running with a lot of older sheep in the big Long Plain paddock. Anticipating the problem of getting them out of the waterlogged gilgai country, I put up several small netting yards in different places, hoping to avoid being tied up all day with little lots during mustering. What a picnic! They were weaners from the wrinkly NSW rams. Most were wool-blind and nearly as many flyblown. Drover Tom Duffy, horse-breaker Claude McDonald and old Spinifex George were all part of the mustering team. It nearly drove us mad — there was nothing you could do with them. They'd scatter and charge off full gallop when they heard you coming and, being wool-blind, ran over the dogs and under the horse without seeing either and into trees and upside down in gilgais full of water. The only sheep we got into the yards were those we ran down and carried back in front of the saddle and threw over the fence. It was dangerous too because the blow-away grass was knee-high all through the gilgai country, making it impossible to see some of the small circular, deep gilgais and melon-holes. Wind blew the feathery top off the dry grass and deposited it as a thick mass held in place by mud and water in every gilgai as if growing there. Sheep were racing everywhere. We couldn't even keep them together in a mob. The dogs and horses knocked up and tempers were well and truly frayed.

I came out on a small leopardwood (*Flindersia maculosa*) plain and saw Claude's horse covered in mud standing with its head down on the other side of a gilgai. I galloped over, expecting to see Claude stretched out somewhere with a broken neck or something. I eventually found him when the dogs started barking. His hat was gone and he was plastered with mud. He had one of the wool-blind weaners by the hind leg, swinging it round and round his head and thumping it on the ground. Don't know how long he'd been at it before I turned up, but the sheep was certainly very dead with its black and blue tongue hanging out of the corner of its mouth. I wasn't game to say a word because we all felt the same way; sheep are quite capable of driving you to distraction in these circumstances. Claude had been trying to run down the weaner and cart it back to the yard. Wool-blind, it had been under the horse and over the dogs several times without seeing either when Claude's horse went end-for-end into a gilgai that looked like a thick patch of blow-away grass but was all mud and water underneath. We had to knock off mustering and wait for the country to dry out by shearing at Thrushton first, but we lost a lot with flystrike in the meantime.

The small railway terminus town of Dirranbandi is midway between St George in Queensland and the New South Wales border at the one-horse settlement of Hebel. These three centres were important outposts servicing major stockroutes along which travelling stock worked their way south into New South Wales from the 1860s onwards. They were to become the main trading centres for that vast area of country as these districts were subdivided into pastoral holdings as settlement spread. Two main streams drain the country to the north and east. These are the Condamine River heading in the Great Dividing Range near Warwick and flowing west where it becomes the Balonne River just east of Surat. This major stream is joined by the Maranoa River coming down from the north where it heads in the sandstone ranges of the Central Highlands and drains the southern slopes at the junction of the Chesterton and Carnarvon Ranges. These two streams meet twenty miles north of St George and continue south past the town, still as the Balonne River.

A few miles south of Dirranbandi, the Balonne River becomes distributary and breaks up into numerous channels. Here it becomes the Balonne Minor, Culgoa, Bokhara, Narran and Ballandool Rivers and Quartpot, Little Quartpot and a maze of other small creeks and flood channels. This major drainage system carries a heavy run-off in good seasons, bringing extensive flooding from Dirranbandi south into New South Wales and producing some of the best agricultural country in south-west Queensland and north-western New South Wales. The variable nature of Australia's rainfall means that torrential rain commonly falls in a spasmodic patchwork, one series of heavy falls over one region often being isolated by hundreds of miles from the next. When heavy rain falls across the upper catchments of these streams, hundreds of miles away to the east and north, watersheds are saturated. The rapid run-off can bring widespread flooding along the braided channels that meander through the drought-stricken country lower down. These may not have seen a drop of rain for perhaps six months or more. Raging droughts can bring dust-bowl conditions to thousands of square miles of country. When this happens, a narrow line a few yards wide at the outskirts of the flooded country often separates dusty drought-stricken wastes where scrub has been cut to feed starving stock for months on end. The dusty half-dead country on one side of a narrow dividing line gives way to a veritable Garden of Eden on the other, with lush herbage and waist-high waving green grass stretching away into the distance with bees humming and birds singing everywhere. The spectacle defies belief until we begin to understand what Australia is all about — and this in itself is a fascinating lifetime study.

I was privileged to have been part of this amazing spectacle during the Second World War when on the road droving stock to the trucking yards in Dirranbandi. At that time I was with Vince Kirby and his wife, Pommy, droving a big mob of full-wool wethers over there for trucking. Pommy drove the horse and cart and put up the ropes to hold the sheep at night and did the cooking, while Vince and I with our dogs handled the mob. Dirranbandi is the end of the line in south-west Queensland and from here we were trucking the sheep to the Cannon Hill meatworks in Brisbane. There had been no rain for ages and we were about to start cutting scrub. Carrying too many stock coming into a drought, we decided to off-load the best of the wether portion, leave the older breeding ewes on Clonard, take the young stock in strong condition over to Thrushton and start cutting scrub to feed them. Full-wool skins were bringing a good price and mutton wasn't too bad either, so rather than knock the aged wethers about during shearing while being held in small paddocks with little feed, we decided to sell them as they were. We heard of good rains in towards the coast and over the Darling Downs a couple of months earlier but, having no contact with outside happenings while camped away mustering and shifting stock about between the two places, what happened was completely unexpected. Nearing Dirranbandi and hoping to make the Culgoa watering reserve the following day, we got into camp pretty late with the sheep spread out all over the stock route in the hope they'd find an odd tuft worth eating in the drought-stricken surroundings. Just before dark as we bumped the mob together in the direction of the rope yard Pommy had put up, the leaders started to bellow and gallop on ahead of the others, which were soon infected by the same madness. It was nearly dark, and we couldn't handle them — they ran over the dogs and round the horses and kept going at full gallop. As it was a dry camp, we thought they must have smelt water and taken off. We had to let them go, intend-ing to get round the outside of the tracks early next morning and push them all together again.

Starting away from camp just on daylight as soon as the horses had finished their nosebags, we'd gone less than a mile when we noticed a green line away ahead, but thought our eyes were playing tricks. As we approached, it turned into a waving green landscape as far as the eye could see across the flood plains. Our horses had gone mad too. Stock hitting this for the first time had never seen anything like it and nothing was going to stop them from getting into it. The flood must have come down a month or so earlier like a surge from a cloudburst and rapidly drained off again. The grass was long and vivid green while *sesbania* formed thickets along the water tables and flood chan-nels. The further we went, the more stock we saw and most of them weren't ours. Every drover on the road had the same thing happen and the country for miles, right up close to town was full of cattle, sheep and horses with bells ringing everywhere. When we got to the river, camps lined both banks. Having let their stock go, the droving plants decided there was nothing more they could do, so settled down to do a bit of fishing while their mobs fattened up on all this feed. There was no possibility of getting ours out either without mustering the whole stockroute for ten or fifteen miles and drafting everything up, so we shifted camp to the river and settled in with all the others after getting rations from Dirranbandi. In the following weeks, we all got together and put up a big set of wire and netting yards in the stockroute and eventually mustered and drafted up all the stock in the area. Strike, what a job! Drovers and their dogs were everywhere and spare horses with bells flogging away seemed to come from all directions. There was no shortage of manpower and dogs. I rode the sixty odd miles home and got Dad to camp with us and give a hand. We were a few sheep short, but got most of them on the trucks and were pleased to get home and be finished with them. What a contrast to get back into that drought scene and start straight into cutting half-dead mulga scrub, with everything as dry as chips and dust blowing along every pad!

The owners of flooded country were very fortunate, because it was always the best land and their good seasons didn't necessarily have to rely on rain in their district. If good falls had been registered over the upper catchments, they were assured of a good season on their flooded country lower down, even if a drought was raging everywhere else. But there are always two sides to a story and you get the other side when talking to the men who work the flood country. Pulled out of bed in the middle of the night to shift stock to higher ground is not uncommon, as are heavy stock losses when trapped by flash floods from isolated wild storms that flatten flood gates and fences. It only needs one big log to get going in a main channel and 'bang' goes every floodgate until the log eventually gets jammed somewhere lower down. Miles of flattened fencing has to be dug from under sticky black mud and river silt, sometimes feet-deep near a river, with barbed wire and netting tangled up with debris underneath. It's not that this kind of thing rarely happens — it's the standard work program after every major flood and can be enormously costly in time, labour and material, sometimes repeated several times in a single wet year. Yet people are always prepared to put up with this in order to get the best country.

CHAPTER 15

The Big Smoke

IT wasn't until after we were married that I began to realise just how lonely it must have been for a young girl accustomed to much better things to be suddenly landed out in that dry mulga country with little outside contact. I'd known nothing else and it didn't bother me, so I hadn't realised it could bother anyone else. But it suddenly sunk into my thick skull one day with a bang. We were camped in some beautiful coolibah flooded country down the Moonie River from Nindigully. Moodgie had set out a bit of lunch on a bag under a tree and was sitting on a log alongside, giving the flies a hammering with a switch, while I waited for the billy to boil.

I'd have been gaping round at the beautiful open coolibah (*Eucalyptus coolibah*) country, paradise after Thrushton's mulga scrubs.

'You know, mate, I'd love to get hold of twenty or thirty thousand acres of this,' I said.

Don't think I was meant to hear the reply, but the mumble from the log said —

'I'd rather have my throat cut!'

Well, that knocked the stuffing clean out of me to think anyone could say such a thing about this wonderful piece of country. Light at last began to dawn that this dry western country wasn't the place for my old mate and I'd have to do something about it. But what? I'd known nothing but rough land and stock work all my life. But, by then, I was starting to get thoroughly sick of the constant battle with droughts, the hard axe work and no money. I couldn't see much future in the land any more either, so was ready to get out and try something else. Also, Moodgie had not long returned from Lismore with our first baby, Keith — a beautiful little boy we were so proud of and couldn't take our eyes off. They surely were owed a better and easier life than the one I'd had up until that point. There must be something a person could do in less trying conditions that offered greater scope for higher learning and cultural activities than horse-breaking, scrub-cutting and roo shooting.

As heavy machinery seemed certain to play a major role in all future fields concerning the land, I thought I'd better learn something about it and maybe get into something of that kind. I began studying diesel engineering by correspondence from the Diesel Engineering College in Sydney, but was often so tired at night after being on the end of an axe all day that nothing seemed to make much sense. I doubt if I'd have finished the three-year course without Moodgie's help. She taught me a great deal. We eventually left Clonard, bought a broken-down house in St George and moved there so I could get some workshop experience before going to Sydney to attend night lectures at the college leading to the final exams. The house was an awful contraption, probably one of the first huts built in St George — a single room about ten feet by ten feet, which became the kitchen when many years later a second hut with three small rooms was tacked on to the first part.

The two portions were joined together at the ground, but were more than two feet apart at the top because of the lean that had developed over the years. Two long sturdy rails had been sunk in the ground about ten feet out from the floor and anchored just below the roof as stays to stop the whole outfit falling over. The slab pine doors were uneven and several inches off the floorboards with old motor lorry tyre tubes nailed along the bottom to stop the wind and sand blowing underneath. The place had been up for sale for one hundred pounds for ages before we inspected it, but everyone said it was too dear! We looked round for the bathroom. It turned out to be a corrugated galvanised iron shed about eight feet by six feet with a dirt floor outside in the yard surrounded by bottles, rusty tins and galvanised burr. Taking up the whole of one side was an enormous bathtub nearly three feet deep made out of parts of a corrugated galvanised iron water tank, wired together and cemented inside.

The house belonged to someone from the local butcher's shop. He had used the bathtub for washing all the dung out of cattle guts before making tripe for years before we turned up. We held our nose and looked inside. Here was a pile of guts, blown up with air from underneath, floating amongst the contents which had formed a green scum an inch thick over the surface, with moss and slime growing a quarter of an inch thick up the cement sides and across the bottom. The two-inch outlet pipe was stuffed with old newspapers to hold this delicate brew from bolting down the paddock. The only water supply was boiling hot from the local artesian bore, with a very strong smell of sulphur. The toilet was a similar but smaller shed down the paddock under a pepperina tree with a pad leading to it from the house through loose sand and a foot-high dense cover of galvanised burrs. With very little money, and most of that coming from the sale of kangaroo skins, we bought the house and cleaned it up. Moodgie and I then cut cypress pine trees from sandhills off the Thallon road. We rolled the logs up skids on to the back of the old truck and carted them to Grady's sawmill and had them cut up so I could build two verandahs. One was at the side of the old leaning section at the back and the other at the front of the second addition. The powerhouse was only a couple of hundred yards away and hammered and clattered night and day with lights blazing. Our new abode was unique, to say the least.

The floor was so uneven inside you couldn't leave Keith's pram anywhere without putting a chock under the wheel to stop it taking off and crashing into the wall. The whole floor seemed to slope steeply away on all sides from the one central point. We pulled up the floorboards to see what was wrong and found the old house had been

built over an enormous carbeen (*Eucalyptus tessellaris*) stump about
three feet in diameter. The only thing that hadn't sunk was the stump
that now propped up the whole house from underneath.

We had to sell the truck and the old Harley Davidson and sidecar
to help pay for the house and things we didn't have. Dad bought the
truck for the fifty pounds I'd paid for it several years before just to
help us along. He didn't ever drive it. A very special kind of technique
was needed and old Pap didn't have that! It wandered all over the
road and every now and then jumped the selector gate and got locked
in reverse and low gear at the same time. When this happened you'd
have to take the top off the gearbox and lever the gears into the correct position again. It was the sort of outfit you had to know a good
bit about and have a fair kit of tools with you all the time if you
wanted to get to where you were going. We kept the Auburn because
we needed a car until we left St George, even though we couldn't
afford to run it far. It was in immaculate condition for a 1927 model,
with solid high quality leather throughout and not a mark on it —
one of the few cars on the road in 1927 with four-wheel brakes. It
was very powerful and had the biggest engine I've ever seen in a car.
Stopping at the roadside tin garages with hand-pump petrol bowsers
was always amusing. The mechanic who was covered with oil and red
dust would come sauntering out with a bottle of oil after filling up
with petrol and lift the bonnet. He'd freeze there for a bit staring, and
then exclaim 'Jesus Christ', before yelling to his mate out the back of
the garage: 'Come an' 'ave a look at this — biggest ingin ever I seen
in a motor car — aughter be in a bloody train, not a car — want a
bowser in the back seat ter keep 'er goin.'

The Auburn only bailed me up once. I'd been putting up gates
with Dad at Thrushton and was about to return home to Clonard.
The engine made a rattling noise as I pressed the starter button and
refused to start. The loose timing chain had jumped three or four
teeth on the camshaft sprocket and put the valve timing out, but
not realising this at the time I asked Dad to tow me back home. I
should have known better because he was a woeful driver and the

twenty-five mile track was narrow and winding with ten or twelve gates to open and close on the way. We only had the one heavy twisted, but well-worn cotton rope. I explained the importance of taking up the slack in the rope before starting the pull each time we stopped but his mind was on filling his pipe. So I sat in the car and waited while he filled her up and got her going properly. I could tell by the smoke coming out the front that the action was about to start — and how! He put the Chev utility in low gear and just took off and bang went the rope, nearly jerking the front end out of the Auburn. We tried numerous times but ended up with more knots than rope in the finish. So I cut a long box sapling and bored a hole in each end, twitching one end to his back axle and the other to the Auburn — he couldn't jerk me now! So away we went.

The dust was so thick I could hardly see where he was and kept hoping I didn't hit one of the hundreds of stumps a few inches from the single wheel tracks. I'm sure he'd forgotten I was behind, the way he was driving. I was standing on the brake every now and then to slow him down. We conquered the first few gates successfully, then the wire holding the pole to the front axle of the Auburn broke. Away Dad went for miles along the dog netting fence, dragging the pole along behind, while I roared laughing at the ridiculous spectacle of that log with nothing on behind bouncing about as it disappeared up the track through the dust. He eventually came back with a sheepish look and told me he went about five miles to the next gate, opened it and drove through. As he got out to close it, he fell over the rail and barked his shins. It was only then that he remembered something should have been attached to the other end. Poor old Pap — he sure was a larrikin. He'd have been sucking away on that stinking old pipe and singing songs all the time and had obviously forgotten all about me till he fell over the rail that was only halfway through the gateway.

With the move from St George to Sydney coming up, we had to sell the old girl. We had to think hard about this though because there was only one other straight eight Auburn of that model in Australia and I'd become so attached to the old thing I didn't like parting with her. She'd be worth a packet today.

It was still dark, an hour or more before daylight, early one morning not long before we moved to Sydney. I heard someone walking round the outside of the house. The footsteps went past several times so I went out to see who it was and found Billy Lock, the bullocky who used to delve our bore drains standing at the door. He'd come to borrow my rifle and some bullets to shoot a kangaroo or an emu to feed all the dogs and cats out at Boolba. He seemed pretty vague so I sat him down at the stove while I lit the fire and made him a drink of tea and some toast. The morning wasn't cold, yet he couldn't stop shivering and shaking as though it was frosty winter weather. Poor old Bill was in a bad way. He had not long started living with the de-facto wife of one of our former married couples at Clonard. He wanted to start a new life away from bullocks and mud-larking and become an owner with better prospects for the future now he had a wife. He sold the wagon and his team of bullocks and bought the old FortyMile store (now Boolba). It was almost abandoned, only being camped in at odd times by passing drovers or roo shooters. His newly acquired wife had plans to clean the place up and start a tea and scones service under a bough shed they were going to build out the front for travellers on the St George to Cunnamulla road. Bill also bought an old International lorry and did a bit of wool carting and bush work when he could get it to help keep things going. Being halfway between Bollon and St George, nobody ever stopped at Boolba — they'd be hurrying into town on business or taking the kids to the dentist or the doctor. Also it was a dirty dilapidated old place perched out in the middle of an open flat with no garden and surrounded by rusty petrol and jam tins, bottles, old spring carts and galvanised burrs in amongst a horde of dogs and cats of every colour, shape and size. If stopping there for some reason, dogs jumped all over you with feet covered in black mud from the nearby stock-watering tank.

Bill was going downhill fast. He was just a rough old bushman whose whole life had been with 'bullicks, 'orses an' dorgs', so he was soon in trouble with the International truck that kept breaking down as he knew nothing about engines and mechanical things of that nature. When delving the drains, the only vehicle I ever saw him with was an old worn-out 1927 model Whippet utility. It was more often dragged behind the bullocks or the wagon than it was driven, a rail tied through the spokes of the steering wheel to keep her in a straight line.

He couldn't see the point of refinements like mudguards on a vehicle, even in black soil country. 'I got caught in a bit of a storm across the SevenMile one day and the black mud packed up that tight under the mudguards it stopped the car. The ingine wez roaring, the radiator wez whistling with steam an' smoke blowing an' th' mud wez like plasticine. Every fifty yards I clawed out all I could and struggled on for another fifty but yer couldn't get yer fingers inter th' stuff. Every time I tried to start, th' ingine roared but the wheels weren't going round and smoke was coming outer th' clutch. What's a man want mudguards for anyway. It never rains out here an' when it does, it's only to annoy a man,' he grumbled, 'so I got th' axe outer th' back, cut th' bastards off an' chucked 'em on th' sider th' road under a tree an' 'ad no more trouble from then on.'

He gradually lost all the wool carting given him by people he'd known all his life who were trying to help him along. Things were going from bad to worse when his wife suddenly contracted meningitis and was dead within forty-eight hours. It was a dreadful shock for Bill. His whole life, that so recently had been full of promise, collapsed around his ears and left him lost and frightened. He'd just come into St George from Boolba and came straight to me. The funeral had been the day before. As soon as it was over, he went back to Boolba to feed and water all the cats and dogs and feed several poddy lambs they were rearing at the time.

'When I got home I nearly went mad,' he told me. 'All the animals raced out to meet me. The dogs jumped all over me yapping and wagging their tails. Then, just as suddenly, all sat down around me, put their heads in the air and started to howl as they stared up the road in the direction they'd seen the ambulance taking her away.'

I didn't know what to do. He was so obviously in a state of shock and needed medical attention, but since he'd never been to a doctor, it would have been like a red rag to a bull to even mention that. He just kept asking for my rifle and a couple of bullets to knock over a roo for the dogs and cats. The hours went by and it was long past the time when I should have been at work. Moodgie and I both kept trying to get through to him but he wasn't listening — all he could talk about was the rifle; it was the only thing he could think of, poor old bloke. He wore us down in the finish. I gave him the rifle and a box of bullets, and away he went in the old truck with a few bales of wool he was taking over to load on the rail at Thallon. He drove out about twenty-five miles and pulled off the side of the road. He put his hat on the seat and his glasses and tobacco on top, then walked a few feet away, put the rifle muzzle in his mouth, pulled the trigger and shot himself.

I had the dreadful job of trying to calm down his old parents, George and Mrs Lock, both in their seventies, who lived not far away. Moodgie had to stay home with the baby while I made them endless cups of tea and struggled to stay awake all night talking to them. I listened for hour after hour as these two sad lonely old bush folk recounted the good times and all the amusing little things that happened to them out in the bush. Most of them seemed to be when Billy was a toddler riding up on top of the wagon or on the delver away out in the bush somewhere delving drains. Each story would be abruptly broken every now and then as they burst into bouts of tears and wailing at some little thing they'd just thought of for the first time in years that suddenly had touched their heart. Then the police came round and wanted to know how Bill had got the rifle — had I given it to him or had he just taken it. It was a terrible night — one I'll never forget. I don't think the old people lasted long after that. Billy was their one and only child and, after working together for so long knocking around the bush with the bullocks, their lives had all but drawn to a close.

We sold our house in St George and moved to Lismore where Moodgie stayed with her parents until our daughter Lyn was born. I continued on to Sydney to get a daytime job and attended night lectures and practical demonstrations for some months at the College and on large stationary diesel engines. There was so much maintenance and operating detail to digest, including start and shut down procedure before sitting for the final exams. I couldn't believe the size of some of these monsters. Practically every moving part had to be lifted by endless chain or crane. Some were twenty-five feet tall — like a small house. Most of these giants were in large overseas cargo vessels and oil tankers we visited privately by appointment, others were in powerhouses. Later, when employed as a diesel fitter, the importance of methodical workshop practice and safety precaution was drilled into us, especially safety-control when calibrating high-pressure diesel injectors. Most injectors broke (injected) at from 2,500 to more than 3,000 lbs per sq inch and at such pressures the injected diesel mist can penetrate right through the skin and into flesh and cause blood poisoning — even death. We also had to learn how to use Doby Maginnis Indicators, an instrument fitted with a diaphragm which was screwed into each cylinder, each of which was called an engine. It was a spring-loaded mechanism with an arm holding a very fine lead pencil that moved up and down across a sheet of graph paper, recording changes taking place in each engine. These lines could then be read off and compared with those in each of the other cylinders (engines) so that the suction, compression and combustion ratios could be synchronised for identical performance and power. Everything was calculated in 'Atmospheres', one atmosphere being the unit of pressure equivalent to 14.69 lbs per sq inch. Air on the compression stroke at 'top dead centre', the point at which fuel injection takes place, had to reach a minimum of 400 lbs per sq inch with a corresponding temperature of 1,000 degrees F. for the flash point (combustion) of diesel fuel.

Houses to rent were very hard to find in Sydney at that time so every weekend was spent house-hunting. The only place I could find in our modest price range was a deserted boatshed away out at Prince Edward Park, hanging out over the bank of the Woronora River, a tributary of the Georges River. The owner was in the middle of renovating it when I inspected it. It was pitifully small — only about eighteen feet long and eight feet wide with a four-foot wide, open balcony along part of one side. The hut acted as the roof of the boatshed directly underneath the floor. As soon as Moodgie could travel with the new baby she travelled from Lismore to Sydney by train with the two children, Keith and Lyn, and we went straight out to the boatshed. This involved a train trip from Sydney to Sutherland and then a bus trip down a steep winding gravel road to Prince Edward Park. We left the bus just before the terminus and climbed down ninety-seven loose sandstone slab steps from the gravel road on top to the boatshed almost directly below.

The owner said we could have the place rent-free for a few weeks if I built a bathroom, laundry or toilet. With very little money, this suited me, so my first job was to build a shed for this purpose and arrange for the nightman to come once a week to collect the can. In the meantime, if we needed the toilet, it meant climbing back up all the steps to a neighbour's house, the owners kindly allowing us to use their toilet until I'd finished building ours. Because of the danger of the children falling off the verandah into the swirling river a few feet below, I built a railing round the narrow verandah and netted it right to the floor. Moodgie had her work cut out looking after the children in such cramped and uncomfortable conditions. With high tide water only a few feet below, everything the children pushed through the netting or threw over the top ended in the river. If it sank, Moodgie scraped it out of the mud at low tide. If it didn't, it floated away on the swirling tide with the jellyfish. Watching the nightman, poor bloke, struggling up the ninety-seven loose sandstone slabs with the can on his shoulder to the nightcart parked on the gravel road on top used to give us the jitters. It was easy to imagine him losing his footing up near the top somewhere and letting the can go. It would have just about come straight through the window to end up all over the floor.

After passing the exams, I became a diesel fitter in the machine shop at Leyland Motors plant in Redfern, reconditioning used diesel engines and assembling new ones. It was a huge factory with well over an acre of cold damp concrete floor. The whole place was hopping with fleas and stank of cat urine from all the Redfern alley cats that assembled there at night to fight and participate in all the other activities alley cats seem to be so good at doing. Having spent my life on the land, and rarely off it, I was bushed the whole time, especially with the electric trains. At first, I couldn't understand timetables or the lights on the boards at railway stations and was forever asking people for directions. Getting to Leyland Motors in Redfern via the underground from the Town Hall station to start work at seven-thirty on my first morning was an experience that gave me nightmares. Straight out of the bush with riding boots, beaver-moles and big hat and my heavy toolbox on one shoulder, I started out early — in the dark, of course. Probably looked just as out of place in Sydney as I felt. I was in a blind panic and a lather of sweat with my heavy load after the half-mile gallop up Bathurst Street hill from where I was staying to the Town Hall station. I wasn't going to be late for work on my first morning. I forced my way into a train that had just pulled in. It took off like a horse stung on the arse by a wasp before I even had time to put the heavy toolbox on the floor amongst all the shift-workers, trying not to squash their toes. When it bolted straight through the first couple of stations without stopping, I was panic-struck that it was heading non-stop straight out miles into the bush somewhere, so decided to bail out as soon as it slowed down a bit somewhere. Its speed suddenly dropped off to about fifteen miles an hour. I looked both ways up the inside line to make sure nothing was coming then jumped straight out through the door with my big heavy toolbox. It was much further down than it looked and I went end-for-end on the sharp blue metal between the lines. Both knees were torn out of my riding trousers and hide off knuckles and knees. Knew I'd have to get off the line fast before another train came, so grabbed the toolbox and, as I looked up, there was the last carriage of the train nearly alongside me where it had stopped at a station. Blow me down if the station wasn't Redfern!

I climbed up to the platform and raced up the long concrete steps from the station. Across the street stood a giant of a policeman with helmet on. Had no idea which way to head for Leylands so I asked the policeman where the taxis were. He looked me up and down, with bleeding knees gaping through torn riding trousers and blood over hands from torn knuckles.

'Where did *you* sleep last night?' he demanded. 'You've been fighting, 'aven't yer? What you got in that tin box there?'

'The train bolted and I thought she wasn't going to pull up anywhere, so I bailed out,' I explained. 'My toolbox is getting pretty heavy so I thought I'd get a taxi if you can tell me where to find one. I've got to get to Leyland Motors to start work at half past seven.'

'So you're from the bush then, are yer? Well yer not in th' bush now. Yer gotter be careful in the city, or you'll get yourself killed. Yer'll find one down the next block at the rank. It'll cost yer about 'alf a dollar an' don't give th' bludgin' bastard a penny more — he'll smell the gum leaves all over yer a mile orf with that big hat and riding boots, an' run you round all over th' bloody place if you give 'im half a chance.'

With those words of warning, I found a taxi and paid him off right in front of the big roll-up doors through which I made my grand entry into Leyland Motors. Talk about stage fright — everyone just stood and gaped at this strange object with a tin toolbox on one shoulder. Fifty pairs of staring eyes followed me to the works manager's office. Mick Sheehan looked up from his swivel chair and pushed his hat back as he gave me the once-over.

'Ah, so you must be the young cove from Queensland that rang me about a job. Looks like you could do with a bit of clean-up — did you get run over or something?'

Mick called the foreman over and told him to show me where to have a wash and got the first-aid cove to dress my knees and knuckles; then gave me a pair of spanking new white overalls. I was taken round and introduced to the engineers, mechanics and welders, then shown over the lathes, surface grinders and planers in the machine shop. The final stop was the tool shop that housed all the valuable workshop tools and gear, with a storeman in charge. It was a great relief to find such a friendly atmosphere. Everyone was asking questions at the same time and offering help if I ever needed it (which I certainly did on many occasions). They couldn't take their eyes off me — my clothes were so different from anything they'd been used to. The hat and boots had them foxed. 'Can we have a go of your hat,' they asked! One wanted to know why I wore women's boots — he'd never seen a pair of high-heeled riding boots before.

I didn't stay long at Leylands. I hated the city and the factory, but, above all, it was the constant travelling that really got to me. Being on the river at the bottom of the Woronora Gorge, I hardly ever saw home in the daylight except for a few weeks in the summer and even then we lost the sun by mid-afternoon. As work started at seven-thirty, I'd often charge up the rickety sandstone steps in the dark with a bit of breakfast hanging out the corner of my mouth just in time to see the lights of the hourly bus disappearing up the road in a cloud of dust. When this happened, it meant climbing a couple of miles up a three or four hundred foot sandstone scarp on a goat track around cliffs to reach the Sutherland station. At the station at last, with tongue hanging out from the two-mile gallop up the hill, the train was often a dot in the distance away up the line.

Even when you caught the train at this hour of the morning, it was generally packed out with early morning shift workers. You'd stand with toes on the step and the rest hanging outside, while hanging on precariously by a finger along with several others hooked through a ring inside until you forced your way in. All the carriages were the same, with a similar cold draught the full length of the train — must have been doors or windows open somewhere. Everybody coughed constantly and seemed to have dreadful colds.

You needed a pretty strong stomach charging up the long flight of steps leading from the Redfern station. Hundreds of early morning workers, most of them on the run and certainly too sick to be at work in such draughty conditions, coughed up and spat out great dollops of yellow pussy phlegm as they raced up the stairs. Both sides were lined with a continuous coating of horrible yellow jelly. They couldn't afford to be sick — all had precarious jobs to hold down, children to feed, rent to pay. There were few generous government handouts those days.

CHAPTER 16

Back to the Bush

WE decided the city wasn't the place for us. We wanted to get back on the land again as soon as possible, but in better country this time with a more reliable rainfall. I found employment in the Wellington district, first as overseer of the two Pine Park Antrum Shorthorn and Armagh Poll Shorthorn Studs, then as manager of Illgingerry, the adjoining sheep property for the Killen and Marr Pastoral Company. These were the two top shorthorn studs in Australia at that time and the stud master, Andy Dollar, had on several occasions won the annual stud master's award at Sydney's Royal Easter Show.

The Pine Park homestead and garden layout, where the Killens at times had entertained visiting royalty, was beautiful, set on the bank of the Cudgegong River, fifteen miles west of Wellington. Many notables had been wined and dined there over the years. The Duke of Gloucester came out of the homestead one morning to where one of the jackaroos was holding the horse they'd saddled for him to ride along the river. It was in the middle of urinating with back legs stretched out behind and you know what dangling down nearly to the ground.

On observing the situation, the Duke said, 'I say, I say, will someone please kick the jolly prop out from under him before I mount.'

Princess Anne, so the story goes, was a young girl always interested in horses. Mr and Mrs Killen were showing her around the animals and buildings one morning when there was a hell of a commotion and dust coming out of the blacksmith's shop. They went over to see what was going on, Princess Anne all eyes. Looking in through the open door of the galvanised iron shed, Mr Killen saw that the black-smith was battling to tack a set of shoes on a big toey colt inside.

'You having a bit of trouble in there Bob?' he called out.

And Bob, not realising anyone else was there, announced, 'Orr, 'es 'ad two or three shits and a couple of pisses an' I jist striped 'im across th' bloody pizzle with the shoeing rasp — 'e's startin' to settle down a bit now.'

The homestead and entrance driveway nestled below the nearby steep slopes of Pine Hill. Rising directly above the whole station complex, Pine Hill provided a picturesque backdrop of light and dark greens as the dense cypress pine thickets stood out from the steep slopes, streaked occasionally by tall straight trunks of white box trees. The entrance was via an imposing archway which gave way to a winding white gravel drive leading to the homestead through tall pines and ornamental terraced gardens, all kept neat and trim by a permanent gardener assisted at times by a jackaroo.

Quite out of place amidst all this grandeur, within a stone's throw of the homestead garden complex surrounded by white-painted wooden fences, were several acres of cattle yards, bull feeding stalls and the stud master's cottage. Close to all that was the huge galvanised iron woolshed and separate shearers' quarters, a big set of sheep yards and several corrugated iron hay, harness and machinery sheds. Also in the same group was a blacksmith's shop, pump shed, old drays, spring-carts and headers. These were surrounded by great heaps of coiled fencing wire, rolls of rabbit netting, dog kennels and grain silos — like a rambling corrugated iron township.

Standing like a statue in the middle of all this was the contraption later to nearly drive me mad at times: the old twelve horsepower steam traction engine that drove the woolshed's six-stand shearing plant. It was straight out of the 1850s, a museum piece that, try as I would, I couldn't get the owners to part with. A mountain of logs, cut into four-foot lengths to feed the boiler, was piled alongside. The story of the steam engine was that Eric Killen's father had bought a big back-country station from Sir Sidney Kidman out near the South Australian border. The steam engine was part of the station plant and Kidman, being the rogue he was, decided to take it with him when he sold the place, thinking nobody would be any the wiser. But the Killens got wind of it somehow and in the ensuing court battle, which they won, Kidman was ordered to turn his bullocks around and drag the thing back to the station. How it got from there to Pine Park was a bit of a mystery. Eric Killen's father must have taken a shine to the lumbering old thing that ate half a ton of wood a day to keep it going. Whatever it was, I ended up with the antiquated great contraption. It spluttered and hissed steam, occasionally bucking backwards and forwards in its block-hole and breaking the long belt driving the overhead gear — with shearers going crook very time it broke down which was fairly routine most days.

Pine Park (the cattle studs) and Illgingerry (the sheep section) combined to form about 17,000 acres carrying up to 25,000 head of sheep before the rabbit plagues took over that country and two large cattle studs — a very large property indeed for that area. Eric Killen initially purchased a number of adjoining blocks on both sides of the Cudgegong River in the late 1920s and 1930s. Amalgamation of these blocks formed the Pine Park and Illgingerry aggregation, the former owners being retained as station hands living in their huts and homesteads along the river.

Before coming to New South Wales, Eric Killen's grandfather had selected a big belt of country in the Northern Territory about the turn of the century and nearly went broke when the Top End was ravaged by the bovine disease, red water fever. Importation of Asian buffalos to northern Australia in the early 1870s brought with them the blood-sucking parasitic cattle tick carrying the fever. A second import of Asian cattle to Glencoe on the Adelaide River in the 1880s further exacerbated the problem. Cattle ticks rapidly spread right across the Top End as buffalos moved from swamp to swamp,

infesting the British breed herds of the big unfenced Territory runs
as they went. Travelling stock, generally in lots of 1,000 to 1,500 head
of 'ticky' station fats and forward store bullocks completed the catastrophe as drovers worked the mobs down stockroutes to distant
railheads or fattening country closer in. Stock had no in-built resistance to ticks and red water fever that created dreadful havoc among
the Territory and North Queensland herds. Cattle ticks have since
spread right across tropical Australia and south throughout the humid
eastern regions of Queensland and into Northern New South Wales.
Cattle ticks gradually built up immunity to arsenic and other chemical dips designed for their eradication while the hundred-year battle
to contain their impact has cost the country and its cattle industry
billions of dollars and considerable hardship. So the Killens sold
out and shifted to Central New South Wales and started all over
again.

The new Illgingerry homestead, the manager's residence, was spacious and surrounded by wide verandahs. The home was built on a
rise directly above Illgingerry Creek fifty yards distant. A windmill
lifted water from the creek up to a large tank high on the ridge
beyond the homestead from which it fed water by gravity to all
points below. From our verandah there were lovely views across the
adjoining Pine View rolling grassy downs to Black Mountain on one
side and the Cudgegong Range (Harvey's Hills) on the other,
Illgingerry Creek and homestead midway between the two. The
house was built two feet off the ground on brick and concrete with
all new modern amenities including water laid on to all points,
phone, flush toilets and 32-volt lighting plant. The mailman came to
within a hundred yards of the house every second day. I was so
pleased to at last have a lovely home for Moodgie and the children.
Being new, there was no garden, but within a week or two Moodgie
had started planting one; with her green fingers, it was soon flourish-
ing with flowering shrubs, vegetables, young fruit trees and masses of
huge strawberries. Each of the original selections which made up the
Pine Park/Illgingerry aggregation were connected by phone to the

Pine Park and Illgingerry homesteads, which were five miles apart. This meant hours on the phone every night as the men rang in to discuss that day's work and to get instructions for the next day. Mr Killen phoned me every night too, generally from Pine Park, but sometimes from Sydney or from one of their other places away out in the west somewhere, and talked for an hour at a time. The talk often had little relevance to what was happening on the place. He just seemed to be starved for a yarn. I'd often get home late, dog-tired and just have time to drag the saddle off the horse as the phone started ringing. Tea was often eaten with the receiver held to one ear. Only when the sessions stopped at about 10 o'clock was there any peace and a person could have a bath. We had no life of our own during the week and looked forward to Sundays when we were involved in tennis tournaments with neighbours at villages scattered throughout the Dubbo, Wellington and Gulgong districts.

We have always had good neighbours on the land and Clive and Marj Hough on the adjoining Pine View property were among the best. Marj was a tiny, quiet, refined little lady who fitted comfortably under Clive's huge armpits. In contrast, Clive was a hard-working uneducated yet soft, kind, giant bushman six feet four and weighing over seventeen stone. He was a man of few words — all of them with the 'h' left off the start and the 'g' left off the end. When talking about *anything*, it was always a 'he' with the 'h' missing, all in a slow old drawl. When I told him his paddock of young oats was looking great just now, and he replied, 'Yeh, 'e's a nice oat, aaaaa.' Clive came from a big family of local bush workers who rarely moved outside the Wellington and surrounding districts. He was a ringbarker, rabbiter, roo shooter, horse-breaker and shearer.

It was while shearing at the Pine View shed that Clive and Marj met. Marj's father, Hilbert Tucker, owned the place. She and Clive were young, quiet and very shy, but fell in love over smoko as she mended a tear on the knee of her jodhpurs, snagged as she got through the barbed wire fence. She had no sooner sat down on a stump with needle and thread, when Clive came round the corner of the shed with a pannikin of tea and offered to give her a hand. 'After a while he traced his finger over the V-shaped tear and said it just reminded him of a beautiful butterfly,' Marj recounted. 'That was it — I was swept off my feet!'

For years they worked hard and saved every penny, eventually buying Pine View after Hilbert and Mrs Tucker died, then two other adjoining properties for the boys as well. They were a good team — Clive and the two boys, Lawn and Lindsay, were good sheepmen and able managers and Marj's clerical skills efficiently handled all the financial side.

Being a typical bushman, Clive couldn't cope with the modern trend of women dressed in men's clothes. 'Women aughter be ladies an' men aughter be men,' he always maintained. 'You'd 'ave to undress 'alf th' buggers today an' stand 'em on their 'ead to find out which was which.'

He said — 'I don't go much on these 'ere 'alf-bred men-women done-up in men's clothes gallopin' about th' 'ills chasin' cattle and wearin' their puss out on the pummel of th' saddle'.

A year or so before Clive died, a specialist in Dubbo checked him over. When I asked what the verdict was — (he had Peripheral Neuropathy) — Clive said, 'Orrrr, I forgit wat th' bloke said it was now — I'm not much good with them big long words mate — can't git me tongue round 'em yer know. But 'e wez a big long bugger, cut 'n 'alf' — bringing his enormous arm down with a swish to show where Peripheral Neuropathy was 'cut 'n 'alf'.

As Mr Killen's health wasn't the best, and he'd been confined to bed for a week or so, I rode over one day to see how he was getting on and to give him a run-down on what was happening on the place. I think he often got lonely for a bit of male company in a house full of women! He started off telling me about a tennis party he went to as a young man from one of his father's properties years before and laughed till the tears ran down his face all the time he was telling the story. Every now and then while the story was in progress, one of the girls or Mrs Killen came into his room to see how things were going and he'd immediately put on a straight, serious face and interrupt the story with —

'Now Jim, about all the stock you've got out the back there. Do you think we'd better shift them over to some agistment country somewhere while they're still strong enough to travel?' — and on he'd go until whoever it was had left the room and then straight back to the story again!

This is how it went —

'Father and mother were away on an overseas trip and one of the neighbouring properties with some smart looking daughters, put on a big tennis party, and of course I was invited. As your appearance was more important for impressing the young ladies than how you played, I spent two or three days getting my cream gaberdine trousers washed and ironed with knife creases and ironed the creases out of a new cream Fuji silk shirt. I got a cake of Bonami and gave the sandshoes a few good coats and boiled up a pair of white socks and found a white Panama hat. I was going to be the star turn at this tennis party! The next thing was to check out the racquet and paint the strings with gut-reviver, then wash and polish the sulky and grease and wax the harness. I shined up all the nickel buckles and stud ornaments in the leather till they hurt your eyes to look at them. Father had recently bought a beautiful new high-class sulky, painted with the latest red scrolls along the sides and on the dashboard and wheel hubs. It really was a dandy turnout, upholstered in fine yearling black leather. I was all excited at the thought of arriving at the front gate of the big homestead in this sparkling new outfit with the classy chestnut thoroughbred I'd been feeding up on green oats and cracked corn, stepping out elegantly between the shafts. Bound to create a stir amongst the district's young ladies at the party. The big day at last arrived and away I went in great style, leaving before daylight as it was a fifteen-mile trip and a good few gates to open and close on the way. It wasn't long before all the green oats I'd been pouring into this flash, high-stepping filly began to have an effect. Being fresh and soft from not enough work, the horse was full of go and soon became a 'lather of sweat and froth that blew back all over me and mixed with the red dust thrown up by wheels and hooves that settled on my snow white gear. Every half mile or so, the horse cocked it's tail and blew out a shower of liquid green scours from the exhaust end that plastered the dashboard and showered me from head to foot in a bright green rain of liquid oats. I was getting to be a rare old sight but the thought of the stylish arrival at the front gate to be greeted by a wing of charming young ladies kept me going. I pulled up to open the last gate, led the horse and sulky through and tied the reins back to the wheel while closing the gate. Before I'd finished, a mob of emus with a couple of dogs in behind, charged out of the scrub full gallop, and with feathers flying, nearly ran over the outfit. The horse took fright and the reins were ripped apart as it bolted away through the scrub, then back onto the track again with me flat out and panting a long way behind. Half of my beautiful Fuji silk shirt with one sleeve still attached was left dangling from a mulga limb as it was ripped from my back as I tore past following the trailing dust of the bolting horse and sulky. Then my heart sank as I came onto trees at the side of the track with the bark knocked off them. And a bit further on, a sulky wheel was jammed half way through the fence and round the next corner, here was the whole outfit upside down across a log at the side of the track. One of the shafts was gone altogether and so was the horse and all the harness.'

'So the tennis party was temporarily forgotten while I circled the upside-down, one wheeled outfit minus the horse, a shaft and all the harness. What the hell was the old man was going to say when he came home and saw what was left of his beautiful new turnout? As this was the horse paddock, the alarming prospect was that instead of the intended grand entry to the front gate, the horse was probably already galloping past the tennis court dragging the shaft along the road through the dust attached to stray bits of flapping harness a bit further behind!'

'My ego suffered a major blow when the girls waiting at the front gate in their fashionable snow white tennis gear doubled up with roars of laughter as I came trotting up the road splattered in green scours and red dust and only half a shirt. My racquet and Panama hat had parted company with the rest of the outfit back in the scrub somewhere. So I rode home bareback with wounded pride and aching heart on my high stepping flash filly. To hell with the lot of them, I didn't want to go to that tennis party anyway!'

The bulk of the two properties once comprised well-grassed hills on slate formation with white box, yellow box, currajong, cypress pine, rough-barked apple and ironbark trees. Most of it had been picked-up and burnt years before with very little regrowth since. This was beautiful sweet country that, before the rabbit plagues took over the district, comfortably ran a sheep and a quarter to the acre on natural pastures. A number of small frontage alluvial flats along the Cudgegong River were farmed with oats and occasionally wheat, which was harvested and the grain stored in silos near the bull yards and feeding stalls to augment purchased hay and grain for the stud stock. Some fifteen years before I took over, a large quantity of green oats and wheat, seasoned with molasses, had been packed into scooped-out earth trenches as ensilage, covered with soil and left to cure. The trenches had been buried for years and nobody seemed to know exactly where they were, because most of the men of that period had either left or died.

During the 'rabbit droughts' when little edible feed was left on the place, the top foot or so of soil was scooped off and eventually the pits were found. It amazed everyone to find that after digging away the top part of ensilage, which had been ruined by moisture over the years, the rest was in excellent condition. It was a thick sticky mat of rich, nutritious, well cured fodder that smelt like rum — you could smell it half a mile away. Though the two cattle studs and the sheep section were conducted on the same aggregation, they were worked as separate units with a stud master in charge of the studs and a man-ager in charge of the sheep section, which involved practically the whole place. As all the young show bulls and some of the breeders and foster mothers were housed and fed in stalls, the only country used by the stud stock were several small paddocks along the river close to the yards and feeding stalls.

Foster mothers are good milking cows used for keeping the milk up to the young stud bulls. When the cows calved, the calves were sold or knocked on the head, and the cows, full of milk, were bailed for one of the young bulls to suck dry every morning — sometimes two or three cows to each bull if the cows were drying off. It nearly made me sick to see these great gluttonous slobbering young bulls nearly as big as the cow, butting into their udders. They nearly lifted them off the ground each time they hit them, saliva running out the corners of their mouth and forming a frothing pool under the empty udder.

This was great stone fruit country and all the old timers, stockmen and miners (there were gold-diggers' holes everywhere on the alluvial levees above the river) had a beautiful orchid of peach trees and big fig trees. Even though the huts, which had originally been at intervals along the river, had fallen down over the years, orchards often loaded with the most beautiful peaches and figs still flourished. Coming from the dry western Queensland country, I couldn't get used to just riding up and picking big ripe juicy peaches off the trees without even having to get off the horse. I'd never tasted anything so delicious. The seed was loose inside and the skin slipped away on your hands while the juice ran down your arms as you broke open the fruit. It was a very hot day the first time I came onto one of these old orchards. The huge, ripe pink peaches hung all over the trees — it was an absolute picture. I got off the horse and gorged myself full for about half an hour — couldn't seem to stop eating. After eating all I could hold, I continued mustering. What with the heat of the day and the rough motion of the horse in and out of stony gullies and up and down hills, the gutful of peaches started to blow up or whatever and I got so crook I thought I was going to die. I tied the horse up and lay down in the sandy riverbed with the most dreadful stomach pains. Serves you right for being such a pig, I kept telling myself, but I've never felt so crook and just lay there for hours. Continuing the muster after the pains wore off, on the way home I half-filled a sugar-bag with peaches to take back for Moodgie. But as home was about five miles away over rough range country, the bag over my shoulder soon became an oozing squelching mess with juice running all over me and the saddle and down the side of the horse. We were like a glue pot and I had to dump the lot. On arriving home, a sticky mess, an excited Moodgie showed me what the mailman had brought us as a treat: three enormous pink peaches — just like the ones that had nearly killed me that morning. I turned green at the very sight of them!

By the time we left Pine Park and Illgingerry the rabbit plagues had taken over both places and eaten out the country. In 1859, grazier and sportsman Thomas Austin of Barwon Park imported twenty-four English rabbits to cater for the sporting needs of his English guests. Like so many introduced plant and animal species — cats, foxes, cattle ticks and prickly pear to name but a few — they inflicted devastation on the new colony. Those two dozen rabbits found their new environment so much to their liking that their population explosion began to approach geometrical progression. With a gestation period of only one month's duration rabbits can produce several litters per year of up to six or eight young per litter. Before long, the young are producing litters too. A few rabbits in favourable conditions can rapidly breed themselves into plague proportions, running into millions in a few years. By the time we arrived in the 'rabbit-country', they'd done just that.

Rabbit plagues soon spread throughout south-eastern Australia, devastating the country wherever they went. They flattened netting fences hastily erected in the path of their migrations from place to place as they followed the storms or other rainfall occurrences. They filled paddock earth tanks as the hordes, in their hopping, crawling millions swarmed on like a wave eating every edible plant before them. They eventually contributed more to land degradation in

Australia than any other introduced pest. Rabbit plagues, in conjunction with excessive land clearing, over-stocking and general over-use
of cropping land in the wheat belt, have all combined to produce the
agricultural industry crisis we are still grappling with today.

The release of the myxomatosis virus in the early 1950s was
most successful and, at least temporarily, all but wiped out rabbits
on the tablelands. One year after we left Pine Park and Illgingerry,
our neighbour Clive Hough on the adjoining Pine View property
phoned, to tell us that the clover and marsh mallow were a foot high.
'Grass is waving up to the stirrup irons on your horse everywhere
and not a rabbit to be seen,' he reported.

With the rabbits gone, the constant pressure was immediately taken
off the previously degraded country and a period of rapid recovery
followed. Prior to this, most farmers in the hill country had to
become rabbiters. They were forced to do little except poison, trap
and ride fences and flood gates over gullies and creeks and dig out
rabbit burrows, in order to survive. This was always at the expense of
normal farming, infrastructure maintenance and stock work. As most
of the Wellington district farms were only 1,500 to 2,500 acres, with
the help of a couple of permanent rabbiters, the problem was generally kept under some sort of control. But on a place the size of Pine
Park and Illgingerry, about 17,000 acres, it was quite impossible.
Fences proved totally inadequate to contain the movement of rabbits
about the country. They had 'pop-holes' dug underneath the netting
everywhere. While you were filling in one hole, they'd be digging
several others behind you. This was a couple of years before the
release of myxomatosis. You could hit two petrol tins together and
the whole hillsides would literally move.

The country on all sides was stripped of every blade of grass till
there was nothing left but tobacco bush, moss and rabbit pills. During
heavy rain, water raced off the bare stony hills like water off the
roof of a house, taking everything before it. Sheer-sided gullies, up
to twenty feet deep in places near the river, were gouged out by the
torrent of racing water, while gullies carved up lucerne-farming

paddocks on the river flats, roads disappeared and wells were filled with rabbit pills and debris. It was impossible to get over some of the gullies on foot, let alone on a horse. I had men for days digging out fences buried underneath rabbit pills and rubbish after an inch or so of heavy rain one night.

By the late 1940s, rabbiting was a big industry in the Wellington and surrounding districts and contributed in no small way to the prosperity of the towns. We had a varying sized mob of professional rabbiters on the place most of the year trying to whittle away the ever-increasing hordes. To keep them going during the summer months when skins had no market value, the station paid threepence a scalp bonus for every rabbit poisoned. As there had to be evidence of ear numbers before payment could be made, I had the rabbiters deliver all the scalps with both ears attached in bags to the homestead, where I gave a jackaroo the job of counting them out before burning. In the hot summer weather the stink of the bags would nearly knock you down. All the fur would have come off the putrid pile of ears and they'd be crawling with maggots by the time we got them. The jackaroo eventually bailed up and refused to handle any more, so I took the average weight of each bag and paid out on that figure. But nothing works for long when you're dealing with people. It was no time before old axe heads, stones and bottles began to appear in amongst the piles of ears in the bags to be weighed out as ears at threepence a time. The gun rabbiters (and, of course, there were plenty who weren't) became spoilt in the finish — they had so much choice. They wouldn't come into an area unless they were sure of poisoning several thousand rabbits a week.

They were masters of their trade and knew little else. The bonus ceased to operate when the price of rabbit skins rose in winter. Good skins often brought high prices and plenty of rabbiters bought houses and new cars, all with rabbit money. The only method used in that country where rabbits were so thick was poisoning with strychnine and oats. It was a real education to watch the way they went about their work. The station bought first-class oats in several ton loads at a time and tins of powered Carnegie's strychnine in twelve dozen lots packed in strong wooden boxes. Both the oats and strychnine were supplied free of charge to the rabbit gangs at the station's expense to keep them going — must have nearly bankrupted them in the finish. The rabbiters boiled up the oats in forty-four-gallon drums until each grain was soft and on the point of bursting open, then poured the drums out on big tarpaulins where the oats was raked out evenly to dry in the sun. It smelt just like a big batch of rolled oats porridge — made my mouth water as I rode past. Most of the professional rabbiters worked on foot but some had an old quiet horse they used for laying the trail.

The trail was simply an unmarked course along which the poison was laid. In preparation for poisoning, the rabbits were fed with the boiled oats for two consecutive nights so they got used to eating it, then the next night was missed, and the following night the poison was laid out. If riding, one of the rabbiters sat on top of a split-bag. This was a chaff bag or corn bag with a slot cut across the middle of the bag. At each side of the saddle seat (or shoulder, if walking) both ends formed a pouch which was filled with the boiled and partially dried oats. In this hill country, the course of the trail followed a general pattern. The man on foot or horseback followed the flat country along a valley, continuously broad-casting oats backward and forward, a handful at a time each side as he rode or as he walked along. He'd turn up a spur to the top of the ridge after about half a mile, broad-casting the oats evenly all the time. Then he'd turn along the ridge for perhaps another half mile or so (depending on the length of the trail) and down another spur to the valley floor again and back along the flat to the point of commencement.

These rabbiters, generally three or four in a camp, would often have several such trails laid at a time in different parts of a couple of paddocks if these were available and free of stock. These long trails were only worked when the skins had no sale value during the summer months when no skinning was involved. Large numbers could be handled in the summer because only the scalps were taken for the bonus money. When the rabbits were skinned for their pelts during the winter and each skin put on a wire bow to dry in the sun, shorter trails were laid because skinning took much longer and only smaller numbers could be handled each day. Poisoning followed the general procedure, using the standard bush measurements for both oats and strychnine. After missing one night following the two consecutive feedings, a seven-pound treacle billy was filled with boiled oats, the same as used for feeding. One cardboard matchbox lid full of powdered strychnine (about one large heaped teaspoon) was then stirred thoroughly into the billy of boiled oats until evenly mixed.

Riding or walking exactly the same route, the rabbiter threw out a pinch of oats (about six or seven grains to the pinch), now thinly coated with pink strychnine powder, where he'd previously thrown out a handful when feeding. I'd never seen anything like it. The rabbits were there in thousands and as there was nothing much else to eat, not a grain would be left half an hour after dark. Next morning there'd be a string of dead rabbits all along the trail, as far as you could see in either direction. The men started running the trail as soon as it was light, making great piles of dead rabbits as big round as a room every few hundred yards. They'd sit down at the piles and scalp or skin rabbits for hours on end, stiff with blood and smothered with fur and flies. Most of them wouldn't even bother having a wash before going to bed or having a meal at night. They lived their whole rabbiting life almost like walking mangy fur coats plastered stiff with dried blood and covered with flies.

With such piles of dead rabbits everywhere and all the strays wandering off to die down a gully somewhere, it was only a question of time before your dogs got poisoned. It was a nightmare because you couldn't watch a dog's every movement while mustering every day and as most dogs won't work properly in a muzzle, they generally weren't used. Every time you sent your dog round a mob of sheep in that hilly country full of ridges and gullies, it was out of sight for some time — long enough to have a feed of dead rabbit on the way and before long it was throwing a fit. If you caught it on the first or even the second fit, you could always save them if you knew what to do; but after that, the fits came so close together that death generally occurred while you were still working on the dog. I always carried two small bags in the saddle pouch — one of pipe tobacco and the other of ordinary fine table salt — and had a thin piece of pine board six inches long and two inches wide hanging on the saddle 'D'. This was the survival kit and you had to work fast. The second the dog went into a fit you'd have to fly off the horse and hold the dog between your legs. The next step was to force the board through its mouth between its teeth and turn the board sideways so its mouth was wide open and you couldn't get bitten while forcing half a handful of tobacco and ordinary table salt down it's throat. It worked every time, providing the dog wasn't past about the second fit; it would be vomiting as you let it go. After bringing up everything it had just eaten, the dog carried on working all day as if nothing had happened. All my dogs had been saved a dozen times or more using this method. I'd tried many other concoctions, but this was the quickest of them all and never failed. The mixture of salt and tobacco was the result of trial and error, all the other methods being discarded in its favour. If either salt or tobacco was used independently, the result was much slower.

In spite of all the precautions, I eventually lost my best dog. It was a Sunday afternoon and, not liking to see dogs chained up all the time when not working, I let him off for a run. As I did, the phone started ringing. After finishing talking maybe ten minutes later, I raced out and whistled him up for half an hour or so before seeing him away over the other side of the creek dragging himself along in between fits while trying to reach me. I raced for the gear on the saddle but knew from one look that I was too late. While I tried frantically to ram the tobacco and salt down his throat during a continuous series of fits, he just quivered all over and his eyes glazed over as he died while I was still trying to force the concoction down his throat.

The rabbiters were the filthiest creatures imaginable. I was bad enough myself when roo shooting, but nothing even approaching this crowd.

They treated a potent poison like strychnine with such contempt, I couldn't understand how some of them didn't poison themselves. Some did, of course, as Eric Killen related:

I had one old cove in a hut down on the river long before rabbits were anything like they are now. In those days, they only poisoned with chopped-up thistle roots or plum jam. As plum jam was cheap and easy to use, old Tommy used nothing else. But he also ate it on his damper, so he had two tins going at the same time and kept both tins, the poisoned one and the good one, in a hanging safe tied to the ridge-pole in the hut to keep the ants away. I was always on to him about this silly dangerous habit, but he said he opened each tin in a different way so he'd always know which was which.

　One of the jackaroos came galloping up to the office one day yelling, 'come quick, old Tommy's down there in his hut throwing fits.' I grabbed a tin of mustard out of the store and galloped the half mile down the river to the hut and after stirring half a cup of the mustard into a pannikin of water, tried to get him to drink it. By now, the fits were coming so close together, every time I'd get the pannikin up to his mouth, he'd throw another fit. I said, 'You drink this now Tommy or you'll die.' He knew it too — but the fits were almost continuous and there was nothing I could do to make him swallow the stuff. A few minutes later, he went into a long spasm and stiffened out as he died. As Tommy's life faded away, his old lop-eared red kelpie, Rice-puddin, came and sat beside his bunk, put his head in the air and started to howl. He wouldn't leave the hut and, several days later, was found dead beside Tommy's swag. Half of him died with old Tom and the other half just faded away, from grief I suppose.

Tommy had been one of the older generation of illiterate station hands devoted to his daily routine of work on the place, preferring his own company in his slab and bark hut high up on the riverbank under a big spreading pepperina tree. His old mate, Rice-puddin, sitting alongside him at the fire while he smoked his pipe after tea before turning in, was all he seemed to need in life.

Noticing a fresh car track on the road to his hut and wanting to find out who had called in, Eric quizzed him on the brand of car, because people were known in those days by the make of their car.

This was a pretty tough question and Tommy needed time to think before answering. He scratched away at his old pipe for a good while, filled her up and began lighting her. 'Orrr,' he said, 'she wez a big bugger.' Then as an afterthought when he'd got her going properly with smoke everywhere, he added, 'With red wheels!'

This district was full of history. It had been one of the early settled regions where camps of Chinese fossickers had honeycombed the alluvial flats with diggers' holes as they rooted up the country looking for gold. There were stories of bushrangers, gold thieves and fights. It also was one of the early key pastoral districts with the remains of old slab or bark shepherds' huts scattered here and there. It was an education to read some of the things scrawled on the bark and slab walls in charcoal or blunt indelible pencil. The remains of a dog-eared faded Mae West calendar hung from a nail on the slab wall of Tommy's hut on Illgingerry Creek. Back in the 1930s, Buckley's Canadiol was all the go for treating coughs and colds — in fact, it was claimed it would cure anything from ingrown toenails to crooked noses. Some dag had scrawled across Mae West's reclining half-naked carcass stretched out on a white satin sofa in large unsteady letters, 'Before Canadiol, my missus was that crook I couldn't sleep with 'er, but after a snort or two of Canadiol any barsturd can to.' And at some later stage a footnote had been added in charcoal on the wooden slab alongside, 'Bugger yer bloody missus. I got me lamps on Mae West.'

One of the old settlers whose run had been incorporated into the Pine Park group found a convict leg iron under a tree on the bank of the Cudgegong River near the homestead. After heavy rain had washed soil away from an old campsite, I found the battered and flattened-out part of another one. Convicts were known to have escaped at times and lived for years with blacks that had befriended them. The part I found had been laboriously flattened out and eventually broken off by hammering with stones.

Pine Park and Illgingerry homesteads were five miles apart over very rough country separated in between by the Cudgegong River and Cudgegong Range. As the woolshed, yards and other facilities were all on the Pine Park side, stock had to be mustered and driven back and forth from the Illgingerry side for shearing and crutching. The station had a long bridge made of oregon timber in eight foot numbered sections, which had to be assembled for erection over the river to get stock across every time the river had a fresh in it. Anchored to trees high up on the banks by wire rope, the bridge was difficult to put up. It was an even bigger job to get stock across with the river swirling along underneath. When you'd finished with it, it had to be dismantled, sometimes several times a year in a wet season, because you never knew when another fresh was coming down the river from higher up to wash the whole thing away, and you couldn't take the risk of leaving it there.

Mustering and shifting stock from paddock to paddock every few days when the rabbit gangs finished one paddock and were up your ribs to be given a fresh one to start poisoning in straight away meant a lot of extra work. The policy was that sheep had to be shifted out before rabbit poisoning began, to avoid poisoning sheep along with the rabbits. There were rabbit duffers too. A jackaroo came back one day saying sheep were hanging round the empty water troughs because the mill wasn't pumping. I went out to assess the problem and could hardly breathe for the stink coming out of the well. Rabbit duffers had sneaked in and poisoned the creek flats surrounding the mill a couple of weeks earlier and had also poisoned some of the sheep. They had dumped them down the well to cover their tracks and it was now half full of dead woolly sheep that had reached the disintegration stage. A thick scum of maggots was literally moving on the surface. The foot valve was packed hard with loose wool on the suction side, blocking water entry to the pump. We had to use five-gallon buckets attached to long ropes to bail out the filthy stinking mess — and the well was very deep. The worst part was staying down there in the foul air long enough to fill the buckets each time so they could be hauled to the surface by the man on top. You had to get down there with ropes and buckets and fish out every last bit of wool, bones and maggots by hand, climbing to the top regularly for a spell of fresh air.

While on Pine Park, I had a couple of good lessons on quality breeding versus quality fodder intake in animals. (I'd go for the good feed every time.) All stockmen know the importance of good feed, of course, but I hadn't realised the full extent to which these extremes could affect fleece and frame development. Breeding for quality stock is important but a lot of stud breeding can be, and often is, a lot of status hogwash. Better quality stock can sometimes be found in good grade herds with a good culling policy. It was demonstrated to me in two classic examples, one with sheep and the other with cattle, and, as is so often the case, both were pure flukes.

It was just about dark one shearing time when I was yarding a big mob for drafting up next day. Forcing the wing round towards the gate with the dogs, a lamb peeled off the side of the mob and disappeared along the rails through the dust. Being so late, I kept on yarding intending to throw it over the rails into the rest of the mob when I'd finished yarding but forgot all about it and rode home late in the dark. When riding past the bull stalls about six months later, I noticed a big woolly lamb with its tail still on, as big as a full grown sheep, standing up in one of the feeding troughs, tucking into the concentrates with the young bulls.

Andy Dollar claimed it just turned up one day and started living with the bulls. 'Sleeps with them, eats with them and drinks with them — can't flog the thing away!' he said. 'We've taken it out into the paddocks and put it with other sheep, but it won't have anything to do with them, and after a day or two, it's back with the bulls again!'

It was only then I remembered the lamb that split off from the mob I was yarding for shearing. As it wouldn't leave the bulls I left it there till next shearing, then took it over and had it shorn. It was only twelve months old, but I'd never seen such a fleece. The clean even staple of medium/strong merino wool (about 64s count) was six or seven inches long and the fleece weighed out at nearly twenty pounds. The comparisons with the fleeces from the rest of the same sheep competing with rabbits for a bare starvation diet said it all. Most were dog-poor with about two inches of matted wool, much of which had died on the sheep and had to be literally plucked out by the handful because the machine couldn't be driven into the tightly compacted dead fibre. Average weight of those fleeces was just over three pounds, all because of rabbits. After shearing was finished, I sent samples of the average compacted fleeces from the starving rabbit country sheep to Mr Killen in Sydney to compare with the beautiful, evenly crimped, snow-white, six or seven inch staple from the concentrate-fed lamb, explaining the circumstances. He got as big a shock as I did and phoned straight back asking me not to show this to anyone or talk about it to other people around the district. What with the escalating running costs and the devastating drought brought on by rabbit plagues, he felt ashamed of the way things had gone on the place, from bad to worse, and there was nothing you could do about it. I'm sure the worry of all this contributed to his failing health.

The other example of the power of good feed was with young reactor bulls. All the stud bulls had to be tested regularly for CAB (contagious abortion) and TB (tuberculosis). Those showing a positive reaction to the tests (reactors) had to be isolated before coming back for retesting. Some ended up being left out in the back paddocks as culls to compete with the rest of the stock and rabbits for whatever meagre feed was available. They'd be top quality solid beef with guts about a foot off the ground when taken away from the foster mothers and concentrates. A few months later they were unrecognisable — just boof-headed hat-racks with protruding eyes and lustreless hair turned back to front. They were the same quality-bred beasts, the only difference being the quantity and quality of what went down the gullet in the form of feed — or, in this case, what didn't.

I had a funny yarn with the Prime Minister of New Zealand (Mr

Holland) early one morning. Both of us thought the other was mad. I was trying to tell him that while mustering sheep in the paddock joining his place, I noticed some of his sheep in the mob I was driving — they'd evidently got through a hole in the fence somewhere. I'm holding them in the woolshed yards I told him — can you come over to get them? Dutchy Holland owned the adjoining property and like us, was also connected to the Wellington exchange, but in Australia, not New Zealand. When I phoned, notifying him about the sheep, the girl in the exchange put me through to the wrong Holland in the wrong Wellington in the wrong country. But we had a good laugh about it — I asked him if he'd like a few head of rabbits but he reckoned he had enough problems of his own!

As the Cudgegong Range formed a high rugged divide between the two places, moving stock from one side to the other, especially if they were low in condition or had young lambs, was a slow and tiresome business. As the woolshed was on the river flats, freshly shorn sheep from the previous day had to be driven up over the range to distant paddocks on the other side. This was to keep them away from the smaller holding paddocks around the shed and yards that housed sheep waiting to be shorn, so the two lots didn't get mixed up. Crossing the range from the river flats was negotiated via a steep single-file pad along the rocky side of a narrow gorge, to a saddle between two higher points in the range. Being a narrow pad one sheep wide along the side of the very steep gorge, there was no way of hurrying the mob. You simply sat at the butt of a tree and waited half an hour or so for them to slowly string along the pad till the last one disappeared over the top. Once over the saddle, the country levelled out and the stock were more easily handled.

It was while driving several hundred freshly shorn sheep out by this route that I had a most remarkable experience. I left the shorn sheep in the yards overnight and headed off with them early next morning after shearing commenced. Before starting the climb up the gorge, which was three or four miles from the yards, a sudden heavy rain squall passed over, followed immediately by a bright cloudless sky in full sunlight. Everything was washed clean and sparkling in a rugged red and slate-grey landscape of jewels. The rays of bright sunlight lit each raindrop in pure gleaming crystal as they hung like strings of diamonds along fence wires and from the tip of every silver-grey leaf of the black-stemmed ironbarks, angophora and white box trees. Silhouetted against the purple backdrop of the retreating storm was a line of big white floaters. They delicately hung above the saddle at the rear of the storm with the winding string of freshly shorn snow-white sheep in single file, as they worked their way slowly up the gorge at the centre of the most beautiful picture I have seen. The leaders seemed to pass out of sight below the fluffy white floaters above the saddle and enter the purple veil of the distant storm.

With not the slightest breath of wind, we were a small silent group. The horse and dogs with ears pricked and unblinking eyes, and me with my pipe and thoughts, we became transfixed by the incredible silence and beauty of a scene so powerful it seemed to weigh us down. It was a long time before any of us made a move — we were all affected in the same way, by the same feelings, which anchored us to the spot as if planted there.

The Government gave notice that both Pine Park and most of Illgingerry were to be resumed by the Water Conservation and Irrigation Commission and gazetted as part of the Burrendong Dam Catchment Protection Plan. The selected dam site was at the junction of the Macquarie and Cudgegong Rivers close to the Pine Park boundary. Before resumption, both places and all fixed improvements on them had to be valued to form the basis of compensation claims against the Commission by the Killen and Marr Pastoral Company. A great deal of wrangling had gone on for the previous twelve months. The Company finally had about three months in which to reduce the rabbit numbers to a sufficiently low level to allow a growth of feed to take the bare look off the stony hills before valuation commenced. As a good body of feed was important to land valuation, rabbiting gangs were increased and we began fumigating individual burrows with chemical gas and systematically ripping the rest with tractors in an effort to reduce the rabbit population in the shortest possible time.

We sold all the remaining sheep and grade cattle off the place because very little remained except rabbits and tobacco bush. The two shorthorn studs also had to go from Pine Park. The whole out-fit was being wound-up. In the meantime Eric Killen bought an excellent small pasture-improved property on the Lachlan River flats, three miles upstream from Cowra opposite Edgel's asparagus farm, as a window for the cattle studs until a new permanent base could be found for them. Neal Killen, their only son, who had a property near Willow Tree, helped me load all the concrete water troughs from windmill watering points and cart them to the new Cowra property. It was a terrible job, as eight-foot concrete troughs are very heavy and most of the lifting was done in rain, with slippery mud everywhere making loading-up dangerous work. With both lorries slipping and sliding on the narrow paddock tracks in the ranges, and bogged much of the time in the lower country, it took several days to get the loads off the place. It was sad to see such beautiful sweet currajong and white box slate country abandoned under such conditions and in such a state. It ran a flock of 25,000 head of pure Peppin blood merino sheep and the two top shorthorn cattle studs in the country before the rabbit plagues arrived. The whole Pine Park homestead, gardens and out-building complex eventually went under a hundred and thirty feet of water when the Burrendong Dam filled.

While at Illgingerry, Ian, third in the family, was born in Wellington in 1950. This was a very wet season with numerous floods in Illgingerry Creek, making it difficult to leave the property. When Moodgie had to be rushed into the Wellington Hospital to have the baby, the creek was half a banker and running very strongly. As it was pitch dark and pouring rain, neighbours from an adjoining property came down to the other side of the creek and shone car lights on the crossing, already bogged up with mud and badly washed out. I put the chains on the utility but got bogged before we even reached the creek. So I got Moodgie up on the seat of the tractor, stood on the turning brake pedal on the upstream side, put the tractor in second gear and the steering wheel on full lock upstream and opened the throttle full bore. Holding Moodgie on the seat as best I could with the raging water halfway up the gear lever, I fought to keep the front wheels on full lock upstream. We were washed well downstream for a while, with Moodgie hanging on to the dashboard as if frozen there. It was a relief when we made the other bank, with the upstream rear wheel locked and the other eating into the mud and stones, while trying to stop the whole outfit going sideways down the creek with the flood.

Not long after Moodgie's return from hospital with Ian, the new baby, we heard that her father, who'd not been well for some time, had died suddenly in the Lismore Base Hospital. This was a great shock and a very difficult time for her, with three young children and me away from home each day organising work with all the men on the place.

A manager's job on a grazing and farming property of this size was no easy task. So much was happening all the time which couldn't be put off, and relationships between the men and between individual men and me had to be kept on an even keel. With the exception of one jackaroo, I was by far the youngest person on the place. I was twenty-six and had put my age up to twenty-eight to have a better chance of getting the job. Some of the men resented the fact that I'd been brought in from another State and put in charge of them and the place when they were so much older and had been there for years. In these circumstances, your home life and family often had to take second place to the smooth and efficient running of the property. This was often a sore point with both of us, but there wasn't much we could do about it.

We stayed on until the valuation of both places was completed in conjunction with local agents, George Paul and Co. from Wellington, and the official Government valuer and representative, Mr Brown from Canberra. Mr Brown was one of Nature's old time gentlemen with not a single particle of bigotry or humbug in his entire make-up. With a mind as keen as mustard, he was interested in everything from classical music to socialism and from the power of the mind to soil conservation. A recently retired High Court Judge, he said he got sick of sitting on the Bench day after day listening to evidence and getting fat. He was a qualified surveyor in the early part of his life before studying Law and, since retirement, took on odd surveys and valuation jobs for the Survey Office and Valuer General's Department to keep his body active and his mind alert. We became good friends during his short month or so stay with us in our home at Illgingerry. He was meticulously thorough in every aspect of the valuation. I had to take him round fences to check their condition and get their bearings and inspect all the other improvements and observe the state of the country from all angles. We seemed to have so much in common and I've always felt honoured to have worked with him throughout the valuation and to have got to know him so well in that short time. Valuing a complex farming, grazing and stud stock place of this size was a big job. When I heard the constant arguing between George Paul and Mr Brown over the value of buildings, yards and watering points, I was glad the final decision was theirs and not mine — though they often did ask me what I thought. There were five houses including the two homesteads, many huts and sheds, silos, woolshed, yards and plant and a host of other buildings.

When it came to valuing the homestead gardens, none of us had any idea what value to put on it. It was a huge garden but it couldn't be taken away and put somewhere else, so what price *could* you put on it? I think George Paul valued it at 65 pounds and Mr Brown, after a lot of thought, went a bit higher with the sum of 85 pounds. I went in between with 75 pounds. When I phoned Mr Killen in Sydney with these figures, he declared them ridiculous. There were hundreds of pounds worth of bulbs in the beds around the sun room alone, he insisted, and dispatched a landscape architect to put a proper valuation on it all. Mr Brown told me later that the garden had been valued at, I think, 970 pounds! No wonder old Eric put on a performance.

I appreciated very much a book Mr Brown gave me when he left. It was one of the very early manuals on soil conservation published by the Agricultural Division of the Rural Bank in league with the Soil Conservation Service. I've only recently handed it on to our son David who is now involved in some of this type of work with his students.

Moodgie's heart was always back on the North Coast around Lismore where she'd grown up and gone to school and on to university, so we decided to stay with Moodgie's mother until we could find a suitable property in the area to buy.

Moodgie and I went back to visit the old Pine Park homestead site in 1995, camping with our former kind neighbours Clive and Marj Hough on their adjoining property Pine View, and again in 1998, a couple of years after Clive had died. The Burrendong Dam, one of the largest in the country, some seven and a half times the volume of the Sydney Harbour (the standard comparison for dam capacities!), was nearly dry after a prolonged drought. We looked out over the expanse of dry cracked mud on the floor of the empty dam at the abandoned Pine Park homestead complex on the other side. The sheep and cattle yards, lanes and paddock fence posts that had been covered by a 130 feet of water for the past forty years, were standing high and dry like ghosts from the past. All the big dead pines along the homestead drive, and the tall stark trunk of a big palm tree that grew beside the front entrance, were standing proudly erect like white beacons from the past as if to beckon the way. All was clearly visible for the first time as the water dried back and exposed the old Pine Park homestead and out-building foundations. Wandering through the ruins, I kicked off the dry cracked mud that had covered the coloured ceramic tiles and red concrete floors and walkways for so long. It was like returning from the dead — everyone was gone but the original atmosphere and memories still vividly remained. Walking round the ruins and across the dining room and lounge room floor to the room we stayed in when we first went there from Sydney gave me an uneasy feeling — like prying into someone else's privacy, their secret places. For a brief moment it all came back to life, though Mr and Mrs Killen were long since dead. I visualised people scurrying about the homestead and cattle yards, and the old steam engine blowing steam, while dust rose from the woolshed yards as freshly shorn sheep were counted out of the let-go pens and stud cattle were being fed over in the feeding stalls. It all had a most unreal feeling about it. I couldn't help thinking: Man proposes, God disposes.

CHAPTER 17

A New Outlook

As Moodgie and I were reluctant to start all over again at Clonard, Dad and Doolie, after battling to keep the place going for years, decided to get out too. The place was put on the market and sold almost before we had time to digest what had happened. So with Moodgie and the children temporarily settled with her mother in Lismore, I went out to help Dad give delivery of the place and muster the stock for sale. I expected to be out there for about a month but ended up stranded at Clonard for three months, with more water over the country than anyone had ever seen before.

I could get no further than St George as the Balonne River was feet deep over the bridge. The only way across the flooded river was by rowing boat. As I looked out over the sea of swirling muddy water, the boat could be seen coming back in the distance from the other side with people sitting up in it. The people turned out to be my brother Frank and his wife Pam on their way back to Brisbane after a short holiday with Pappy and Doolie. They left the station utility on the other side of the flood for me to take back. Leaving my utility in someone's back yard, we loaded the small boat to get my gear across and, just in case, I threw in my heavy skid chains, axe and shovel as well. Before Boolba, I ran into heavy storm rain, which set in during the night with sheets of water running everywhere. I put the chains on before tackling the brigalow and belah gilgai country in Boomerang Reserve. The utility finally came to a halt in a gilgai down in the water table with the axle buried in mud underneath.

Nothing I could do without a light in the pitch dark, so I curled up on the seat listening to rain thundering down on the roof. (Horrible sound when miles from nowhere by yourself without tucker and hopelessly bogged.) My memory went back to an earlier time when similarly bogged in the old Auburn between Talwood and Boomi, only fortunately there was no river here to flood me out this time. It was all surface water running everywhere but was nearly as bad. By mid-morning the rain had eased off. As Dad had put in the winch, I hooked one end to the front of the car and the other to the iron telephone post of the Bollon/St George telephone line, the only thing close enough for the wire rope to reach. After winding away for ages and out of rope, I went back to see how far the car had been pulled and was alarmed to see it hadn't moved at all. I'd been dragging the telephone post through the waterlogged black soil and it was now nearly three feet out of line! It stayed that way for years until new posts were put in.

I was about to start walking when Dad and our neighbours arrived in a truck. Knowing I'd left town the day before, they thought they'd find me on Boomerang Reserve. Nobody could get through from either direction and as the rain started again, we left the utility where it was bogged and all came back the following week to winch it out. Everything came to a standstill and it seemed the rain would never stop. Vehicles were bogged in their garages under houses and horses and cattle were bogged in the paddocks, while the mosquitoes and sandflies almost ate us alive and swarms of pestering little bush flies nearly drove us and the horses mad. Green feed was knee-high everywhere and even the spinifex, now in full seed, was over the top of six-foot dog netting fences. We started mustering for delivery. The horses bogged and knocked up. I tried counting the few hundred sheep we'd mustered, but the ground turned to jelly all round the counting gate with sheep struggling over the top of one another half buried in squelching mud. So we waited for a few more weeks of sun.

The traffic bridge over the Balonne River at St George was washed away, cutting all access to the east and nothing could get along the roads to the west or south either.

All the flooded channel country for miles around Dirranbandi was under water and remained so for several weeks. The only river crossing near St George was Sturt's Stony Crossing, which was twenty feet under water and was impassable for three months. With no way of getting out and nothing to do until the country dried out, I started roo shooting on foot and wherever a horse could go without getting bogged. As skin prices were three times higher than in previous years when I was shooting, I made more money from skins in that couple of months than I'd made in the previous twelve. When the floods drained off the Culgoa channels and flood plains, we loaded Dad and Doolie's possessions on a lorry to be railed from Dirranbandi to Brisbane. Taking the light stuff with us in the two utilities, we crossed the Balonne River at Sturt's Stony Crossing near St George with water halfway up the doors and said goodbye to Clonard for the last time.

I returned to Illgingerry to collect the rest of our gear and belongings before starting to look for a place to buy so we could get back on the land again. I cleaned up the house and garden and recharged all the lighting-plant batteries and loaded the Stewart utility. I thought we'd taken most of our stuff on previous loads but was now overloaded as the last bits were rammed in. This always happens. You think there's nothing much left until you begin getting all the stray bits and pieces together — and, of course, you can't do without *any* of it. Anyway the job at last was done and I headed off for Lismore to meet up with Moodgie and the children, arriving there two days and two new tyres later. The passenger side in front of the utility was loaded to the roof so my two dogs were tied in the back under a tarp with just the tip of their noses poking out. It was so hot and stifling and both dogs were choking in thick dust and whining to be let out. So, out of kindness to them, I let them ride out on top of the load for short intervals of fresh air. The dirt road between Coolah and

Gunnedah was so rough and dusty, with great potholes and corruga-
tions, that two of the tyres blew out under the heavy load. When I
stopped for the second blow-out, I found poor old Ginger, my
favourite of the two border collies, had over-balanced, fallen off the
load and been dragged by his chain for some distance. He was still
alive and breathing and wagged his tail as I picked him up, but died
shortly afterwards. Great sadness and many tears, for it had been my
fault. I buried him beside cypress pine and white box trees at the base
of a little pointed pine hill near the road some 20 miles out of
Gunnedah. I still stop the car there for a few minutes silent thought
whenever I pass that way. Ginger was a kelpie/border collie cross —
a wonderfully kind mate and a sheep dog a long way above the average. Bell, my last border collie, died from tick paralysis only days after
unloading our stuff at Moodgie's parent's place in Lismore. So I had
lost all my dogs in a matter of months.

I knew Moodgie's favourite place was the North Coast and since she
had introduced me to this area before we were married, I began to
have similar feelings about it. So with wool prices booming (up to
240 pence a pound) and western sheep country now well outside our
financial capability, we began looking for cheaper country closer in.
After inspecting numerous farms we decided on a very cheap run-
down abandoned dairy farm between Kyogle and Nimbin. From all
parts of the property were magnificent views of the mountains at
each side of the Tweed Valley and Mt Warning and Numinbah Gap in
the Border Ranges at the centre, like a framed picture. Also, a little
one-teacher school and teacher's residence was on top of the hill a
quarter of a mile from the house. With four young children of school
age, this was a big advantage.

  As fat lamb prices had been high for a number of years and looked
like holding up, we decided to breed Romney Marsh sheep. This
breed would probably handle the wet humid climate as well as any of
the other British breeds and produce a higher priced fleece than

other crossbred types. I knew nothing about dairy farming and it didn't appeal to me much as an occupation either. Also the country on the North Coast certainly wasn't cereal-cropping agricultural country, so on a farm of 320 acres and limited finance, there were few options. While prices of wool and fat lambs held up, we'd run sheep on one side of the place and beef cattle on the other. This arrangement would probably be as good as anything else — there obviously wasn't going to be a fortune in any of it, but I preferred to accept a lower income than to work for someone else.

There were few better places which offered so many choices in ways to make a living by working for yourself as did this area of the Northern Rivers, we discovered.

When I started buying cattle through Ray Gordon and Sons in Lismore, Tim Gordon told me: 'You won't find any of your big western sheep station millionaires here, Jim, but you'll find everyone's got a bob. The cockies run those cows through the yards twice a day and there's a bob in 'em every time they hunt the last one out the gate.'

High rainfall, good water and predominantly young basalt soils created the kind of diversity which allowed the country to be successfully subdivided into small farms with potential to enjoy similar amenities to those in the villages and towns that sprung up every few miles.

Italian and young Australian smallcrop farmers began renting portions of traditional dairy farms and building packing sheds. Many of the Italians worked together as families and shared the produce and expenses. We were puzzled at first by lights that danced about the hills all night. Only much later did we realise what great small-crop farmers the Italians were. When most Australian cockies were sleeping on cold frosty winter nights, the Italian farmers were walking the hills with hurricane lights pegging out all the little warm, frost-free pockets of country. The colder and frostier the night, the easier it was to pick them out. As they moved about the country they came on small but quite warm airpockets like a vacuum in amongst the frost, generally in hollows along hill slopes. They pegged out these small areas, then approached the farmer to rent each little plot to grow vegetables susceptible to frosting that could not be grown on the alluvial creek and river flats. This gave them a head start in the markets.

I had the first Ferguson tractor and hydraulic gear in the district and was pleased to help these hard-working smallcrop growers who had so little to start off with. One of these families of growers was Charlie and Mrs Yuss, both Italians in their late twenties. Their eldest boy, Joseph, was at school with our children and very bright too. They started growing tomatoes, beans and peas on their little plot several miles from our place. It was obvious they didn't have much and were just struggling along although all worked hard and for long hours — Joseph, too, as soon as school was over. Charlie very timidly asked if he could pay me in instalments to dig the holes for his new fences with my Ferguson posthole digger and cart all the posts on to the line in the trailer. I was pleased to help, of course, and wouldn't take any money for the work because they had so little. To say thankyou they insisted on putting on a huge dinner and kept handing out all kinds of liqueurs. I tried to politely explain that I was not a drinker, but felt obliged to sample this and that special drink. Every time I took a sip, I could feel tingles running right through my body and rattling up and down my legs. Don't know how I ever got out of the room — it seemed to be all doors and huge windows that were going up and down and in and out. The next thing I remember was being on the tractor and trying to work out which way to follow the fence to get home. The thing seemed to be running upside down on its back without wheels. How I ever got home I have no idea!

A little later we were swamped by a big cyclone (2,960 points of rain at nearby Mt Burrell in one day and one night). Enormous floods and landslips everywhere. Right in the middle of it all, with visibility down to about a hundred yards, the Yuss family arrived like drowned rats. A big landslip had opened up a huge crack almost a foot wide right across the hillside within a couple of yards of their small house, so they left in a hurry without anything. They stayed in our home until the cyclone was over and I could take them all home. Fortunately, unlike so many other landslips that took whole hillsides all the way down to the bottom of the valley, this one didn't go any further.

Although an enormous amount of work was obviously needed to turn our new farm into the kind of place we wanted, the fact that a vehicle could be driven over most of it was a big advantage in this hilly country. Also, clear sweet water gurgled along in all the creeks, shaded by rainforest trees towered over by tall hoop pines. It was in fact a very scenic farm. The purchase price was only four thousand five hundred pounds, walk in walk out, most of the money coming from the sale of Clonard. We developed and worked this farm for eight memorable years, becoming very much part of this dairy farming community. We weren't accepted for a long time, because we'd broken into their quiet, simple and fairly poverty-stricken lives (by comparison) from the inland grazing country. This, to them, meant wealth and toffy noses — things instinctively to be shied away from at all costs. But, carefully sounding us out in subtle little ways that we took very seriously, they gradually came round to accepting us as one of them. From then on, we all became friends, their simple kindness and acts of generosity in so many ways winning us over completely.

They were amongst the most congenial neighbours we ever had in all our time on the land. They were a happy, extremely funny group. Poor as they were, they saw the funny side of everything, and, whether you felt like laughing or not, you were caught up in the constant mirth and pranks.

At our first school function, just after we bought the place, one of the farming women, rough as bags, but with a heart of pure gold, came forward to introduce herself.

'Are yous religious?' she asked.

When we said we weren't, she replied: 'Well, that's all right then, because I wes jist goin' to tell yers there's only two things interests men — one's their belly and the other's wot hangs on the end of it!'

Our new farm was a long-neglected mess. Everything on the place was falling down, including the big old spacious homestead built from local teak and red cedar. One glance told of a prosperous past when

all was new and the lovely garden, along with the rockery with foun-
tain and fishpond, had created a former showplace. Outbuildings,
saw-bench, slab and picket fences, old concrete paths, water troughs,
bridges and a gravel quarry were further evidence of the industry and
workmanship of old Ed Parry who took up the country. Almost as if
to emphasise the two extremes, a couple of young locals had 'looked
after the place' until we bought it. Too lazy to cut a bit of wood for
the stove, they'd started on the house, pulling off the verandah rail-
ings and anything else that looked loose enough to be shifted without
using too much energy before moving on to the wooden fence and
gates surrounding the house. The dilapidated dairy and pigsty on the
other side of the creek had been considered too far away, so they'd
run a length of netting around the house stumps, which were about
three feet high, and put in a mob of pigs underneath, pulling up a few
floorboards through which to pour their slops and corn cobs. The old
leaning wood and galvanised iron thunderbox out the back near the
woodpile had seemed too far in the rain too, so what should have
gone into it had probably dropped straight down the hole for the pigs
to clean up.

Dad came down from Brisbane and camped with me to help clean
things up. The whole house and underneath too stank like a vast rubbish tip and was literally crawling with rats and fleas. Until everything
was put in order and the house painted inside and out, I didn't want
Moodgie and the children anywhere near the place. But the land was
good and getting it cheap allowed us to rebuild, re-fence and improve
the farm. Every day stray horses turned up and wandered aimlessly
around the house, eating everything they could find. You couldn't
leave a loaf of bread or a box of groceries anywhere for five minutes
before it was torn to pieces and everything inside was eaten except
tins and bottles.

One of the neighbours, Jim Browning, rode over to introduce himself. He told me not to worry any longer because a mate of his was a

champion with a lifetime's experience of shifting horses and all those sorts of unwanted things. This turned out to be Jim's uncle, Freddy Grey, who lived with Jim and his wife, Nessie, on the adjoining farm.

So, a bit later, over rides a shrivelled-up, hook-nosed scrawny, cockatoo-like old cockie, answering the title of one Freddy Grey. He was about six foot three long, as poor as a crow, and half turpsed-up with rum. A greenish-brown high-water mark round his legs between ankles and knees showed the depth of cow dung and mud in the milking yards. The cockies never knew the feel of a pair of boots and all went barefoot except at funerals, dance hall functions or calf days at the saleyards when they all went to town. Even then, the boots had a free ride in and were pulled on with agony just long enough to see the ordeal through, then another free ride home again as soon as the show was over.

Freddy climbed unsteadily off the horse, nearly fell down a couple of times, then staggered forth with an out-stretched hand dangling from the end of a long skinny arm, a bit like an emu's leg. Pappy couldn't believe it — just stood there with his mouth open — hadn't seen such a specimen since the old days!

'Jimmy tells me yer bin 'avin' a bit er trouble with 'orses, matie,' said Freddy, addressing me. 'That no bloody good — man got enough to put up with without them buggers hangin' around under yer bloody feet all day an' gittin' in th' road.'

True, I thought.

'I'd fix 'em up for yer meself, matie, only I'm 'avin a bit of a blow gist now.' (Freddy's 'bits er blows', we found later, were generally under a shady tree down on the creek bank surrounded by empty beer bottles!), 'But yer can do it yerself easy enough, yer know, matie. Jis go down [to Nimbin] and tell Johnny Winning [the chemist] to give you a bottle of Sendem, matie.'

'What the blazes is Sendem?' I asked.

'Buggered if I know, matie, but you jist run a 'orse inter a corner an' ketch 'im. Tie 'im up an' lift 'is tail over yer shoulder an' shake a bit outer the bottle on 'is arse'ole. But by crise, matie, git outer his bloody road quick — it'll lift 'im all right — 'e'll travel real quick an' yer won't never see 'im no more.'

Hell, I thought, what a mighty idea and easy too!

So down I went to see Johnny Winning, careful not to let on I was a new chum to all these cunning cockies' devices for 'shiftin' bloody 'orses'. I leaned on the counter, pushed my hat back and started to light my pipe. Out came an immaculate looking gentleman, all togged up in a starched white coat and looking very professional — not a bit like the Johnny Winning I was expecting to see. Of course, what I didn't know — and what Freddy didn't know either — was that this was a Sydney chemist relieving while Johnny was away on holidays, a bigger new chum than I was.

Unaware of this, I looked at him through the smoke and said in the local lingo, 'Give us a bottle er Sendem, will yer, mate.'

He looked at me vacantly for a bit and asked, 'A bottle of what?'

'Sendem, mate, jist a bottle er Sendem.'

'*Sendem*, never heard of it. What's it look like?'

'Buggered if I know.'

'Well how do you spell it?'

'Buggered if I know — S-E-N-D-E-M, I suppose.'

'New one on me,' he said. 'You'd better get the label off the old bottle and bring it in — what's it for? Is it an ointment or do you take it or sniff it up your nose?'

'No, mate,' I said, 'you just sprinkle it on a horse's arse and he travels!'

'Oh, that's a freezing agent,' he said, when I took the label back. 'I'll soon make you up a bottle of that.'

So away I went eager to try it out. I had no trouble finding a candidate. At the back of the house was a big old rangy looking half-draught black horse with two white hind legs, snoring off under a silky oak tree with a mob of flies hanging out the corner of his watery eyes. I put the halter on him and tied him to the tree, then walked round the back and lifted his tail over my shoulder as directed. Then, following instructions, shook some of the innocent-looking fluid in the bottle over his arse and dragged the halter off in a hurry before the action started. But nothing happened. He just stood there with a stupid look on his dopey face. So I gave him a stripe over the butt end with the halter and he trotted away along the track leading down the hill towards Webster's Creek, every now and then giving his tail a bit of a twitch as he happily trotted along. I thought, this is just a hoax — bloke might as well have used bore water.

Then all hell suddenly cut loose. Hooves on the end of long black and white legs began clattering and rattling together about six feet over the top of his head as he began kicking up and farting. *Fart*, you never heard anything like it in all your life. Propelled along rocket-fashion by the frightening roars exploding from the exhaust end and the clatter of hocks, he charged off like a black dart. A couple of dogs came over the brow of the hill to investigate the roaring farts and dust and promptly joined in the race. He was just hitting top speed when the creek loomed ahead. It had a sheer drop of eight feet off the bank to twenty yards of water-worn stones in the creek bed below. He flew off the bank at about thirty miles an hour with a clatter of stones as he hit the middle of the creek and then silence. I went cold with panic — hell, he's broken his blessed neck and I figured he was one of the neighbour's cart horses too, he was so quiet. Sneaking down as if someone was watching me all the time, I gingerly peeped over the bank expecting to see him stretched out there among the stones. But no, not a sign of him and not a sound either.

So I waited, and, sure enough, early next morning a stranger arrived on the scene with a mob of dogs —

'Yer woulden a see ole Darkie over 'ere pokin' about, would yer, mate?'

'Old Darkie, who's he?' I asked, acting all innocent.

'Orrr, 'es me ole black horse that pulls th' slide an' me cream out to th' road — 'e always comes up to th' kitchen winder about daylight an' Vera gives 'im a bit of bread t'eat through the winder. Don't seem to be about this morning.'

In Darkie's headlong flight and broadjump off the bank and

through the loose stones on the creek bed, he'd kept on going. Ploughing his way through the dense lantana thicket along the creek, he planted up in the rainforest running back into the Tweed Range and didn't show up for days. When he did, nobody could get a halter or a bridle near him — he'd just kick up and fart in your face and take off. As Freddy forecast, we never saw hide nor hair of him again!

I soon found that Sendem was Jim's and Freddy's chief entertainment, much better than picture shows and things that other *Homo sapiens* often found so appealing — and always accompanied by roars of laughter as they relived their latest conquest. They were a terrible pair of larrikins, always full of mirth and mischief, and had Sendem down to a fine art — there was practically nothing in the district they hadn't tried it out on. Fowls just kicked about, squawked and then fainted. Goats galloped round the yard on their front legs with their back ones stuck out in front beside their cheeks as they rubbed their arse along through the grass. Pigs charged up and down the troughs kicking up and squealing. Dogs took off across the flat with bristles standing on end, at speeds they hadn't known they possessed — and we've seen what happened to 'orses!

We bought 330 Romney Marsh stud ewes from Colonel White's Romney Marsh and Aberdeen Angus 'Bald Blair' stud, between Guyra and Ebor. Two semitrailers left with the sheep at night, expecting to arrive mid-afternoon the next day. But storm rain had fallen over the range between our farm and Kyogle and the heavily laden lorries with wheels skidding on the slippery clay and gravel road surface couldn't get up the range. They eventually phoned to say they were being towed up by a tractor and wouldn't arrive till late that night. Hoping to keep the dingoes away, we unloaded the sheep at last in netted paddocks and began our course of disaster with sheep. From the very beginning we had trouble with dingoes and stray dogs killing lambs and tearing grown sheep about. They had started on the cattle too. Then the tick eradication campaign was launched which meant dipping everything on the place except the kids and ourselves every second week. Full-wool stud ewes, many with twin lambs inside, seemed just as happy sinking to the bottom of the dip and staying there as they did coming out the other end. We battled on for about eighteen months but, with wool prices rapidly falling, the writing was on the wall. Not wanting to move yet again after having just netted the boundary with expensive imported Belgian netting, we sold the sheep in twos and threes and in little lots as lawnmowers. What we couldn't sell we ate until we'd worked our way through the last few, and then shifted over to beef cattle, dairying and pigs.

When we took delivery, the farm was overgrown with scrub and most of the old rusty barbed wire fences had fallen down with wire tangled up in lantana and cockspur thickets. So when taking delivery, you could only count the cattle as they charged from one patch of scrub to the next, hoping you hadn't counted the same ones twice.

I bought a new wheel tractor and all the necessary hydraulically operated implement attachments and a trailer for carting fence posts and rails and ploughing up small paddocks for oats and ryegrass. With heavy dews on the compacted paspalum pastures on the hillsides, wheel tractors are extremely dangerous when pulling trailers, especially if heavily loaded with posts. You can't touch the brakes because this locks the wheels. The only way is in low gear to keep the wheels slowly turning to avoid complete loss of traction. But if the grade is steep and the grass wet, the outfit just takes off with both back wheels skidding and the further you go the faster you go with no control over the machine. You have two alternatives: bail out and let the lot pile up in a heap at the bottom, or open the throttle to keep the wheels turning while holding the tractor in a straight line and ride her out hoping she'll still be on her feet when you hit the flat at the bottom. After a few too many close shaves, I decided to buy a Caterpillar bulldozer to drag the trailer loaded with posts. Also I'd built up a spray plant with drums of hormone spray attached and with 100 yards of hose on both sides. This was dragged up and down the hills to poison regrowth after clearing the scrub. It also safely pulled the big wheeled fertiliser spreader up and down the steep hills and the renovator to prepare the country for improved pastures after clearing. As regrowth thickened up in the cleared areas, these were hormone-sprayed and the place was fenced into seventeen paddocks. We installed a new pumping plant on one of the five creeks and a large holding tank in a high central position from which water gravitated to every paddock, the homestead and dairy.

Shifting over from sheep to beef cattle, dairying and pigs meant starting from scratch. We had to build a new dairy and covered-in concrete yard, outside holding yards and loading ramp, new combined piggery and grain shed, all with new cement floors to government specifications. Then there was the purchase and installation of new engine, vacuum pump and milking machines, separator, stainless steel vat and all the additional gear necessary to start a modern dairy. Everything had to be new as all the old stuff had fallen down and had to be cleaned away before we could start rebuilding. It would have been much easier if we'd been able to just buy a block of undeveloped country with nothing on it at all. We went to several clearing-out sales and bought sixty or seventy good quality dairy cows, a couple of stud bulls and started producing.

We hadn't seen the inside of a dairy before and knew nothing about machine-milking, so it was all a new adventure — and how. I was feeding the pigs one day and saw maggots along the drainage trench where water flowed away after the pigpens were cleaned out. After a long experience with sheep and maggots I thought they might start on the pigs. In a bit of a panic I caught a horse and galloped over to Jim Browning's farm to see if he had maggots there too and to ask what he did to get rid of them. Even though we went to no end of trouble to keep everything spotless, I began to feel guilty that the yards and floors may have been dirty after all!

'Have you blokes got maggots in your pig yards, Jim?' I asked.

'Orr, bloody maggots,' he said — 'I'll give you a wheelbarrow full of th' bastards if you like and, if that's not enough, I'll give you another one out of the dairy too!'

I soon learned that dairying, pigs and maggots went together. There was nothing you could do about it because everything was wet and sloppy outside in the long kikuyu grass where the yard cleanings drained away when dairy and pigsties were washed out every morning. Blowflies were simply part of the game as well.

David, our youngest, was born in Kyogle in 1953. Young as the children were, they were a great help on the farm. Keith always drove the cows into a new paddock after each milking and helped take the cream cans out to the road in the tractor. Lyn and Ian checked the water troughs and threw in corncobs for the pigs as skim milk was pumped from the dairy 100 yards to the pigsty. David often came with me on the bulldozer while I was clearing country under contract. When he went to sleep, I put him on a corn bag under a bush, and told him not to move.

'That's what will happen to you, mate, if you shift off that bag and I don't see you,' I said, showing him logs crushed flat by the tracks.

He didn't ever leave that bag, and when awake, just sat there until I knocked off for lunch and we had the big thermos of soup Moodgie had prepared for us. Even though she had so much other work to take up her time, especially establishing a garden and keeping fowls and ducks, Moodgie was always there at milking time, as were the older children. We couldn't have got by without them. Lyn especially, even though she was such a little thing, had excellent hands with animals and loved being with them. She knew all their names, and there were a lot of them. I can't remember her missing a single milking.

Some city people came to visit us one time. Lyn was showing them all the young pigs. Straight out of the city, immaculately dressed and with little clean pink fingers holding her nose, one woman said, 'Dear me, don't they smell?' A little voice down below responded, 'Yes, that's why they call them pigs!'

A cranky old cow with a young calf took to David one morning as he was on his way from the house to the dairy. He was very small but could run like a rabbit. He was poking along minding his own business, when there was a snort from behind. I opened the door for some reason and David flew through the opening like a dart, with so much pace up he nearly went out the other side of the dairy. The cow propped alongside me at the open door with a silly look on her face. The calf hadn't moved!

For about a week, the radio had been reminding everyone to watch the western sky, where it should be possible, if there were no clouds at night, to see the first satellite, Sputnik 1, as it started to orbit the earth. Few people, including us, believed it was possible — sounded like science fiction stuff that was exciting to read or dream about, but nothing more. As it was a glorious chilly cloudless night, we all climbed a hill near the house, got a good fire going in a big log and cooked a pile of potatoes in the coals to eat with butter, salt and pepper while we kept vigil. The only sounds were the chirp of crickets and the croak of frogs down in the creek and the occasional swish of an owl's wings as it scurried past in the dark. Full of excitement because they'd heard all about the satellite at school, the children, in their pyjamas, stood around the fire with us, eating potatoes, with eyes glued to the western sky. It was certainly a night to remember. The crystal clear night was studded with a million brilliant stars. With not the slightest breath of wind and smoke from the log trailing skywards like lengths of wispy rope, you felt you could almost reach up and pluck out each twinkling little gem and put it in the palm of your hand for a better look. Don't know who saw it first, but, at last, there at the rim of the western horizon appeared a tiny red light, slowly growing upwards like a living plant reaching for the sun as it rose. We silently watched in disbelief as the tiny red beacon continued its unwavering course across the sky above us and gently subsided, ever so slowly, into the east above the Pacific Ocean.

We'd hear packs of hunting dogs chasing the cattle around the paddocks at night. Some of the big yearlings had even been pulled down with holes eaten out of them and tear marks from enormous teeth across their back. I used to fire the .303 in the air to scare them away, but very often we didn't hear them and only saw the evidence next

morning. The dogs crawled and scratched their way under the netting on creek crossings. Every time it rained, and there was no
shortage of that with a 60- or 70-inch rainfall, the netting was washed
out and the dogs crawled in underneath. If the sheep were to survive
more than a few months, I'd have to start poisoning. So I phoned the
Nimbin Police who advised me to put a notice in the paper warning
neighbours to tie their dogs up, and then to be on the safe side, to
ring them up as well or ride over and tell them. That would put me
in the clear and I could start poisoning straight away.

The only ones not on the phone were a couple of beat-up share
farmers on derelict farms about a mile away, so I rode over and told
them to keep their dogs chained up at night while I was poisoning.
Like most share farmers, they had a hell of a swag of dogs (most of
them useless), racing around everywhere barking and jumping all
over you, and probably never fed either.

'Our bloody dorgs aren't eatin' your bloody sheep, mate,' they
protested. 'They're at th' back er th' 'ouse wen we go ter bed an' the
buggers is still there wen we git up at daylight ter git th' cows — they
never ever leave 'ome.'

Yes, I'd heard it all before. So I killed a couple of big calves and
dragged them all round the farm with the tractor, chopping off sections on the way and poisoning each bait with strychnine I'd brought
with me from the Illgingerry rabbit country. Caught the horse at daylight next morning and galloped round the trail hoping I'd got a
couple of dingoes, but nearly passed out when I came to the first calf
leg that had four dogs dead on it and three of them had collars on.
At the next bait were a couple of half-bred beagles, then a bit further
along on the next bait were another four or five dogs, some with bits
of hemp rope round their necks. Strike, there's going to be trouble
here, I thought. By the time I'd ridden right round, I counted fourteen dogs and none of them was a dingo. Most were local dogs that
met up at night and hunted in packs. In a bit of a panic, I dragged
them all together and rolled the pile down a big crack in a landslip
near the boundary fence and covered the pile with sticks and

branches and rode home to await the storm — which wasn't long coming. We'd not long finished breakfast when the first of them rode up — with no dogs, the first thing I noticed.

What they weren't going to do to me was nobody's business. They got onto the police sergeant 'Bloody Gasteen's poisonin' all our bloody dorgs.'

'How many of yours has he poisoned?' the sergeant asked.

'Twelve — good dorgs too.'

'How many have you got left?' continued the sergeant.

'Only two.'

'Well, that's one too many. If he poisons one of them, you'll have the right number, and make sure you tie it up at night and feed it properly too!'

Over the next few weeks I poisoned a total of thirty-two dogs (these were the ones I found — there would have been more.) A lot of them were half-bred beagles and a big half-bred Alsatian, but only one dingo — the rest were farm dogs and other semi-domesticated dogs that roamed about the forests like dingoes. Good farmers only had a couple of working dogs and were pleased that I'd whittled down the hunting packs that had given them trouble for ages. The police were on side too, because it got farmers off their back to do something about reducing stock losses from hunting dogs.

We had eight good years on the farm, surrounded on all sides by wonderful neighbours. On one occasion, I got very sick and had a spell in the Lismore Base Hospital — they thought I had scrub typhus. One of the neighbours who'd been in the war in New Guinea said in typical straightforward farming lingo: 'Ah well, that's th' end a ole Jimmy. Don't last long wen they git that one. I seen 'em before!'

Well, it wasn't scrub typhus, but as we had a bad bout of *Leptospirosis* in the cattle and pigs at the time, which I'd been trying to treat, it's very likely I'd picked it up from them. Anyway, it made me pretty sick. Jim Browning used to get up at all hours in the morning, milk his own cows and then gallop over and give Moodgie and the children a hand with ours. One of the neighbours drove Moodgie and the children to the hospital in the Buick to pick me up. We didn't get back till late in the evening and, typical of the kind of people they were, Jim and Nessie killed one of their turkeys and baked it with a huge pile of roast potatoes, pumpkin and other vegetables and gravy, and prepared lavish dishes of sweets too. The neighbour phoned from Lismore to let Nessie know when he was leaving to bring us home. As we got to the house, I noticed a horse galloping away down the hill. Jim had just set the table and laid out this beautiful hot meal for us to simply walk in and sit down to. The cows were all milked and the calves and pigs fed and the yard all washed out. In fact, there was nothing to do but have tea and go to bed. This was typical of the kindness meted out by these wonderful people in times of trouble. Our children were fortunate to have been surrounded by such kindness and to have grown up and gone to the little one-teacher school on our boundary at the top of the hill during their early schooldays.

The country between Kyogle and Nimbin, like that between other major centres, is broken up into smaller communities like Stony Chute, Lillian Rock, Wadeville, Homeleigh, etc., which generally meant there was once a school there and perhaps a telephone exchange/post office as well. Over the years with changing times, most of these gradually disappeared but the names remained. All the farmers in these small communities were fairly close neighbours and knew one another well. When something happened anywhere in the district, it became the business of the whole group.

So it was a sad day when we heard that Wag Emery, who was a farmer not far from us, had committed suicide. He had a lovely wife and several young children and, being such a good person and good neighbour, was immediately liked by everyone he met. He often seemed to go through periods of depression. I had recently sold him a mob of weaners and, as my neighbour Jim Browning and I walked across a paddock with Wag to inspect the stock, Wag bent down, picked up a stick and, grinding his teeth, broke it into several pieces and threw it away. Although Jim and I looked at each other in surprise, we said nothing, realising he didn't want to talk about whatever it was that was troubling him. While milking that afternoon, he sent the young lad who was helping away on the horse to get a cow he said was missing. When the lad returned to say there were no cows missing, he found Wag hanging by the neck from a rafter by the long V belt he'd taken off the vacuum pump, the stool he'd stood on kicked from under him upside down alongside. We all searched our minds for weeks wondering whether we could have done anything to change the final outcome. It seemed Wag had made an instantaneous decision to end his life and not even his family understood why.

Good neighbours are so important on the land and Jim and Nessie Browning were among the best. Jim and I worked together on both farms in perfect harmony, helping each other in all kinds of work that needed an extra pair of hands. Our joint boundary fence bisected a fifteen-acre plateau of good heavy soil. As it was good level corn-growing country, we cleared the timber and pulled the boundary fence down so we could farm it as one unit and go halves in the cost of clearing, ploughing and planting. The crop would also be halved and go into our grain sheds for pig feed. By this time, Jim had bought a tractor too. We coupled both of them together to snig away the big trees and logs too heavy for one tractor to shift. It was all new country and the crops were heavy and of excellent quality. We doubled up on a lot of the fencing work too. When clearing a fence line on our place, Jim had a bad accident with his tractor. There was only one remaining large log to be snigged off the fence line and, as my tractor was coupled to the trailer with a big load of posts waiting to be laid along the line, he used his tractor. When snigging a heavy load, the drawbar, as close to the ground as possible, should always be used for pulling to avoid the possibility of the tractor rearing over backwards from a high pulling point. We'd been using his tractor to bore all the postholes and the borer was still attached. But he'd left his drawbar in the shed back home, so I was on my way over to get my tractor and unload all the posts and uncouple the trailer so the drawbar could be used for the pull, the only safe way. But Jim, think-ing the log wouldn't be too hard to pull, disconnected the posthole digger and hooked the chain to the three-point linkage pin high up behind the seat — the worst possible place — and started to pull. Sensing what was about to happen, I raced back to unhook the chain but was too late. It all happened in a flash. The front of his tractor went straight up in the air and reared over backwards, the bonnet slamming into the ground alongside me, showering me with battery acid and flying tools with Jim underneath. He'd seen the bonnet coming at him and kicked himself sideways just missing being crushed underneath by a hair's breadth. But his arm, still on the steer-ing wheel as it dug a hole on impact with the ground, was torn wide open from the elbow to the wrist, with fragments of bone sticking out through the torn muscles all the way along. With petrol running everywhere, the first thing I thought about was fire. I'd just lit a big log under the bank of the creek directly below and expected the whole outfit to explode at any moment.

I got Jim out from under the thing somehow and Moodgie phoned the ambulance that we met halfway along the road while racing him into Lismore. He was out of action for several months. The arm was a real mess and had to be held in place by a length of thick wire that went in at the elbow and came out the other end in the palm of his hand. I'll never forget the day the wire was to come out. The four of us, Jim and Nessie and Moodgie and I, all went in to see our vealers sold in the Lismore saleyards. Jim's appointment with the doctor was for twelve o'clock and the sale of our stock was not long after.

The doctor had a good look at the arm and tried to line Jim up for the anaesthetic at the hospital the following week.

'No bloody fear you won't — I want the bastard out now,' Jim insisted. 'What's more, I've got stock over at the yards and I want to be there when they're sold. So get hold of that wire with those multi-grip things you blokes use and drag the bastard out. I haven't got time to bugger round with it any longer.'

'I'm telling you, it'll be very painful. You won't be able to stand it once I start to pull,' said the doctor.

'Never you mind whether it'll hurt or not,' said Jim. 'Just get into the thing and drag 'er out or I'll do it meself.'

So the doctor started to pull. Jims' mouth flew open and he started to holler, and couldn't stop. He kept on bellowing until the doctor stood back with it still stuck in the end of his pliers. He felt cold all over and had the shakes — had to sit down on a chair for a while.

The doctor looked at him for a bit and said, 'I told you it would hurt.'

'When I came out of the surgery, still shaking and as white as a ghost, there's a couple of old girls in the waiting room waiting for their turn. You should have seen the look on their faces,' Jim told me. 'They must have thought he was cutting my throat — I think they were just about to get up and leave!'

Soon after we bought the farm we became close friends with two farming families from nearby districts. They were the Flowers from Findon Creek and the Griffiths from Homeleigh. Of all the people we'd met on the North Coast up till that time, we seemed to have a lot in common with these two families.

Frank and Mary Griffiths were brother and sister, neither of whom had married, but lived together on the farm and jointly worked it. They took our four children under their wing as a substitute for the children they would have liked but didn't have. They had a jersey stud on their Homeleigh farm towards Kyogle, which was worked by a share farmer and his family who lived in a cottage near the homestead. The Griffiths were a fascinating old pair, quite unique in a dairy-farming district. A strong artistic flair had run through the family from a long way back. They loved music and literature and Frank always played his piano with great gusto every time they asked us over there. They had a beautiful big garden and pet black ducks and wood ducks swimming around and waiting to be fed in a waterhole in the garden specially designed for their convenience. Every time one of their old stud cows died, they fenced off a little square plot on the side of one of the hills surrounding the farm and planted flowering shrubs and trees in it. Over the years, many such plots were planted as memorials to the old champions and beautified the farm by providing distinctive splashes of colour dotted about the hills as jacarandas, bougainvillea and flowering shrubs came into spring bloom in each little plot to keep the memory going. Mary was a great cook and spoilt us all, especially the children. She always had a huge roast meal prepared followed by lavish sweets of all kinds, pressing the children to have helping after helping before they'd even finished the one they were on.

They loved telling us about their champions and paraded their show ribbons. Top of their famous jersey blood lines were 'The Daphnes', all V.H.C. (Very Highly Commended) butter fat cows. Frank had a great sense of humour and got a real kick out of telling me about his ill-fated evening with his favourite old Daphne — the most highly decorated of this fine jersey blood line. Frank suffered from asthma and tried to avoid climbing the hills where possible but Daphne had come in season at the age of fourteen, down on the creek, right at the bottom of a long hill running away from the house and yards. Wanting to mate her with one of the top bulls to produce another champion, a chip off the old block as it were, he walked down to drive her up to the house and put her in the yard. It was a full afternoon's job, as they only went a few yards at a time between spells. They were both old, Frank gasping with his asthma and Daphne all burred up with arthritis. Keeping well behind in case Daphne took the line of least resistance and headed back down the hill, they'd got about halfway up when Daphne stopped for another blow. At that moment, there was a rattle in the lantana thicket alongside as one of the neighbour's mongrel-bred, down-horned, licorice-all-sorts bulls, made all the more grotesque by the fine sleek lines of the pure bred Daphne, arrived on the scene.

'He even had an undershot jaw and a down rump as well,' said

Frank. 'The brute, this ill-bred uncouth creature jumped the fence and served poor Daphne right under my very nose. What a jolly insult — like casting pearls before swine!'

Harry Griffiths, Frank and Mary's elder brother, was as large as Frank was small. He was an old man when we knew him and must have weighed close to twenty stone. The pine fruit box he carried around with him as a stool while attending the district show and cattle sales used to be so bowed out at the sides when his weight was let loose on top that you expected the explosion at any moment — but he seemed to have it all under control. He had a large collection of seashells of every colour, shape and size. He'd been exchanging shells locally and with collectors from overseas countries for years, he told me. He must have had hundreds of them resting on cotton wool in long polished timber cabinets with hinged glass-topped lids along a closed-in verandah.

Harry had taken up a block of wild, only partly cleared bush country between Kyogle and the New South Wales–Queensland border years ago when the country up in the hills was still being opened up. Out of this he carved a dairy farm for himself from the scrub just below the border fence. When the railway line from Sydney to Brisbane was being laid through the McPherson Range linking the towns of Kyogle and Beaudesert at opposite sides of the border fence, Harry made a living selling milk, eggs and vegetables to the railway workers. Fettler gangs had major construction camps at Grady's Creek and The Risk not very far from Harry's farm, so supplying their needs kept him going.

As the country was steep and rugged in places, progress was slow and required considerable engineering skills to get the line over the McPherson Range into Queensland. This was accomplished via a maze of difficult creek crossings on high concrete bridges linked by deep cuttings and tunnels from the opposite side of hills and ridges. When surveying the line, it was found that the last steep pinch a few miles south of the range crest was so steep it could only be negotiated by constructing a loop round a hill, with the line passing over the top of the one below. Thus, in conjunction with tunnels, rail gradients were kept within the prescribed safety limits. Moodgie's grandfather, George Pearce, had been chief draftsman for the Queensland Railways for many years and was instrumental in much of the initial design and construction work. This landmark, now known as The Border Loop, can be seen from The Border Loop Lookout. Completion of the loop line created a real problem for Big Harry because it was all on his farm and, when completed enclosed, denied his stock access to a considerable area of choice grazing country.

Harry wasn't about to be 'buggered around by a bunch of city shiny-arses that wouldn't know "B" from a billy goat's beard'. So he wrote numerous protest letters, all to no avail. Being an old bushman used to taking daily decisions to keep afloat, he decided to dig a hole under the line. Such was the local support for Harry's illegal tunnelling that the rail authority constructed a walkway under the line for the exclusive use of Harry's cattle — and the cattle on Harry's old farm still go under the line! But Harry had bad memories of those early trains. He was halfway across the line with his team, snigging a big red cedar log to the Grady's Creek sawmill. Before he could get the bullocks across the line, an unscheduled goods train came out of a tunnel and ploughed through the team of bullocks killing some and dragging the rest away down the line each side of the engine.

Long before Moodgie and I came to the North Coast, the Flower and Griffiths families knew each other well and were good friends. The old people were farmers down the South Coast for many years before moving to take advantage of the cheaper country in the Northern Rivers districts. They took up undeveloped forest blocks, cleared them and started dairying, both families eventually buying farms in the Kyogle district. Jim was one of the Flower boys and a most unorthodox one at that — a mixture of rough-as-bags bushman and intellectual — read poetry, drove a bullock team, studied history, went to the war and was mentioned in dispatches. It seemed he had a funny story on every cocky, dead or alive that ever hit the North Coast.

Returning from the war, Jim studied veterinary science at Sydney University, got his degree and set up practice, working from the family farm at Findon Creek, midway between Kyogle and the Queensland border. Mrs Flower had died some years earlier so the three men — Fred, their seventy-year old father, Jim, about forty, and Harry, some years younger — all batched together in the house. Our first meeting was a strange one to say the least. It was in the middle of a cyclone with rain coming down in buckets. Shifting cattle out of a paddock along the rising creek, I noticed a cow with a dead calf partly hanging out of her and, as you'd expect, looking pretty stressed. Looked like she'd been trying to calve for a week or two and the dead calf was decidedly on the nose. I put her in the yard and phoned the only vet in the telephone directory under Kyogle. It happened to be Jim Flower. Jim had already decided to get into bed with a book and call it a day when my call came. He had just finished saying to his brother Harry, 'I bet I just have time to pull this blanket up and start reading when some dopey bloody cocky rings up with a cow with a dead calf hanging out of her, that's been dead for a bloody fortnight.'

Sure enough!

So over came Jim, pitch dark and pouring rain, in a little red Volkswagon car he could only just squeeze into with head bent forward to avoid dinting the roof! When the rain had eased off a bit we got in my utility with a Tilly pump-up lamp and Jim's gear and just about floated over the flooded creek to the yards to start on the cow. She was as wild as a hawk with long spike horns and it was blowing a gale, but we got her in the crush. A couple of hours later when the filthy job was over, we let her back into the holding yard. She was pretty toey by this time so, as we walked back towards the car along the rails, she gave a bellow and a snort and came charging straight at us, full gallop. With the dip directly behind, there was only one way to go — straight into the draining pen through the six-foot-high slab rails. She was right on us. I tried to go through between the lower rails, but Jim and his thirteen stone hit the top ones at the same time at about thirty miles an hour. The whole lot, plus Jim, collapsed on top of me and the light went out in a shower of broken glass. The cow was slobbering all over both of us.

In the pitch dark and pouring rain, I had no idea where Jim was, or the cow, so yelled out, 'Don't move or you'll end up straight down the dip with a gut full of arsenic.'

The cow must have got one hell of a fright, too, and, fortunately for us, went back to the far corner of the yard. With no light, we didn't know this, so crawled out and gingerly felt our way round the rails with our ears cocked for the sound of flying hooves and splashing water till at last we came to the car. Over at the house Moodgie had a steaming hot drink of tea ready and a big batch of hot scones and golden syrup, which we demolished after washing some of the stink off us. Miraculously, the cow survived and so we met Jim Flower.

Although it was about eleven o'clock, we talked on for another couple of hours and found we had similar thoughts on many subjects. He stayed the night.

'Would you like to borrow a pair of Jim's pyjamas, Mr Flower?' Moodgie asked.

'No, I've had malaria but I've never had pyjamas!' he replied.

From then on, he often called in for a yarn and a meal when in our area and sometimes stayed the night. Next morning he'd be gone. Often we'd be halfway through dinner — Jim would have downed his first, and walked out. At first, we thought he was just going to the toilet — then we'd see the car going up the hill. He had finished, so simply decided to go. We thought this most strange, but got used to it over the years — there was only one Jim Flower.

He often brought old Fred, his father, over too. We'd just finished dinner one time when it started to rain and as we had a greasy black soil hill the car had to climb to reach the main road. They took off, but got stuck halfway. With Fred and I pushing, the red terror finally got a toehold and took off, with Jim leaning forward over the steering wheel inside. He didn't look back — just kept going! We couldn't believe it — he'd forgotten he'd brought his father with him. After about half an hour, it was obvious he wasn't coming back, so we walked home and finished dinner, wondering what to do with old Fred. Jim came back eventually.

Having had so many meals with us, they decided to return the compliment and asked us over for Saturday lunch. I can imagine the hectic cleaning up that must have gone on before we arrived. They had got up early and milked the cows and killed two Muscovy ducks, rolled them in corn bags and poured boiling water over them to loosen the feathers while they had breakfast. When they came back to start plucking, there were feathers everywhere and no ducks, but three very fat dogs! It's just as well Moodgie had prepared a full meal to take over for the batching trio.

Mechanical things like engines were foreign territory to Jim. I told him it was just as well his degree was to do with animals and not motor cars, or he'd have starved to death. It was raining and we'd just finished tea when in walked Jim covered with mud —

'Have you got time to have a look at the Volkswagon? It just cut out and won't move — might have a broken axle!'

Away we went in my utility and there she was with the rear end jammed against a road cutting. He'd been reversing to turn round and had backed into the bank, filling both exhaust pipes with compressed mud like corked bottles that killed the motor!

'I never bother much about what's behind — whatever it is it generally pulls you up!' he reckoned.

I cleaned out the mud, got him going and gave him a bed for the night. Before leaving next morning he asked us over for Sunday lunch. The kids were all hungry as usual, of course. He had prepared a stew.

'The eating irons might be a bit light on', he apologised, as he tipped the cutlery drawer upside down on the kitchen table and gave the bottom a thump with his fist.

Out fell a shower of mouse dung and a few dead cockroaches, half a knife, a teaspoon, a fork and the end of an egg slice with the rivets sticking up to show where the handle had once been.

'SHE says it should all be scalded before we use it!' he said, pointing to Moodgie.

We hadn't thought to bring bread and Jim only had a quarter of a loaf — just enough for his tea, so he decided to keep it well away from our four hungry kids. He'd rolled it up in brown paper and put it high up on top of the kitchen cupboard in a 'safe place'.

Keith was about nine and, like all growing boys, still hungry. Looking round to see if there was any more tucker lying around anywhere, his sharp eyes suddenly latched on to the parcel. 'What's in that brown paper parcel up there, Mr Flower?' he asked.

'Orr, you'll be all right till you get home, won't you?' said Jim.

As we poured the tea, Jim dragged a two-gallon bucket half full of 'green' milk from the fridge. When I commented that his cows must have come off very rich clover to produce green milk, he admitted, 'The wrong end of the cow got over the bucket at the wrong time, but its good Findon Creek protein, so get into it.' One of the first things he'd been taught at vet school, he told us, was that dairy cows produced milk and manure with equal facility, but as both of these commodities came from the same end of the cow the difficulty facing the dairying industry was how to keep the two products apart!

I sometimes gave Jim a hand with jobs in our area. A year or so and a couple of capsized Volkswagons later, he phoned one night to ask if he could bring a migrant over to meet us. We thought this must be someone he'd met during the war in the Middle East or perhaps in Borneo. We couldn't believe our eyes as a very tall distinguished English lady stepped out of the little car and was introduced as 'my fiancée, Barbara.' Jim was togged up to the nines with spotless white shirt and red tie, sharp creases in new gaberdine trousers and, of all things, a gold wristwatch. There was no cow dung or blood on his clothes or shoes — they even had laces in them. Barbara, an English nurse, had been on a working holiday in New Zealand, before coming to Australia to visit her aunt who lived not far from the Flowers' farm. Barbara and Jim met there and that was that.

Just before they were married, Jim invited us over to inspect the farmhouse in which he was batching while renovations were in progress to turn it into a comfortable marital home. Entering the living room to begin the inspection, we nearly tripped over an enormous cured pig about six feet long all wrapped up in mosquito net stretched out on the floor in front of the fireplace. The mosquito net had been torn away over the pig's flank, exposing a great hole from which Jim had been carving off bits of pig every time he wanted a feed. A butcher's knife stood upright where it had been last driven into the carcass. The fireplace was full of charcoal that had overflowed out across the floor and a bit to one side was a great pile of discarded eggshells. No broom was in evidence anywhere.

We wondered how this cultured young English bride would shape up amidst all this chaos and just how long it would take Jim to flatten out some of Barbara's refinement. But she proved as resilient as she was adaptable and we have been great friends since the first day we met. Imagine my surprise to find it was Mr Winslow who was to marry them. He was the Queensland Bush Brother who took me on my first holiday to Sydney when I was fifteen and married Moodgie and me at Tabulam in 1944. We hadn't seen him since, but, in the meantime, he'd been moved to Kyogle.

CHAPTER 18

Selling Up

AFTER eight interesting years on Dalgonally, our Stony Chute farm, we decided to sell out and move to Brisbane. We had spent a lot of money improving the place, most of the improvements were new, most of the scrub was cleaned up and the place was now properly fenced into convenient paddocks. But the income wasn't there. Being what was termed 'good scrub country' with a high rainfall, it was prone to regrowth ('dirty country' in the local lingo) of original scrub species as well as pest plants like lantana, crofton weed and cockspur. These sprang up through the grass, literally while you slept. If you stopped for any length of time to do other things, the regrowth soon got away and involved a lot of extra work and expense just to get the country back to the condition it was in the year before. I got sick of this ongoing non-productive exercise and wanted to do something more meaningful in life than become a scrub turkey scratching out weeds to exist in a failing industry that was rapidly going downhill.

Because of the general deterioration of the country, low butter prices and rising overheads, dairy farming had been declining for years with more and more dairies being condemned as lack of viability left nothing over to spend on maintenance. Improvements on many farms had reached the falling-down stage from years of neglect, where the cost of renewing and updating infrastructure outweighed the value of the country. Most farmers simply didn't have the money and banks weren't prepared to increase already over-stretched accounts. The country had been over-cleared and over-used for years, with a declining nutrient base brought on by soil compaction and severe leaching. Thousands of heavy sharp-hoofed animals in that high rainfall area had been walking out from the yards to feed and back to the yards to be milked, twice a day every day, since the turn of the century. This concentrated mass movement of heavy stock had compacted the surface soils to the stage where torrential rain was no longer absorbed rapidly enough to restrict heavy run-off, which hastened the deterioration. There were no underlying hardpans to hold the leached nutrients close enough to the surface to be used by shallow-rooted plants, and not enough mulch and humus to protect and enrich the surface soils. These factors, combined with the high rainfall, brought on a steady decline everywhere except on the river flats.

Productive native grasses like kangaroo grass, *Themeda australis* (on the hills), and forest blue grass, *Bothriochloa species*, began to disappear as did the better introduced species like *Paspalum dilatatum*, often replaced by useless bladygrass and serrated tussock. In time, the vastly inferior, prolific-seeding *Paspalum compressum* became dominant at the expense of the more productive pasture plants. Its short growth habit formed a dense mat of inferior low-fodder-value grass that carpeted the surface, exacerbating the already poor soil moisture infiltration. The cost of bringing this country back to a viable healthy fertile state far outweighed any benefits likely to accrue from the extra work and expense. We got out while we could, before the total collapse of the industry.

We also had the children's higher education to consider, since we expected they would go on to university. Keith was already attending Kyogle High School, leaving home early by bus and getting to Kyogle about morning tea break, and Lyn was to follow the next year. When heavy rain fell in this landslip-prone country, the school bus wouldn't run at all. Children from the land are always at a disadvantage where higher education is concerned and we certainly wouldn't have been able to afford the additional cost of boarding them in the city, nor did we want to. So we sold the farm and moved to Brisbane. Moodgie's choice was to live in Longman Terrace, Chelmer, the Longmans having been old family friends whose home she had often visited with her parents when young. So we bought a *Courier-Mail* and what luck — there was a house for sale just five doors along from old Mrs Longman's place.

We jumped in the Buick as soon as milking was finished and raced up to Brisbane, bought the house and raced back to the farm and finished milking halfway through the night. The house was on half an acre of land 300 yards upstream from the Indooroopilly Bridge in Chelmer. Nudgee College Junior was directly opposite the house on the other side of the river. It was a beautiful block of land with lovely views looking both ways, up and down the river from high up on the outdoor patio. But the Queenslander house built in the 1930s had been neglected for years; paint was peeling off it and it was full of white ants. The previous owner must have had a fixation about dogs dressed up in men's clothes. Portraits of dogs playing drafts, in swimming togs, smoking cigars and driving vintage cars covered the walls of every room. Narrow trenches nearly one metre deep had been dug in the dirt under the house so you didn't thump your head on the floor joists on the way to the rusty gas copper and the dripping tap on the other side of the house. Within a few years we had fixed it all up — dug out and cemented under the house and put in new facilities. I got a dozer and put in a beautiful full-sized tennis court on a lower level between house and river. We also built an entertainment area and a jetty thirty feet out into the river. It was a most picturesque setting for a tennis court and parties on the riverbank under big spreading poinciana, jacaranda and mango trees.

We went into partnership with my brothers, Keith and Frank in their established dry cleaning businesses. I knew the offer of a partnership was only out of kindness to me since I knew nothing but land work and would probably still be there if it hadn't been for their help. The business could well have done without me tacked on.

So leaving the land winds up the story of what Dad and Doolie started so long ago and a little of our life on the land since those earlier days. I've tried to illustrate the hardships faced by those older settlers who started with nothing but their determination to leave a mark for others to follow. Their lives were isolated and the work was hard and constant as they battled with isolation, droughts and financial worry. It gradually wore them down. Many became embittered with age and felt they'd wasted their life. Though there *were* good times too, these so often tended to be clouded by memories of loneliness and heartbreak. Some were incapable of enjoying themselves any longer and simply withdrew in solitude to live out the rest of their life. Few left any written words behind for they saw nothing worth writing about in the perpetual drudgery and boredom of hard sweaty work that changed little from day to day or from season to season. They had plenty to do just staying alive, bogged down by work and financial worry, as they tried to cope with nature's seasonal processes.

We had many regrets at leaving a way of life we knew so well in exchange for a new life in an uncertain city environment. And this was made no easier by the large send-off at the Stony Chute Hall. We said our sad goodbyes, rolled our swags, loaded the truck, packed up the Buick and headed for Brisbane.

Leaving the land put a great hole in our lives that nothing seemed to fill. As one of our Stony Chute neighbours said to his mate when he heard I was going into dry cleaning in the city: 'Jesus Christ, Jimmy Gasteen ironing bloody pants. Be like tryin' ter carve a silk stockin' outer a sow's ear — 'e'd be like a fish outer water, wouldn't 'e?'

'E was too — we all were.